The Legal Obligations of th

turned on or before

ɔw

ɔ3

LIVERPOOL JMU LIBRARY

3 1111 00714 1466

The Legal Obligations of the Architect

Andrea Burns, Solicitor

Contributors

Norman Royce, OBE, FRIBA, PPCIArb, FBAE

Darryl Royce, Barrister

Richard Fernyhough, QC, LLB, FCIArb,
   Bencher of the Middle Temple

Kim Franklin, Barrister

Hugh Cawdron, FRIBA, FRSA, ACIArb

Peter Madge LLM, FIRM, ACII, FCIArb

Elizabeth Jones, Solicitor

Butterworths
London, Dublin, Edinburgh
1994

United Kingdom	Butterworth & Co (Publishers) Ltd, 88 Kingsway, LONDON WC2B 6AB and 4 Hill Street, EDINBURGH EH2 3JZ
Australia	Butterworths, SYDNEY, MELBOURNE, BRISBANE, ADELAIDE, PERTH, CANBERRA and HOBART
Canada	Butterworths Canada Ltd, TORONTO and VANCOUVER
Ireland	Butterworth (Ireland) Ltd, DUBLIN
Malaysia	Malayan Law Journal Sdn Bhd, KUALA LUMPUR
New Zealand	Butterworths of New Zealand Ltd, WELLINGTON and AUCKLAND
Puerto Rico	Butterworth of Puerto Rico, Inc, SAN JUAN
Singapore	Butterworths Asia, SINGAPORE
USA	Butterworths Legal Publishers, CARLSBAD, California, and SALEM, New Hampshire

All rights reserved. No part of this publication may be reproduced in any material form (including photocopying or storing it in any medium by electronic means and whether or not transiently or incidentally to some other use of this publication) without the written permission of the copyright owner except in accordance with the provisions of the Copyright, Designs and Patents Act 1988 or under the terms of a licence issued by the Copyright Licensing Agency Ltd, 90 Tottenham Court Road, London, England W1P 9HE. Applications for the copyright owner's written permission to reproduce any part of this publication should be addressed to the publisher.

Warning: The doing of an unauthorised act in relation to a copyright work may result in both a civil claim for damages and criminal prosecution.

© Butterworth & Co (Publishers) Ltd 1994

A CIP Catalogue record for this book is available from the British Library.

ISBN 0 406 03677 2

Typeset by Doyle & Co, Colchester
Printed and bound in Great Britain by
Butler & Tanner Ltd, Frome and London

Foreword by His Honour Judge Newey QC

John Ruskin in his *Lectures on Architecture and Painting* said: 'No person who is not a great sculptor or painter can be an architect. If he is not a sculptor or painter, he can only be a builder.' Later, in *The Lamp of Memory* Ruskin wrote: 'When we build, let us think that we build for ever.'

No doubt it is principally the desire to design and so be the creator of something which will both fulfil its purpose and be beautiful and which may be appreciated for a long period, which causes architects to join their chosen profession. Their training is long, the competition for work is often severe and they are subject to changes in economic circumstances, but a worthy design properly executed must give its creator a great sense of fulfilment.

Unfortunately, architects have never been able to be just designers; they have always had to be many other things as well. Clients have always been a necessary 'evil' and discovering their requirements, the amount of money which they wish to spend and how soon they require their buildings can call for much patience and diplomacy. The client will need advising as to many matters, including, probably, the form of contract which he should enter into with contractors. The architect should be sufficiently businesslike to ensure that he and his client enter into a sensible contract to govern their relations, which among other things limits the architect's responsibilities.

The design of parts of many modern buildings requires specialist knowledge of structural, mechanical and electrical engineering, which the architect cannot possibly possess. He should, however, know the limits of his knowledge and advise his client of the need to instruct specialists from the outset. Similarly, if the works are of sufficient magnitude he should serve his client by recommending the appointment of a quantity surveyor.

Even primitive societies have customs which must be observed and which constitute law. Architects must, therefore, have always had to design against a background of law binding upon them and upon their clients. Supervisory authorities have been with us for centuries. Neighbours have always been alert to complain!

No architect can be expected to have the knowledge and expertise of a professional lawyer, but, if an architect is to perform his own work properly, he must have sufficient knowledge of the sections of the law which bear upon it. He must, for instance, know the details of planning and building control requirements. He cannot recommend a building contract unless he has a sound knowledge of its terms and those of alternative contracts. He will again need detailed knowledge of the contract selected when he comes to administer it fairly and efficiently. When the architect encounters legal problems to which he is not certain of the answer, he should advise his client to take professional legal advice.

This book consists of six separate contributions; each of considerable substance in itself. The information contained in some of the contributions as to law, goes far beyond that which an ordinary competent architect could be expected to know, but not, I venture to suggest, beyond that which many interested architects might think it worth while to acquire – at least in general terms. The book should be of great value to solicitors and others who have to advise architects and others in construction matters.

The first contribution, by Norman Royce, OBE, FRIBA, PPCIArb, FBAE and by his barrister son, Darryl, provides an admirable and in places entertaining short history of architects, comments upon their present position and makes some forecasts as to the future. The second contribution, by Richard Fernyhough QC and Kim Franklin, Barrister, is a succinct and comprehensive description of the existing state of the law applicable to architects. I think that it is quite excellent and worthy to be read right through and then kept readily to hand for reference purposes.

The third contribution is by Hugh Cawdron, FRIBA, FRSA, ACIArb, who, like Norman Royce, is a very experienced architect. Mr Cawdron gives some down to earth advice to architects about contracts which they should enter into with their clients.

The next contributor is Andrea Burns, a solicitor who has long specialised in construction matters. She deals with the very sensitive subject of collateral warranties, explains clearly how they came about, describes and then comments upon them and gives words of warning. That section is followed by a contribution by Peter Madge, LLM, FIRM, ACII, FCIArb, who sets out clearly the professional insurance position.

Finally, Elizabeth Jones, Solicitor, provides a section dealing with dispute resolution. She reminds us that there have always been disputes in the construction industry and she describes methods of resolving them over the years. She does not suggest reversion to trial by combat nor use of the ducking stool, although each of those methods of resolution would be likely to save costs.

John Newey
Former Senior Official Referee

Preface

In recent years, architects have been in the firing line in terms of liability when something goes wrong on construction projects. It used to be the case that if defects were discovered in a building, or losses were incurred due to delays on a project, the owner's main concern was 'how do we put this right?' Now, it tends to be 'whose responsibility is this and are they worth suing?' There are two main reasons for this apparent attack upon the architectural profession. The first is that, especially in the 1980s, innovative techniques were used in building which had not been previously tried and tested. Designs became more adventurous, dictated by the affluent 1980s. If these designs did not work, architects were blamed. The second reason is that, usually, architects have substantial professional indemnity insurance cover and they are thus potentially more attractive to sue than contractors and specialist sub-contractors, who may have shared responsibility for design.

Architects have been asked to sign onerous documentation. In recent years collateral warranties, in particular, have become popular. Architects, usually for no extra fee, have been required to sign collateral warranties making them liable to third parties in addition to their own clients. The influence of professional indemnity insurers has managed to curb these liabilities to some extent, culminating in the industry agreeing standard forms of collateral warranties. The RIBA, too, have played their part in trying to protect architects by producing the new Standard Form of Agreement for the Appointment of an Architect, known as the 'Black Book'.

This book aims to discuss the legal obligations of the architect from several viewpoints.

Norman Royce, Fellow and Past Vice President of the RIBA and Arbitrator provides a historical background with Darryl Royce, a specialist construction barrister.

Richard Fernyhough QC and Kim Franklin discuss the legal obligations of the architect in terms of liability in contract and tort.

Hugh Cawdron is a practising architect and regularly gives expert evidence in court cases and arbitrations. He examines the new provisions of the Black Book.

I then review the controversial subject of collateral warranties.

Peter Madge examines insurance aspects and Elizabeth Jones the disputes procedure both in litigation and arbitration and the various alternatives, such as ADR.

I hope that the book will be useful to all those in the construction industry and especially to lawyers and architects. I would like to thank the contributors for their efforts and for being involved in this work. I would particularly like to thank His Honour Judge John

Newey QC for reading the manuscript and producing a foreword. Judge Newey was obliged to retire from his position as Senior Official Referee in November 1993 due to ill health and everyone who knew him professionally and frequented his court will miss him greatly.

On a personal note, I am greatly indebted to John Newey for all his help and encouragement over the years.

Andrea Burns

The Contributors

Norman Royce
Norman Royce is a consultant architect and arbitrator. He did his architectural training at the Bromley College of Art and the Architectural Association. He is a Fellow and past Vice President of the RIBA. He is Fellow and past President of the Chartered Institute of Arbitrators and also past Chairman of the London Court of International Arbitration. He is a founder and consultant to Royce Hurley and Stewart, Chartered Architects, and served in the Royal Air Force as a pilot in Europe and the East. He contributed to *Construction Disputes: Liability and the Expert Witness*. He was recently awarded the OBE. His hobbies are gardening and flying.

Darryl Royce
Darryl Royce was called to the Bar in 1976 and is a member of the specialist construction chambers at 1 Atkin Building, Gray's Inn.

Kim Franklin
Kim Franklin was called to the Bar in 1984 and practices from Lamb Chambers, Temple, specialising in construction-related work in the Official Referee's Courts and arbitration. She is the joint editor of Construction Law Journal and Council Member of the Society of Construction Law. Her publications include contributions to *Construction Disputes: Liability and the Expert Witness* and *The Architect's Legal Handbook*. She has homes in London and Suffolk and has forsaken motorcycles in favour of fast cars and horses.

Richard Fernyhough QC
Mr Fernyhough is Chairman of the Official Referees' Bar Association and a Council Member of Justice and of the Chartered Institute of Arbitrators. He has been in practice at the Bar since 1970 and specialises in legal problems arising out of the Construction and Engineering industries. He works both as counsel and as arbitrator before tribunals both at home and abroad. He is married, with three children and, when time permits, he enjoys playing tennis and flying.

Hugh Cawdron
Hugh Cawdron is a Fellow of the Royal Institute of British Architects, Fellow of the Royal Society of Arts and Associate of the Chartered Institute of Arbitrators. He has been engaged in private practice since being released from National Service in 1949, thirty years as principal. His work has ranged from heavy industrial installations to local authority housing and the conservation of historic buildings which gained him a Civic Trust award. He now mainly concentrates

on providing expert opinion in respect of building failure and professional liability litigation and arbitration. His other interests include designing and building passenger-carrying, steam-powered launches and church furniture.

Andrea Burns

Andrea Burns is a partner and head of the construction department of Bermans. She specialises in the contentious and non-contentious aspects of construction and property law and acts in major cases in the Official Referee's Courts and in arbitration. She edited *Construction Disputes: Liability and the Expert Witness.* She lectures and writes regularly in the construction and property press. She is married and has two children and spends time in the Caribbean when time permits.

Peter Madge

Peter Madge holds qualifications in law and insurance and has spent all his career in the insurance and risk management fields. He is a consultant in legal liability, liability risk management and insurance and is the Principal of Peter Madge Risk Consultancies, prior to which he was a director of Willis Faber International Insurance Brokers, where he was Managing Director of Corporate Liability and Managing Director of Willis Wrightson Risk Management Services Ltd. He is the author of many books dealing with liability and construction insurance, including *The Indemnity and Insurance Aspects of Building Contracts* and *A Concise Guide to the 1986 Insurance Clauses.* He acts as insurance consultant to the Royal Institute of British Architects and the Joint Contract Tribunal.

Elizabeth Jones

Elizabeth Jones is a solicitor and Fellow of the Chartered Institute of Arbitrators who has practised for many years in the construction industry and the City and was most recently Group Legal Advisor to High-Point Plc. She has contributed a number of articles to the legal and construction press and has been involved as editor and contributor with books on international commercial arbitration and Turkish company law.

Contents

Table of Statutes

Table of Cases

A

B

C

D

N

O

P

R

S

T

Chapter One

Historical perspective

Norman and Darryl Royce

The beginning of the story

The identification of the first architect will no doubt turn on the reader's religious persuasion, but the first mortal who is recorded as practising the profession is generally agreed to be Imhotep, vizier to Zoser, the third king of the Third Dynasty of ancient Egypt. In about 2778 BC a monument to the king, designed by Imhotep, was built at Saqqara using the innovation of small blocks of stone. The result is thought to have been the first pyramid. History does not relate whether there was a loss and expense claim or a subsequent claim against the architect by the employer. Neither eventuality seems likely, because Imhotep was deified in the Late Period (during the 26th Dynasty) as a god of medicine and architecture. Not all of Imhotep's successors have been accorded such distinction and some have paid the price of being too successful: it is said that the eyes of the architect of the Taj Mahal were put out on the orders of Shah Jehan in order to prevent him designing such a beautiful building again.

While modern employers do not take such an extreme view of their architects, it has to be recognised that the quality of an architect's performance is something which continues to generate as much heat as that of the national cricket or football teams. Why is this? Part of the reason lies in the origins of the relationship between the employer and his architect. No doubt Imhotep did pretty much what King Zoser told him to do, but the king would have needed the guidance of an expert on technical matters and perhaps accepted the suggested innovation of building in stone using small blocks from his architect. Of course, the relationship would have been very much one of master and servant, or perhaps more accurately, slave. This aspect of the matter did not change for centuries. Some architects would no doubt say that some employers have yet to realise that it has changed.

The first professional architect we can identify with any degree of certainty in European history was Hugues Libergier, who designed St Nicaise at Reims. His tomb, built in 1262 AD, shows him with a measuring rod, a square and a pair of callipers. Libergier was in fact a master mason, but the tools depicted on his tomb suggest that he was concerned with design rather than execution. The emergence of a separate profession of building designer can be traced to the development of Gothic architecture, which required a degree of complexity and planning not necessary for its predecessor, Romanesque architecture. Many of the stone masons who were architects were, of course, contractors and made large fortunes as a result. They offered a 'package deal' to their clients, assuming responsibility for the supply of stone and other materials. Such accounts as we have of the length of time required for completing a church suggest that the employer was not offered a 'fast track' option.

Gradually, architecture came to be recognised as a separate occupation, and one which a gentleman could undertake. The revolution in English architecture brought about by Inigo Jones (1573-1652) also marks the beginning of architectural practice in a form roughly comparable to that of today. The career of Christopher Wren (1632-1723) is even more recognisable as being that of the profession of architect. This process continued through the eighteenth and nineteenth centuries to those Victorian and Edwardian giants whom the modern reader would regard as exemplifying the architect.

The emergence of a separate profession, entering into a contract of engagement with the employer, perhaps had the result of concentrating the latter's mind on what he was getting for his money. There had always been building failures, but now the employer would look to his architect in law if there was evidence to suggest that the design was at fault. In law, one very important distinction was made between a contract with an architect and a contract with a builder. They would both be required to exercise reasonable care and skill, but the builder, in certain respects such as providing materials reasonably fit for the purpose, would guarantee the result. The architect was a professional and what he was selling to his client was his skill, not the materials which made up the building.

Why an architect?

The whole face of Britain, Europe and indeed the world is changing. Existing towns and cities, many of great beauty and many others of great ugliness, will change in the foreseeable future. Towns which grew up in the day of the horse and carriage have to be drastically redesigned if they are to function and provide for an economical, functional and good life in the day of the motor car and the aeroplane.

Building is the job of the construction industry, but it is still the responsibility of the architectural profession more than anybody else to produce the final shape, character and environment of a city. The architect does not work in a vacuum: he is responsible to the clients who commission him, the users of the buildings, the town planning committees, the climate of public opinion, and to other professionals without whom the understanding of good architecture is very hard to achieve.

The emergence of architecture as a separate discipline from medieval times onwards is a fascinating story, leading to the apotheosis of the profession with the great names of the Victorian and Edwardian eras. Even they, however, experienced problems with their clients and builders.

In the second part of this century, there has been a dramatic change – now being accelerated – in the practice of architecture, from a 'gentleman's profession' to an intricate business exercise. There are so many new techniques to be mastered and, with the increase in the size of projects, the whole matter of the architect's place in the building industry requires reconsideration. Few architects receive adequate instruction in business methods, which are so necessary to efficiency.

Architecture in its full sense is a lifetime's study. The training is long and in itself sufficient to tax the full powers of the average architect. But this is not enough. Projects have to be built and building is a practical necessity of life encompassing contracts, materials, plant, trade customs, negotiations with contractors, management, quality assurance, supervision, building regulations, legal responsibility and professional indemnity.

Every architect has the urge to design yet some design so much better than others. Design inevitably entails innovation. Without innovation design can be very dull. If an architect is not prepared to innovate, he is in the wrong profession. Little stimulation flows from a mundane approach to an exciting profession. But innovation must be measured against the problems which could arise from a design which has not been thoroughly researched. It is a Solomon-like balancing act of the perils of either approach.

The architect's duties

In very general terms the architect's traditional duties consist of the design of the building, the preparation of working drawings and contract documents, the arranging of the contract and interim payments, and examination of the final accounts (including their checking if no quantity surveyor has been appointed).

But traditional methods and duties are being rapidly overtaken by new and more streamlined methods and the great danger that many architects face is the desire for yesterday to return. We should admire and keep the best of the past whilst maintaining a vision of the future.

With the gradual demise of the traditional builder, the large firms of building contractors carry out only about 5% to 10% of the work, leaving the remaining 90% to be done by specialist sub-contractors, working under new management methods.

While an architect is required to supply the fullest possible information to the contractor, he is not expected to provide constant supervision during the erection of the building, but only such periodical supervision as may be necessary to ensure that the work is being executed in general accordance with the contract. Should constant supervision be required, a clerk of works must be employed. The architect usually has authority to give orders on behalf of the client, provided that the contract sum is not materially exceeded, but he must always advise his client if any variations become necessary which will materially alter the scheme.

Although the architect is appointed by the client to look after his interests, he has a very real responsibility towards the building contractor and must act quite impartially and fairly between the building owner and the contractor. This is of the utmost importance and should be made quite clear to the client in the event of any dispute between the two parties to the contract. Maintaining this impartiality requires tact and strength of character and provides the greatest test of the architect's integrity. It is only by such integrity that he can fulfil his duty, both to his client and to the builder whilst retaining at the same time the respect of both.

The architect's relationship with his client

The architect must find his client before he can practise his art. Unlike the painter or sculptor, he is seldom at liberty to choose his own subject. He may be rash enough to design his own house. Very few architects, however, have the confidence or bravado to do this. The late Sir Wilfrid Greene MR must have recalled with some feeling the occasion when he had to sue his architect (an old (ex) friend) when he remarked:

> 'The greater part of my time on the bench is concerned with people who are persuaded by people they do not know to enter into contracts they do not understand, to buy goods they do not want, with money they have not got.'

An architect's relationship with his client is of the utmost importance. It used to be much easier when the client was head of his organisation and able to give a definite decision. Now, with most large concerns headed by a committee, it is far more difficult for architects to interpret their clients' wishes and to provide them with the building they want at the price they can afford.

It is essential that the architect and client should have a mutual confidence in each other right from the outset, particularly as the architect also has certain responsibilities to other members of the building team – responsibilities that some clients find difficult to understand, knowing that they are responsible for paying the architect's fees.

It is the architect's responsibility to take his client along with him from the very beginning, to establish and agree fees and to keep the client informed at every stage of the evolution of the project. This should be done by keeping a record of all discussions at all stages of the development of the scheme, and by retaining the earliest records of the earliest sketch schemes. Some of the most acrimonious disputes have resulted from the inability of an architect to be able to justify his entitlement to fees following the premature determination of his services, because of the paucity of his records of preliminary work done and time spent on the scheme.

The architect and the law

An architect is not expected to be a lawyer and it is not his duty to give legal advice to others, but it is important that he should understand something of his own legal position, his rights and duties and, in particular, he should have a working knowledge of the statutory and common law matters which will enable him to carry out his duties to a standard which may reasonably be expected from the average competent practising architect.

Fine analysis of legal decisions is obviously outside the architect's province, but he should have a reasonable knowledge of the principal cases having a bearing on the work of his profession.

During the last 15 years a formidable spectre has cast its shadow over a most enjoyable profession: liability for professional negligence. The dramatic increase in tortious duties recognised by the courts as being owed by architects to parties other than their clients and the prospect of 'open-ended' liability for latent defects has led some architects to conclude that their feeling of persecution is not simply the result of a complex.

One of the difficulties has been that the law has never really been clear as to the provenance of the duty of care owed by an architect to his client. This difficulty arises because some of the cases suggested that a professional person owed a duty either in contract or in tort. It followed, it was said, that a client could bring an action against his architect either for breach of contract or for breach of a tortious duty of care in respect of any particular act or omission by the architect.

From the late 1970s, a general tendency to recognise the existence of a wider tortious duty, combined with the fact that the architect's position as 'captain of the ship' for a project and the tendency of negligent contractors to fail to avoid insolvency, resulted in a series of decisions which seemed to impose greater and greater responsibility upon the architect. Because the time within which actions could be brought was generally longer for tortious claims, the architect's dual responsibility took on a particular significance.

Recent decisions by both the Court of Appeal and the House of Lords suggest that the tide may have turned and that professional liability will be more closely related to contractual obligations in the future. A firm conclusion cannot be reached at present, but it is not unreasonable to suggest that an architect will be able to evaluate his liability primarily in terms of the obligations which he has assumed to his client. This would be a result which would be welcomed by both architects and lawyers: by architects, because they will consider it good common sense and no more than their due; by lawyers, because they will no longer be afflicted by the persistent grumblings of the more vociferous members of the architectural profession.

That, however, is not the end of the story. Employers and the big institutions have detected the trend of the recent decisions and have taken to demanding collateral warranties under seal to be supplied by the architect, not to his client, but to the eventual purchaser or tenant of the building. These warranties accept that the architect owes a contractual duty of care to the other party to the subsequent agreements. It is not clear how effective these arrangements will be, nor is the position on the transfer of the rights under them to other parties, but they look likely to remain a source of claims and disputes for many years to come.

Forms of contract

Many architects still take little interest in the contractual side of architecture but a practising architect should be able to advise his client on the choice of contract to be made for a project and to be reasonably proficient in administering the contract. This calls for an all round knowledge of different forms of contract.

There are a number of standard forms of contract produced by the Joint Contracts Tribunal (JCT). Much has been said, especially by lawyers, about the many weaknesses of the Standard Forms of Contract, but that is usually when disputes have arisen.

Generally speaking the standard forms have proved satisfactory. Their existence relieves owners and contractors of the necessity of evolving for themselves a form of contract to meet individual cases. Were it not for the standard forms, the employer would be saddled with the expense of drafting an appropriate form of contract for each job, whilst the builder would be obliged to have his solicitor scrutinise the contract in detail to see that his own rights were safeguarded. Standard forms act as a guarantee to both parties. Both are aware that representatives of their own interests have helped compile the documents.

Neither architect nor builder need ordinarily consult his solicitor on the legal conditions contained in the standard forms. They are conditions which they should know reasonably well and upon which the business of building is based. They are based on custom evolved over the years.

Acceptance of the documents involves a certain surrender of rights by the parties to a building contract, but standardisation in reasonably clear and simple language has helped create a confidence that the standard form protects both employer and contractor.

Certainly, a greater confidence did exist 30 years ago than exists now. Both architects and contractors tended to concentrate their activities on getting buildings built, rather than looking for excuses for delay, and the authors believe, arbitration cases were fewer in the industry.

Management contracts

There are a variety of contractual situations covered by management contracts but the term is commonly used to refer to a type of contract where the main contractor is selected at a very early stage and appointed to manage the construction process and include his own expertise during the pre-contract stages. The contractor receives a fee for his services which is agreed between the parties before the contractor is appointed. The contractor does not act in the traditional manner of carrying out and being responsible for the works as he does under the JCT forms but he is responsible to the employer for the construction process. Competitive tendering is the usual method for the creation of the various sub-contract elements so that the final position is a series of sub-contracts being supervised by a main contractor.

Design and build contract

This is sometimes known as a 'package deal contract' or 'turnkey contract'. In this type of building contract the contractor takes full responsibility for the whole of the design and construction process from initial briefing to completion. Architects may or may not be employed by the employer to varying degrees in the preparation of the initial design.

Project management

A project manager may be appointed by the employer to co-ordinate the entire job from its inception to its completion. His relationship with the other professionals must be clearly set out and respective powers and responsibilities established. Since practice varies from contract to contract, it is impossible to define his role precisely. He could be appointed to take over the whole of the architect's traditional management and co-ordinating functions together with those of the main contractor. The concept is still in the process of evolution. It involves the following functions:

(a) Advising and guiding the client, from the moment he considers: building, financing, land acquisition, preparing the brief and appointment of consultants and contractor selection.
(b) The planning, control and direction of the project for the client, in accordance with the client's brief and advising on the form of contract to be used.
(c) The motivation and co-ordination of all participants in order to achieve the completion of the project to programme and within budget.
(d) The provision to the client of a project that fully satisfies his requirements regarding quality, performance and cost in use.

Project management by contractors (Construction Management)

In many projects clients prefer to place the responsibility for the design and construction of a building with one firm, without the separate appointment of the various members of the professional team and the appointment of a contractor. This is claimed as an advantage in using turnkey, package deal and with contractor design forms of contract. Multi-disciplinary firms of contractors provide this service. The client simply places a contract for a complete package with a single firm and that firm assumes responsibility for agreeing the project's objective, design, management and construction.

The changing industry

Historically, architecture developed from a craft base and, with the support of patronage, architects gradually concentrated on the design aspects of projects leaving building and management in the hands of the builder.

In their traditional role architects combined design responsibility with management responsibility and the contractor carried part of the management responsibility.

The architect's duty was (and still is) to interpret the client's requirements and, with an input from other professionals, to design the project and to ensure that it is built in accordance with that design. The architect is the right person to take on overall view of the building and to co-ordinate its construction so as to ensure that the client gets what he wants.

This is, of course, an over-simplification. It is suggested that the architect's role remains but the development process has become more complex. The accountant has now assumed a vital role with a more consistent commercial environment, the increased sophistication of the occupier and the emphasis on speedy problem-free construction and the variety of methods of funding the projects. With the speeding up of contracts and, regrettably, the lack of enthusiasm by architects to take the initiative in assuming leadership in the management of contracts, a climate has been created for management services to proliferate and for the advent of the project manager.

With computer aided design (CAD) facilities the demands of 'fast track' in building can be met. The trend has been to continue to reduce building periods through faster starts on site and shorter construction times. It has its problems and often tends to cause problems but clients are prepared to take risks by moving responsibility from their own shoulders to those of the professional team. The concertinering effect forces the members of the professional team to produce information extremely quickly and to demand equally quick decisions.

Time can be saved by undertaking packages of work – such as excavation, foundations, superstructure, etc – as separate contracts and by enveloping the project for watertightness. Construction advice is usually built into the method of building by management contracting.

This type of contract requires a great deal of pre-planning to co-ordinate each aspect of the work and it requires great expertise both technically and in management by whoever runs the project.

Looking ahead

Practice promotion

With the relaxation of the Codes of Professional Conduct, architects can now take an active part in an enormous field and clients will tend to buy the services they want and not necessarily those which the architect has hitherto been accustomed to offer. With free competition, architects will be obliged to sell their services. In this context architects, with a few exceptions, have a great deal to learn. There is a general reluctance amongst many of the profession to look upon marketing as a suitable activity for a professional person. It is, perhaps, time for architects to start to look upon themselves as business people.

Very few architects have a reputation high enough to attract sufficient good work to keep their practices constantly busy. Most architects have to obtain work by selling themselves and their expertise. Everybody the architect meets is a potential client and if a client is to trust an architect with his fortune, he will want to be reasonably certain that the architect is worthy of that trust.

A great deal can be learnt from the way architects in the USA operate. They have been involved in marketing a great deal longer than their British counterparts. To Americans, marketing is a job for the experts and they are prepared to spend a lot of money on getting results. Until recently advertising by architects has appeared to be a little 'un-English' but it does get results and with the influx of Americans into Europe, architects here should study the principles and underlying psychology of marketing, of how to find clients and which leads produce fee earning work. The great American architect, Philip Johnson, defined architecture as resembling 'the oldest profession in the world – it has only one aim and that is to please for a fee'. What is being done by successful architects in America today is an indication of what the power of marketing may mean in the future for architects here.

For some architects it is a case of a fight for survival rather than a matter of increased prosperity. The assistance of a public relations consultant can often not only identify weaknesses in a practice but make recommendations for improving its image by making potential clients aware of the practice; the services the practice offers; its special expertise and how to generate enquiries. This is especially so in young practices.

Ultimately, the successful marketing of a practice relies on its ability to achieve what it sets out to do but it must be doing the job properly to be successful, and the expert in public relations can skilfully guide the practice in the right direction.

To be accepted by tough business people, architects must present in their offices an air of efficiency demonstrating a professional business atmosphere. With this must be included a practice brochure prepared with great care and highlighting the firm's special expertise in a manner that can be easily and quickly read and which can be easily supplemented by additional photographs. The brochure is the architect's best selling feature but it must be backed up by the architect's ability to gain the confidence of his prospective clients at an interview.

The future

Market trends suggest that there will be many changes in the construction industry in the European Community during the next ten years. These changes will demand new skills from architects. The indications are that practices will become larger with resources on the USM. There will be a tendency for the traditional image of the architect to change even more as architects establish multidisciplinary organisations with financial and legal partners. Indeed, it seems that the trend will be towards the kind of service offered by the American counterparts in managing the design programme and contract procedures. Practices will expand not only in size but also in capability. There will remain a need for some smaller specialist practices able to trade on their specialised reputations, but with a tendency to diversify in order to compete.

The division between designer and technologist will continue to grow, the designer providing the aesthetic and quality requirements and the technologists providing the research and technical ability to get the projects built. Overall, project management and management contracting will continue to grow in popularity. It has caught the public imagination as a means of releasing both the designer and the technologist to concentrate on the design rather than the implementation of the project.

Quality

The requirement of maximum floor space for minimum of cost during the 1950s and 1960s has shown the problems and the ultimate costs that working to a minimum standard can bring. Fortunately, funding bodies are beginning to learn the lesson of this false economy. Many developers however, have yet to learn it.

With the growing awareness of a requirement for better quality in building, quality assurance is going to be a mandatory requirement for the 1990s. With its claims of the benefit to the client, quality assurance will help ensure completion on time, to budget and to the client's requirements.

The Building Research Establishment, in a recent analysis of faults in building contracts, concluded that they are mainly attributable to design errors and poor workmanship on site and only about 10% are due to inadequate products.

Before quality assurance can become really effective, clients must be trained to be aware of the benefits and implications of adopting quality assurance (QA), to appreciate the role and involvement required and to be prepared to accept the discipline required. Contractors must demonstrate their competence and gain certification from an accredited body and architects and other consultants must demonstrate their commitment to QA and must have gained a certificate of conformity.

Education

The present architectural education is geared to achieving a reasonably high standard of design but a fairly elementary level of skills geared to the normal service on a one-off building. Some schools of architecture encourage brilliance but the system as a whole encourages safe mediocrity. The greatest weakness is that the system has become too academic and should be more flexible allowing education and practical work to be interspersed. All architectural courses should include project management.

Conclusion

In some ways, the architectural profession has reached a crossroads. The architects emerged from builders, became gentlemen and succeeded to the privileges and duties involved. Now the builders are taking the architects back. However, the situation is different because the contractors are employing the architects themselves as independent contractors. It remains to be seen whether this is a purely temporary situation or whether the architect will cease to act as 'the captain of the ship' for all time. One result of the building contractors contracting with architects may be increasing attempts by those contractors to shift their liabilities to the client onto the architect.

In addition, there appears to be an irreversible trend towards limited liability. The days of the professional guaranteeing his commitment and integrity through his personal liability seem to have gone. This in itself is not objectionable and reflects the business practices generally adopted by the rest of the building industry and indeed most other industries. It is, however, bound to have an effect on the attitude of those employing architectural companies. In the past, litigants have been known to 'hold off' from pursuing an uninsured architect because of the consequences of personal liability. The same will not apply to companies operated by architects.

The opening up of the European Community to truly competitive practice by architects from one member state in another will raise difficult questions of conflicts of law as well as conflicts of standards.

Finally, the plethora of collateral warranties demanded of, and supplied by, architects means that the spectre of professional liability will continue to haunt the architect for many years to come. We are tempted to remind our readers of Shakespeare's phrase 'that affable familiar ghost', but we fear they may not see things in quite that light.

Chapter Two

The liability of the architect in contract and tort

Richard Fernyhough QC and Kim Franklin

Introduction

An architect is a professional and as such is expected to carry out his
skilled and specialised work to a high standard for its own sake.
Arguably, he owes a duty to the community which goes beyond that
which he owes to his client, and, for example, has a responsibility for
environmental matters and public health. A characteristic of the
professions in Britain is that they are self-governing and independent:
if any profession falls down in the enforcement of its own standards,
public confidence in all professions is undermined.[1]

Beyond this self-regulation, however, the law imposes obligations
and standards upon the architect in the performance of his
professional duties and holds him liable to those who suffer loss as a
result of his breach or failure. In this chapter we consider the basis
for professional liability, the standard to which the architect should
perform his various duties and the assessment of damages in the case
of breach.

Common law liability

An architect should have adequate skill and knowledge to enable him
to originate, design and plan buildings or other works which require
skilled design and arrange for and monitor their construction.[2]
Common sense and experience tell us, however, that success cannot
be guaranteed in every case. Modern design criteria involve

1 Dahrendorf 'In Defence of the English Professions' Journal of the Royal
   Society of Medicine Vol 77 p 178.
2 *R v Architects' Registration Tribunal ex p Jaggar* [1945] 2 All ER 131 at
   134.

innovative technology which contrasts starkly with traditional construction methods so that defects and failures are almost certain to occur.   Even when the architect is operating on more familiar ground, complex matters requiring difficult decisions may defeat him and errors are made.

The courts have approached the question of professional liability in three distinct tiers:

(a) a minimum standard of reasonable care to be exercised in the discharge of professional duties;
(b) a higher duty to achieve particular results;
(c) a different duty for the giving of advice.

Duty of care

The architect, like other professional people, has a duty to use reasonable care and skill in the course of his engagement.   The extent of this duty was described by McNair J in *Bolam v Friern Hospital Management Committee*.[3]

> 'Where you get a situation which involves the use of some special skill or competence, then the test as to whether there has been negligence or not is not the test of the man on the top of a Clapham omnibus, because he has not got this special skill.   The test is the standard of the ordinary skilled man exercising and professing to have that special skill. A man need not possess the highest expert skill; it is well established law that it is sufficient if he exercises the ordinary skill of an ordinary competent man exercising that particular art.'

What, then, is the degree of care required?   The courts' answer can be illustrated by the following two cases decided over 100 years apart. In *Lanphier v Phipos*[4] Tindal CJ told the jury:

> 'Every person who enters into a learned profession undertakes to bring to the exercise of it a reasonable degree of care and skill. He does not undertake, if he is an attorney, that at all events you shall gain your case, nor does a surgeon undertake that he will perform a cure: nor does he undertake to use the highest possible degree of skill.'

In *Greaves & Co v Baynham Meikle*[5] (discussed below at p 17) Lord Denning updated the terminology but adopted the same examples:

3   [1957] 1 WLR 582 at 586.
4   (1838) 8 C&P 475.
5   [1975] 1 WLR 1095.

'The law does not usually imply a warranty that [the professional man] will achieve the desired result, but only a term that he will use reasonable care and skill. The surgeon does not warrant that he will cure the patient. Nor does the solicitor warrant that he will win the case.'

Thus the courts recognise that, in carrying out his duties, the professional man may not succeed and that failure is not therefore conclusive evidence of breach of duty. In this respect the architect differs from the builder[6] and does not guarantee that he will achieve the desired end result.

Duty of result

An architect can assume the responsibility to ensure that the end product will perform as required. This duty is more onerous than that to take reasonable care and it is less common for it to be required of the professional man. Within the field of construction design such a duty usually arises in design and build or package deal contracts. For example in *Greaves & Co v Baynham Meikle and Partners*[7] the contractors undertook to build a factory complex and warehouse supplying all necessary labour, materials and expertise to produce the finished product. The contractors engaged the defendants, consultant structural engineers, to design the warehouse which was to be built according to a newly introduced method of composite construction and used for storing and moving oil drums loaded on to stacker trucks. Within a few months of completion the first floor began to crack: the floors were not designed with sufficient strength to withstand the vibration which was produced by the stacker trucks. The contractors claimed an indemnity from the defendants on the grounds that their warranted that there design would produce a building fit for its purpose. The Court of Appeal explained that the professional man is not usually under a duty to achieve a specified result but went on to say that when a dentist agrees to make a set of false teeth for a patient, there is an implied warranty that they will fit his gums.[8] Lord Denning said:

'What then is the position when an architect or an engineer is employed to design a house or a bridge? Is he under an implied warranty that, if the work is carried out to his design, it will be reasonably fit for the purpose? Or is he only under a duty to use reasonable care and skill? In the present case . . . the evidence shows that both parties were of one mind on the matter. Their

6   *Hancock v B W Brazier (Anerley) Ltd* [1966] 1 WLR 1317.
7   [1975] 1 WLR 1095.
8   *Samuels v Davies* [1943] KB 526.

common intention was that the engineer should design a warehouse which would be fit for the purpose for which it was required. That common intention gives rise to a term implied in fact.'

After setting out the evidence upon which he relied, Lord Denning concluded:

'In the light of that evidence it seems to me that there was implied in fact a term that if the work was completed in accordance with the design it would be reasonably fit for the use of loaded stacker trucks. The engineers failed to make such a design and are therefore liable.'

A similar argument was raised by the plaintiffs in *IBA v EMI and BICC*.[9] In that case the Independent Broadcasting Authority's predecessor contracted with EMI for the design, supply and erection of a television mast at Emley Moor, Lancashire. EMI sub-contracted the design and erection of the mast to BICC. Three years after completion the mast suddenly collapsed as a result of a tension fracture caused by vortex shedding and asymmetric ice-loading. BICC, who were responsible for the design and construction of the mast, argued:

'Firstly, that design is normally the function of a professional man and that the law is clear that no professional man warrants more than the exercise of reasonable care and skill according to the accepted standards of his profession: he never warrants a successful outcome. Secondly, in putting forward designs it was known that BICC were working on the "frontiers of knowledge" and entering into the field of the unknown and with the unknown must go risks which are unknowable. So long, the argument ran, as risks are unknowable no warranty of success can be given or expected.'

The Court of Appeal said that the correct approach was to interpret the contract between the parties to ascertain the extent of BICC's obligations. They considered the position of a builder who builds and sells a house who is under an obligation to ensure that the house is built in an efficient and workmanlike manner and of proper materials, and that it shall be fit for habitation. Why then, asked the court, should the position be any different for the person who designs, supplies and erects a television mast?

'It is not easy to see why, if the builder had been guilty of bad design rather than of the supply of bad materials or bad workmanship, the result should have been different on the grounds that, as has been contended, the matter of design should always be

9   [1978] 11 BLR 29, CA.

regarded as involving no higher duty than that of reasonable care, and that the law should never impose a greater obligation upon the would-be designer than that. Nor is it easy to see why if a builder contracting to build and sell a house is under an implied obligation that the house shall be fit for habitation when completed, a contractor who contracts to design, supply and erect a mast is not under some obligation as to its fitness for the purpose for which he knows it is intended to be used upon its completion.'

The Court of Appeal concluded that the contractual obligation was to provide a mast which would be proof against any meteorological conditions likely to be encountered on Emley Moor.

When the case was heard by the House of Lords the point did not directly arise for decision. Lord Scarman expressed his view, however, that the design obligation of the supplier of an article should not be equated with the design obligation of a professional man in the practice of his profession. Relying upon the case of *Samuels v Davis*[10] he compared the obligations of a dentist who takes out a tooth with one who agrees to supply a set of false teeth and concluded that –

'one who contracts to design an article for a purpose made known to him undertakes that the design is reasonably fit for the purpose.'

The distinction is readily apparent: in the ordinary course of things the professional designer does not warrant the ultimate success of his design. If, however, his involvement is either as part of a package deal to design, supply and erect an end product, or to design something to comply with stated performance criteria then he is obliged to ensure that the finished article is fit for its purpose.

Design and build contracts – the package deal

The 'package deal' contract recognised by the courts in *Greaves & Co v Baynham Meikle*[11] and described by Lord Denning in 1975 as 'a new kind of building contract' has subsequently been adopted by the JCT and used as the basis of their Standard Form of Building Contract with Contractor's Design. The unwary are warned against designating certain types of contract by names such as 'design and build', 'turnkey' or 'package deal' in order to ascertain the precise nature of the rights and obligations of the parties to them and are advised in each case that the terms of the contract have to be examined and the relevant principles of law applied.[12] In the case of

10 [1943] KB 526.
11 [1975] 1 WLR 1095.
12 See, for example, the commentary 33 BLR at 104.

Viking Grain Storage Limited v T H White Installations[13] the
defendant contractors offered a package deal to the plaintiffs who
required a large grain drying and storage installation.   The
contractors' tender which included 'design, execution and
management by a skilled and experienced specialist contractor' was
accepted. The court was asked to determine whether the contractor
thereby warranted that the grain store would be fit for its purpose.

The judge acknowledged that design and build contracts were
becoming an increasing feature of the building industry but went on
to say that various extraneous factors such as the suitability of the
ground on which the store was to be built and the number of different
parts of the structure that were the subject of specialist sub-contracts
drove him to approach the case without any preconceived notion as to
whether a term of fitness-for-purpose should be implied. He found
that there was nothing in the express terms of the contract which
would controvert the implication of a fitness-for-purpose term if
it would otherwise be justified and said:

> 'I turn therefore to the positive question: should a term of
> reasonable fitness for purpose be implied, or is it that in matters of
> design, specification and supervision of the works the defendants'
> obligation is limited to the exercise of reasonable care and skill.
> I confess at the outset that I find it difficult to comprehend why an
> entire contract to build an installation should need to be broken into
> so many pieces with differing criteria of liability. The virtue of an
> implied term of fitness for purpose is that it prescribes a relatively
> simple and certain standard of liability based on the "reasonable"
> fitness of the finished product, irrespective of considerations of fault
> and of whether its unfitness derived from the quality of work or
> materials or design. In my view such a term is to be implied in this
> case.'

The effect of this case has been described as establishing beyond
doubt that a design and build contractor's obligation in respect of
design is that it shall be fit for its purpose.[14] A better approach may be
to heed the warning to the unwary and consider the judge's view:

> 'Whether transactions so called are to be deemed to contain
> implied terms of one kind or another will depend on the contents of
> the package, and the nature of the term sought to be implied. There
> are many possible shades of the spectrum and this is particularly so
> where the term sought to be implied is one of fitness for purpose.'

---

13 (1985) 33 BLR 108.
14 See Cornes *Design Liability in the Construction Industry* (3rd edn, 1989)
   p 160.

Professional advice – duty to avoid financial loss

When the two types of duty described above are compared it can be seen that in ordinary circumstances the architect assumes a duty to take reasonable care in the exercise of his function under the contract by which he is engaged. In less common circumstances he is bound to achieve a specific result and the fact that he exercised reasonable care is no defence should he fail. The importance to the architect of the distinction between the two types of duty lies in the consequences should he be in breach. A duty of care has been described as a 'duty to avoid harm'[15] and is a creature of the law of tort. The scope of the harm to be avoided together with the duty of care expanded dramatically during the mid-1970s and 1980s as a result of the decision of the House of Lords in *Anns v Merton London Borough Council*.[16] The cases that followed it charted an expansion of tortious liability such that an owner who ended up with a building that did not perform in the manner anticipated could make good his loss by an action in tort. Decisions of the appellant courts made in the late 1980s have, however, restricted this development and have marked a return to the more traditional view that if specific results are required they should be contracted for. A more detailed analysis of the development and the inter-reaction between the law of tort and contract is discussed elsewhere in this chapter. The recent decision of the House of Lords in *Murphy v Brentwood District Council*[17] completed the restrictive process and put the final nail in the coffin of the all encompassing duty of care. The court held that the common law duty in building cases was to take care to avoid personal injury or physical damage to property other than the building in question.

Thus the harm to be avoided in cases based on tort is physical damage to persons or other property and not, importantly, financial or economic loss. Prior to the expansion of tortious liability referred to above, economic loss was recoverable only for breach of a duty to achieve results and that loss has usually been within the province of contract. The subsequent blurring of the distinction between the original, and relatively simple notion that breach of a duty of care gives rise to liability for personal injury or damage caused thereby, whereas breach of a contractual duty gives rise to liability for any consequential loss, financial or otherwise, has produced much academic comment and, needless to say, litigation. In the wake of the decision in *Murphy* it is hoped that the traditional distinction will prevail.

There is, however, a significant exception to the tort (physical damage) contract (financial loss) rule in the context of professional

15 Capper *Construction Disputes – Liability and the Expert Witness* (1989) Butterworths.
16 [1978] AC 728, HL.
17 [1990] 3 WLR 414, HL.

advice.   As a result of the decision of the House of Lords in *Hedley Byrne & Co Ltd v Heller & Partners Ltd*,[18] the professional man owes a duty, when giving advice in the ordinary course of business, to exercise care in making his reply, if his advice is to be relied upon by the other, to save that other from foreseeable loss or damage.   The decision is an important one because it transcends the distinction between physical damage and financial or economic loss.   Thus their Lordships held that whenever a special relationship came into existence, such as between a professional and their client, there arose a duty to take care when making statements which, if made carelessly, would cause either type of damage.

Hedley Byrne were advertising agents who asked their bankers to enquire into the financial stability of a company with whom they had placed substantial orders.   The bankers in turn made enquiries of Heller & Partners, the company's bankers.   They gave favourable references but stipulated that they were made without responsibility. Relying upon the references, Hedley Byrne placed further orders.   The company subsequently went into liquidation with a loss to Hedley Byrne of £17,000.   The court held that negligent advice may give rise to an action for damages for financial loss caused thereby, since the law will imply a duty of care when a party seeking information from a party possessed of special skills trusts him to take care in giving the information.   Lord Devlin said:

> '. . . where ever there is a relationship equivalent to contract, there is a duty of care.   Such a relationship may be either general or particular.   Examples of a general relationship are those of solicitor and client and of banker and customer.   Where there is a general relationship of this sort, it is unnecessary to do more than prove its existence and the duty follows . . . I consider that outside contract there should be a special relationship between parties which imposed a duty to give careful advice and accurate information.'

On the facts, however, there was an express disclaimer of responsibility which the court held to be effective and so no such duty was implied.

What then is the liability of the architect to his client?   (The liability of the architect to third parties is considered below at p 40) Is he to be considered by the courts much like the builder who owes a duty to take care not to cause damage as defined by *Murphy v Brentwood District Council* [19] and, in the event of breach liable only for personal injury or damage to other property caused as a result?   Or is he a professional giving advice and owes a *Hedley Byrne*-type duty to keep his client safe from both physical and financial loss?

18 [1964] AC 465, HL.
19 [1990] 3 WLR 414, HL.

This is a point yet to be resolved by the House of Lords. Commentators have remarked upon the potential injustice to the construction profession.[20]   Should a building develop defects, the contractors, who have the greatest commercial stake in the development, have been all but exonerated from tortious liability by *Murphy v Brentwood District Council*.[1] On the other hand, the professional team, with the least commercial interest in the development, may be liable for both the cost of remedying defects and consequential financial losses.

The decision in *Murphy* is too recent for discernible trends on this point to have developed.   Such guidance on the likely direction of judicial thinking as is available can be gleaned from cases decided after *Murphy's* predecessor, *Church Commissioners v D & F Estates*.[2] In *D & F Estates*, as in *Murphy*, the House of Lords were concerned with the type of damage for which a builder could be liable in an action in tort.   The analysis was subsequently qualified by *Murphy* but in the two years between the two decisions several cases against designers were tried at first instance.

In *Frost v Moody Homes Ltd* and *Hoskisson v Donald Moody Ltd*,[3] house owners brought proceedings against the developers and their engineers when their homes suffered heave damage.   They claimed that the engineer had failed to take proper soil tests before designing the foundations and failed to take precautions against heave when designing them.   The judge inclined to the view that the engineer owed a duty to the house owners to take care but that he did not act in breach and was not negligent.   He did not consider whether the duty was to keep the owners safe only from personal injury and damage or to prevent greater economic loss.

In *Portsea Island Mutual Co-Operative Society Ltd v Michael Brashier Associates*[4] the defendant architects were employed by developers to design and supervise the construction of a supermarket for the Portsea Co-op.   There was no contract between Brashiers and the Co-op.   After the Co-op had taken occupation of the supermarket, brick slips fell from the walls threatening injury to staff and members of the public.   The Co-op sued Brashiers in tort alleging that they owed them a duty of care, that they were in breach and that the cost of removing the brick slips and replacing them was recoverable.   Judge Newey reviewed the authorities where the defendant's duty was confined to avoidance of injury to persons or damage to chattels or buildings and went on to consider other cases, including *Hedley Byrne*,[5] where there had been held a duty not to cause financial or economic loss.   He

20 Construction Law Journal (1991) Vol 7 p 67.
 1 [1990] 3 WLR 414, HL.
 2 [1989] AC 177, HL.
 3 (1989) CILL 504.
 4 (1989) CILL 520.
 5 *Hedley Byrne & Co Ltd v Heller & Partners Ltd* [1964] AC 465, HL.

concluded that Brashiers owed the Co-op a duty of care to avoid damage or personal injury. He said that the Co-op could recover their expenditure on removing the brick slips and any other work necessary to make the walls safe as that was 'damage' within the then leading authority of *Church Commissioners v D & F Estates*.[6] They would not, however, be able to recover the cost of re-cladding the wall since such cost was economic loss.

There is little doubt that the *Portsea* case would have been decided differently in the light of *Murphy v Brentwood District Council*:[7] neither of the areas of expenditure incurred by the Co-op can be considered to be 'damage' as defined by the House of Lords. Importantly, however, Newey J held that the defendant architects did not owe a *Hedley Byrne*[8] type duty and were not liable, therefore, for economic loss. The duty owed was the ordinary tortious duty not to avoid personal injury or damage to other property as now defined by *Murphy*.

Other decisions which offer some guidance on this point, including the recent decision of *Midland Bank v Bardgrove Property Services Limited*[9] are considered in *Jackson and Powell on Professional Negligence*.[10] They conclude that, save in special circumstances, an architect will not owe a duty of care to prevent economic loss.[11]

Although guidance from the appellate courts is awaited, it seems likely that they will confirm the trend of the first instance decisions. Such a conclusion would follow from the continual process of restricting tortious liability and renewed emphasis on the importance of contractual liability. Further, it would avoid the injustice of leaving construction professionals vulnerable to tortious liability for both physical damage and economic loss whilst the construction team's liability is limited to contract.

Contractual duties

Formation of contract

The ordinary law of contract applies to the formation of a contract between an architect and his client. Thus, if an offer is made and accepted and consideration passes for the promise then a contract is formed. The agreement may be oral or written, part oral, part written or it may be an oral agreement evidenced in writing. It is a recognised

---

6 [1989] AC 177, HL.
7 [1990] 3 WLR 414, HL.
8 *Hedley Byrne & Co Ltd v Heller & Partners* [1964] AC 465, HL.
9 (1990) 24 Con LR 98.
10 (3rd edn, 1992).
11 *Jackson and Powell on Professional Negligence* (3rd edn, 1992) p 111, para 2-46ff.

truism in the building industry that the documentation relating to the contract between the contractor and the employer may be several inches thick where as that relevant to the contract between the employer and his architect may be no more than a note of a telephone conversation.

Although an oral contract is binding in law, in the event of dispute the terms of an oral contract can only be proved by oral evidence given in court. It is advisable, therefore, for a formal procedure of appointment to be adopted setting out the terms upon which the architect is engaged. This can be done either by exchange of correspondence or by entering into a standard form of agreement.

Simple contracts and deeds

Simple contracts are usually executed by no more than a signature, although even this is not strictly a legal requirement. The limitation period for simple contracts is six years. Thus, a party to a simple contract can not be sued for its breach after six years from the date of that breach. Most contracts, whether by exchange of correspondence or a formal agreement are simple contracts.

Different considerations apply to contracts executed as deeds or contracts under seal. The relevant limitation period is 12 years. Thus a party to a contract executed as a deed is liable for a period of 12 years from any breach. As a result of the Law of Property (Miscellaneous Provisions) Act 1989, contracts executed under seal are now called deeds. There is no longer a requirement that the document be sealed and the words 'signed sealed and delivered' have been replaced with 'signed as a deed'.

When entering into a contract with a developer or employer, an architect should be aware of the difference between simple contracts and deeds and not assume a greater liability than intended.

Letters of intent

Because of the complexities and sophistication of building contract documentation, the parties often resort to a letter of intent, on the strength of which contractors and sub-contractors are engaged. Work is started under a letter of intent on the basis that the contract documentation will sort itself out in due course. Usually, a letter of intent merely expresses an intention to enter into a contract in the future and creates no contractual liability. Such procedure is all well and good if the parties are in agreement and it is a simple matter of filling in the forms. If a contract is entered into subsequently, it may have retrospective effect.[1] If it transpires after several months that

---

1   *Trollope & Colls Ltd v Atomic Power Construction Ltd* [1963] 1 WLR 333.

there are crucial elements of the contract upon which the parties are not agreed such as time, method and amount of payment, time for completion or delivery and the general conditions applicable, then there can not be said to have been an agreement or a contract at all.

Such a situation arose in *British Steel Corporation v Cleveland Bridge & Engineering Co Ltd*.[2] Cleveland Bridge asked British Steel to fabricate steelwork for the Sama Bank in Saudi Arabia. British Steel arranged for the manufacture of the steelwork on the basis of a letter of intent and in anticipation of an order from Cleveland Bridge. The specification underwent five changes and British Steel increased their quoted price accordingly. The parties then negotiated as to whose standard terms and conditions should be incorporated into the contract whilst production continued. British Steel finally submitted a revised quotation and a revised delivery schedule. Cleveland Bridge rejected their conditions and proposed that their own conditions which included a liquidated damages clause be accepted. By that time most of the steelwork had been delivered, the remainder was delivered shortly afterwards. British Steel contended that no contract existed between the parties and that they were entitled to pay upon a quantum meruit. Cleveland Bridge accepted that they were liable to pay for the steelwork but at a lesser price than claimed. They counterclaimed on the grounds that a contract had been concluded and that British Steel had, in breach of contract, delivered the steelwork late and out of sequence.

The court held that there was no contract since the letter of intent asked British Steel to proceed pending the preparation of a contract which was plainly in a state of negotiation, not least on the issues of price, delivery dates and the applicable terms and conditions. Since the parties were still in a state of negotiation, it was impossible to say what the material terms of the contract would be, and by starting work British Steel did not bind themselves to complete the work. Robert Goff J said:

> 'In my judgment, the true analysis of the situation is simply this. Both parties confidently expected a formal contract to eventuate. In these circumstances to expedite performance under that anticipated contract one requested the other to commence the contract work and the other complied with the request. If thereafter a contract was entered into, the work done as requested will be treated as having been performed under that contract; if contrary to their expectation, no contract was entered into, then the performance of the work is not referable to any contract of which the terms can be ascertained, and the law simply imposes an obligation on the party who made the request to pay a reasonable sum for such work as has been done pursuant to that request, such an obligation sounding in quasi-contract or as we now say, in restitution.'

2   (1981) 24 BLR 94.

Therefore, should it transpire that a concluded contract in the legal sense never came into being it does not mean that the architect is not entitled to any remuneration for the work he has carried out. He is entitled to be paid a reasonable sum for such work as has been done at the employer's request. Such entitlement is called a quantum meruit and is usually calculated on an hourly rate.

Express terms

The express terms of a contract are those that are agreed between the parties and expressed either orally or in writing. Subject to the restrictions of legality and public policy there is no limit on the parties freedom to contract. Difficulties arise, however, when the agreed terms are ambiguous or inconsistent or where the parties proceed on the basis that they understand and agree the provisions of the contract and subsequently disagree. For these reasons the use of standard forms of agreement is recommended by the professional institutions. The most well known (published by the Royal Institute of British Architects) is the RIBA Memorandum of Agreement and Schedule of Services and Fees which is available for both standard works and minor works.

'Architect's Appointment'

RIBA also publish its recommended conditions for the engagement of an architect in the form of the 'Architect's Appointment'. The purpose of this document is to enable the architect and his client to achieve a clear understanding of the services required and the conditions concerning the provision of those services together with the basis of the fees and charges to be paid therefor.

The document is made up of four sections. Part I describes the preliminary and basic services which an architect would normally provide. Part 2 describes services which may be subject to a separate appointment. Part 3 sets out the conditions which normally apply to an architect's appointment and Part 4 explains the recommended methods of calculating fees on the different bases of a percentage of total construction costs, time spent or a lump sum fee. A modified version of the Architect's Appointment has been produced for use with Small Works and RIBA have recently issued a variant of the Architect's Appointment for use in connection with historic buildings and a supplement for use in connection with community architect services.

The Architect's Appointment does not, however, constitute a contract by itself. If it is desired to incorporate the standard conditions of engagement it is necessary to agree, expressly, the extent to which they should be incorporated. In *Sydney Kaye, Eric Firmin & Partners v Bronesky*[3] the plaintiff architects entered into a contract with the developer defendant. The contract was set out in a letter, clause 9 of which stated 'the RIBA conditions of engagement so far as it is consistent with the foregoing shall apply'. Clauses 1 to 8 related to the payment of fees and copyright. When the plaintiff architects commenced an action for fees for work done and damages for alleged repudiation of the contract the defendant developer sought to invoke the arbitration clause contained in the conditions of engagement and stay the action for arbitration. The architects argued that the conditions of engagement only applied to matters not covered by the first eight clauses of the letter. The Court of Appeal held that the RIBA conditions did not themselves constitute a contract and they could have no operation as between an architect and his client except by incorporation in a contract. The arbitration clause was undoubtedly incorporated in the contract and it was sensible and businesslike to interpret it as covering any dispute under the contract.

The Architect's Appointment expressly deals with the extent of the architectural services to be carried out, the architect's right to charge for additional services, questions of copyright and the right to terminate the contract. If the exchange of correspondence or contract between the architect and his client refers only to the method of calculation of fees payable under the conditions, for example, then the other matters referred to above may not form part of the contract.

The architect is advised to explain the fee scale to the client and not to assume that he is aware of the current conditions in force even if he is familiar with them generally.[4] If the fee scale is not expressly agreed an architect will only be entitled to be paid a reasonable sum for his services and although the court may gain some assistance from the scale it is not binding. Further it should not be assumed that because a client ought to know of the financial consequences of requiring additional works, he is thereby impliedly promising to pay a reasonable additional fee.

In *Gilbert & Partners v Knight*[5] the plaintiff surveyors agreed to prepare drawings, arrange for tenders and supervise works for the defendant at an agreed fee of £30. During the course of the works the defendant required that additional works be carried out by the builder significantly increasing the total cost from £600 to £2,283. When the works were complete the plaintiffs submitted an account for £135. The Court of Appeal held that the contract had no provision for the payment of additional services and that had the plaintiffs wished to recover for such they would have had to end the original contract and

3   (1973) 4 BLR 1, CA.
4   Males *Architects Legal Handbook* (5th edn, 1990) Ch 5.
5   (1968) 4 BLR 9.

enter into a new one. As that was not done, either expressly or by implication, they were not entitled to the additional payment. Davies LJ said:

> 'Of course in the ordinary way if one employs a professional man to give professional services it is a necessary implication, unless anything to the contrary is expressly said that the employer will pay a reasonable remuneration for those services. But in this case the cardinal point is that there had been a previous agreement to do some work for a lump sum of £30, and I for myself cannot see that there is any necessary implication that, when the work was going to be extended, or increased in the absence of any express mention of it, Mrs Knight should be liable to make any further payment to the plaintiffs.'

Edwin Hill & Partners v Leakcliffe Properties Ltd[6] is another example of the difficulties that can arise if standard conditions are not incorporated and the parties do not define the terms upon which an architect is to act. The plaintiffs, Edwin Hill, Chartered Surveyors, were engaged to provide architectural services for the defendant developers. The parties had worked together before and although there was no agreement for the particular development, there was an earlier agreement that Edwin Hill would be paid 10% of the total cost of the work. In the event the mortgagees of the site insisted on financing the development themselves and engaging their own architects. Edwin Hill's engagement was terminated and they commenced proceedings claiming their fees and damages for breach of contract. The court held that the agreement between Edwin Hill and Leakcliffe gave no right to dispense with Edwin Hill's services where the project was to proceed and that their dismissal was in breach of contract. The judge pointed for the termination of the architects' engagement as the terms had not been incorporated. In those circumstances he relied upon the case of *Thomas v Hammersmith Borough Council*[7] where Mackinnon LJ said:

> 'If, when the plaintiff was appointed architect . . . no special terms as to his remuneration had been agreed, the defendants would have been liable to pay him reasonable reward. Upon this abandonment of the scheme and dismissal of the architect . . . they would have been liable to pay him reasonable remuneration for the work he had done already, together with damages for preventing him from earning payment for the further work in completion of his appointed task.'

---

6   (1984) 29 BLR 43.
7   [1938] 3 All ER 201.

Competition

The contract may come into existence as the result of a competition. The architect who enters an architectural competition should study the rules of entry to ascertain what financial rewards, if any, are likely to flow from success.   The RIBA publish a Model Form of Conditions for single stage and limited competitions.   In *H N Jepson & Partners v Severn Trent Water Authority*[8] the plaintiff architects entered a competition held by a water authority to design new divisional offices. The competition conditions, which were similar to the RIBA Model Form but not identical, stated that no prizes were to be given other than the offer of appointment as architect for the works; that the appointed architect would be paid in accordance with the RIBA conditions of engagement and that if no instructions were given to the winner within three months of public announcement of the award, the winner would be paid a fee of £3,000. The plaintiffs won the competition and entered into a contract with the water authority for the works.   Later in the year the water authority informed the plaintiffs that the project was abandoned. The plaintiffs presented a fee account of £16,000 for work done for the purpose of the competition and a smaller sum for work done after their appointment calculated on the RIBA scale. The Court of Appeal held that they were not entitled to payment for work done for the purposes of the competition prior to their appointment. Sir David Cairns said:

> 'Work done in the hope of winning the competition is not work for which the setter of the competition would expect to have to pay, at any rate if he makes no use of it. Obviously the losers in the competition get no payment for the work which they have done and it is difficult to see why the winners should be in any better position merely because an appointment is made which in the event is ineffective. Further I do not see how the various stages set out in the RIBA document can be considered to have any reference to work done by an architect who, at the time when he does that work, does not know whether he is going to be appointed architect to the building or not. The language of the stages is not appropriate to work so done.'

The water authority agreed to pay the plaintiffs £3,000 as an ex-gratia payment despite their being appointed within three months of the announcement of the result, but the claim for £16,000 was rejected. Had the RIBA Model Form of Conditions applied to the competition it is still doubtful whether the plaintiffs would have been entitled to be paid the full fee claimed since the relevant clauses

8   (1982) 20 BLR 53, CA.

appear to contemplate payment of a fee in excess of the competition prize only if work done after winning the competition justifies it.

Implied terms

There are cases in which the law implies a term in a contract although it has not been expressly included by the parties. A term will not be implied by the court unless it is in all the circumstances reasonable to do so. A term will not be implied, however, merely because it is reasonable, or convenient or improves the contract: the court must be persuaded that the term is necessary. Whether a term can be implied in a particular case will depend upon the circumstances of the case and the terms that are agreed expressly. The more sophisticated the contract and the more experienced the parties to it, however, the more reluctant the courts will be to imply terms. In *Trollope & Colls Ltd v North West Metropolitan Regional Hospital Board*[9] the House of Lords said that its function was to interpret and apply the contract which the parties had made for themselves. Thus, if they had made a nonsense of a contract, the court would not intervene unless it were necessary in order to make the contract workable.

Terms may be implied by one of several routes. They may be implied by operation of law either by statute or more general considerations. The Supply of Goods and Services Act 1982 provides for the implication of a term that where a designer acting in the course of a business supplies a service, that service will be carried out with reasonable care and skill.[10] In many classes of contract implied terms have become standardised and there is a rule established by the courts that in all contracts of a certain type certain terms will be implied unless the contract expresses a contrary intention. For example, it is an implied term of all building contracts that the contractor will carry out the works in a good and workmanlike manner.

The court will imply a term if it appears from the language of the contract that the parties intended the term contended for. Thus a term will be implied if it is necessary to give business efficacy to the contract. In such circumstances the courts will add a term to those expressly agreed on the basis that without their intervention the contract will not work. Similarly, a term may be implied if it was obvious that the parties must have intended it to form part of their bargain. In such cases the court has to be satisfied that both parties would have agreed to it if it had been suggested to them at the time by a third party often referred to as 'the officious bystander'.

A term may be implied from a previous course of dealing. Thus if the parties have consistently on earlier occasions adopted a particular

9 [1973] 1 WLR 601, HL.
10 See s 13 of the 1982 Act discussed further below at p 53.

course of dealing then the terms previously agreed will be implied in a given case.   In *Sidney Kaye, Eric Firmin & Partners v Bronesky*[11] Lawton LJ considered that the RIBA Conditions of Engagement were incorporated into the contract in question, as a result of three years of dealing with the developer on those terms.   But a term will not be implied if it is inconsistent with an express term contained in the contract.

Certain implied terms are of particular relevance to architects.

Co-operation

The courts will imply a term that parties to a contract shall co-operate to ensure the performance of their bargain.[12]   The degree of co-operation required is determined by the obligations imposed on the parties by the contract and not what is reasonable.   Thus where both parties have agreed to do something that can not be done unless both concur in doing it, the contract will be construed so that each agrees to do all that is necessary to be done on his part for the carrying out of that thing.[13]

Termination

In *Edwin Hill & Partners v Leakcliffe Properties*[14] the developer sought to argue that there was an implied term that he could terminate the retainer.   Hutchinson J said:

> 'The most attractive way in which the argument in support of an implied right of termination can be put . . . is to submit that if the officious bystander had asked the parties, "If the development becomes impossible while you, Edwin Hill and Partners, remain the surveyors and architects, what will happen?" they would both have replied, "Well, of course, in that event Edwin Hill's employment can be terminated subject to a reasonable payment being made for work to date".'

He went on to reject that argument however, on the basis that the parties had expressly dealt with what was to happen if the developer was unable to proceed and had not made any arrangements for termination.

11 (1973) 4 BLR 1, CA.
12 *Chitty on Contracts* (26th edn, 1989) Vol I, para 911.
13 *Cory Ltd v City of London Corporation* [1951] 2 All ER 85.
14 (1984) 29 BLR 43.

Fitness for purpose

There is a term implied into an architect's engagement, both by common law and by statute[15] that he will exercise reasonable skill and care. A building owner who discovers that his building is defective may seek to establish that the architect's duty was higher than that of reasonable care and imply a term that the designer warranted that the design should be fit for its purpose.[16] Whether he would be successful in such a contention would depend upon the terms of the contract.[17] The RIBA 'Architect's Appointment' expressly provides, however, that the architect will exercise reasonable skill and care in conformity with the normal standards of the architect's profession in carrying out his obligations under the contract. In contracts where the Architect's Appointment has been incorporated, the express term as to reasonable skill and care is likely to operate in such a way as to prevent implication of a term for fitness for purpose.[18] On the other hand, if there is no express term of reasonable care, the way is clear for the implication of a term of fitness for purpose.

Certification

Where an architect's engagement involves a standard form of building contract with a procedure for the issuing of certificates for payment there is an implied term between architect and employer that the architect will exercise his certification functions according to the terms of the contract. In *Townsend & Another v Stone Toms & Partners*[19] architects were appointed to act in connection with the renovation of a dilapidated farm house in Somerset. The owner was dissatisfied with the quality of the work that was done and with its costs which was more than originally envisaged, and commenced proceedings against the architect claiming damages for defective design, failure to supervise the contractors and wrongful certification. The Court of Appeal held that one of the implied terms of the contract with the architects was that the architects would supervise the building contract according to its terms. The architects were in breach of their duty and certified for work which they knew was not done properly. Oliver LJ said:

'The whole purpose of certification is to protect the client from paying to the builder more than the proper value of the work done,

15 Supply of Goods and Services Act 1982, s 13.
16 See *Greaves & Co v Baynham Meikle & Partners* [1975] 1 WLR 1095, discussed at p 17, ante.
17 See the discussion at p 17, ante.
18 See Cornes *Design Liability in the Construction Industry* (3rd edn, 1989).
19 (1984) 27 BLR 26, CA.

less proper retention, before it is due. If the architect deliberately over-certifies work which he knows has not been done properly, this seems a clear breach of his contractual duty.'

Completion

In the absence of an express term as to when any works contracted for will be completed there is generally an implied term that they will be completed in a reasonable time.[20]   Similarly, in the circumstances described in the supply of Goods and Services Act 1982, s 14(1) there is an implied term that the supplier of the service will carry out the required service within a reasonable time.

Continuing duty

In the absence of an express provision to the contrary, an architect is under a duty to review his design as necessary until the works are complete. In *Brickfield Properties Ltd v Newton*[1] Sachs LJ said:

> 'The architect is under a continuing duty to check that his design will work in practice and to correct any errors which may emerge. It savours of the ridiculous for the architect to be able to say . . . "true my design was faulty, but of course, I saw to it that the contractors followed it faithfully". . .'

In *University of Glasgow v William Whitfield*[2] Judge Bowsher QC held that an architect's duty to design extended beyond practical completion until the building was in fact completed.

Although this duty is not described as arising as an implied term, that would appear to be the contemplated basis of the duty.[3]

Tortious duties

To the client

The scope of contractual duties owed by an architect has been considered above (at p 24 et seq). The fact that he owes his client

---

20 *Charnock v Liverpool Corporation* [1968] 1 WLR 1498; *Franks & Collingwood v Gates* (1983) 1 CLR 21.
1 [1971] 1 WLR 862.
2 (1988) 42 BLR 66.
3 See generally *Jackson and Powell on Professional Negligence* (3rd edn, 1992), para 2.14.

duties defined by contract does not necessarily preclude the existence of an independent duty of care in tort. Both the retreat of the law of negligence and the re-establishment of contract as the vehicle by which parties duties' are defined, have brought the question of whether a professional should owe a duty of care to his client, concurrent with his contractual duties, to the fore.

Over the past 20 years or so many cases have been brought against architects for both breach of contract and negligence and have been resolved without the question of a concurrent claim in tort being explored or decided. In *Tai Hing Cotton Mill Ltd v Liu Chong Hing Bank Ltd*[4] the Privy Council suggested that where there is a contract there should not be concurrent tortious liability. Lord Scarman said:

> 'Their Lordships do not believe that there is anything to the advantage of the law's development in searching for a liability in tort where the parties are in a contractual relationship. This is particularly so in a commercial relationship. Though it is possible as a matter of legal semantics to conduct an analysis of the rights and duties inherent in some contractual relationships, including that of banker and customer either as a matter of contract law when the question will be what, if any, terms are to be implied, or as a matter of tort law when the task will be to identify a duty arising from the proximity and character of the relationship between the parties, their Lordships believe it to be correct in principle and necessary for the avoidance of confusion in the law to adhere to the contractual analysis.'

Why, then, is it important whether there is a duty of care concurrent with a contractual duty? The answer is in relation to the limitation of actions and the amount of damages recoverable for breach. Actions for breach of contract are statute barred six years from the date of breach (12 years if the contract is executed as a deed) and this usually occurs in building cases before practical completion. Actions brought in tort, however, are barred six years from the time at which the damage occurred, which can be many years after completion of the building. It is easy to envisage a situation where a contractual claim is defeated by the operation of the Limitation Acts whilst the claim in tort is made in time. The point is illustrated by the case of *London Congregational Union Inc v Harriss and Harriss*[5] in which the owners of a building brought proceedings against the defendant architects for negligent design of the drainage system which surcharged and flooded the church hall. The Court of Appeal held that the cause of action in contract accrued in January 1970, when the building was completed, thus the proceedings which were commenced

4 [1986] 1 AC 80, PC
5 (1986) 35 BLR 58, CA.

in 1977 were out of time so far as they related to a claim for breach of contract.   The cause of action in tort, however, accrued when the drains first flooded in August 1971, within six years of the issue of proceedings.   The claim against the architects succeeded in tort.

It is evident, therefore, that it is in the professional person's interest for their liabilities to be limited to those arising from contract only.   Lord Scarman in the *Tai Hing* [6] case also recognised the desirability of certainty in this respect when he said –

> 'their Lordships believe it to be correct in principle and necessary for the avoidance of confusion in the law to adhere to the contractual analysis: on principle because it is a relationship in which the parties have, subject to a few exceptions, the right to determine their obligations to each other, and for the avoidance of confusion because different consequences do follow according to whether liability arises from contract or tort, eg in the limitation of action.'

In the light of the above it is increasingly common for defendants to argue that it is not open to a plaintiff to advance a claim both in contract and tort in circumstances where the proximity of the relationship necessary to establish a common law duty of care arises only by reason of the contract between the parties, as did the defendants in the recent case of *Iron Trade Mutual v J K Buckenham Ltd.* [7]   In that case the defendants described the point as a potential 'House of Lords point' and did not seek to base their interlocutory application upon it.   In the second edition of their work, the editors of *Jackson and Powell on Professional Negligence* [8] also considered it to be a 'House of Lords point' and said:

> 'When the House of Lords comes to consider the question of concurrent liability in the context of professional negligence, it may apply the *Tai Hing* analysis to some professions only.   Indeed it may even be held that the "contract only" approach is appropriate only in those cases where there is a detailed contract of retainer between the professional man and his client.'

In the third edition, [9] Jackson and Powell conclude that a professional person probably does owe to their client a duty in tort as well as contract to exercise reasonable care in giving advice or performing services, and that because of the special nature of the relationship the duty often extends to protecting the client against

6   *Tai Hing Cotton Mill Ltd v Liu Chong Hing Bank Ltd* [1986] 1 AC 80, PC.
7   [1990] 1 All ER 808.
8   2nd edn, 1987, p 12.
9   See *Jackson and Powell on Professional Negligence* (3rd edn, 1992), para 1.56 [p 33].

pure economic loss as well as personal injury or damage to property. At the same time, however, they set out the principal argument against concurrent liability – namely that it is wrong to subvert a particular contractual provision that has been expressly agreed between two parties.[10]

At present it is accepted that there is concurrent liability. The correctness of such an assumption has been challenged and given the recent developments in the law of negligence it remains to be seen whether it will survive consideration by the House of Lords.

To the contractor

In the usual course of things there is no contract between the architect and contractor. Under the terms of most building contracts generally, and the standard forms in particular, the acts or omissions of the architect affect the contractor directly. Can the architect be liable to the contractor in respect of the exercise of his function under the building contract? In the absence of a contract such liability would be founded in tort. The question then arises as to whether the architect owes the contractor a duty of care. The existence of a duty of care is the product of the facts from which it arises and the nature of the alleged breach. In each case it is necessary to examine the relevant facts, the relationship between the parties and their responsibility in order to consider whether such a duty is capable of being established. The courts have considered various aspects of the relationship between architect and contractor.

Execution of the works

In *Oldschool v Gleeson (Construction) Ltd* [11] Judge Stabb QC held that an architect did not owe a duty to tell the contractor how to carry out the work. He said:

> 'Not only has [the architect] no duty to instruct the builder how to do the work or what safety precautions to take but he has no right to do so, nor is he under any duty to the builder to detect faults during the progress of the work. The architect, in that respect, may be in breach of his duty to this client, but this does not excuse the builder.
>
> I take the view that the duty of care which an architect or a consulting engineer owes to a third party is limited by the assumption that the contractor who creates the work acts at all material times as a competent contractor.'

10 *Jackson and Powell on Professional Negligence* (3rd edn, 1992) para 1.56.
   See also *Keating on Building Contracts* (5th edn, 1991) Ch 7, p 172.
11 (1976) 4 BLR 103.

Thus an architect is generally under no duty to tell the contractor the manner of performance of his work.[12]   It was suggested in *University of Manchester v Hugh Wilson*[13] that if an architect knew that the contractors were making a major mistake which would involve them in expense the architect would probably owe a duty to the contractors to warn them. The judge said:

> 'In those circumstances the architect would not be instructing the contractors in how to do their work but merely warning them of the probable consequences of persistence in the particular method which they had adopted.'

Personal injury

Clay v A J Crump & Sons Ltd[14] is an example of how the particular facts of a case can give rise to a particular duty. The architect undertook to look into the question of leaving a wall standing to keep intruders out of a demolition site. The architect never inspected the wall but relied upon the advice of the demolition contractors that the wall was safe. Thereafter, no one noticed the dangerous condition of the wall which collapsed injuring the plaintiff. The Court of Appeal held that the architect and both the demolition and building contractors owed the plaintiff a duty of care and were liable. Liability was apportioned 42% to the architect and 38% and 20% to the two contractors. It seems that the architect's duty arose from his promise to investigate the safety of the wall and the fact that he was in continuous charge of the works. Further, the contractors were entitled to assume that the architect had left the site safe.[15]

Certification

In *Arenson v Arenson*[16] the House of Lords opened the way for contractors to bring a claim against architects for loss resulting from under certification. Lord Salmon said:

> 'The architect owed a duty to his client, the building owner, arising out of the contract between them to use reasonable care in issuing his certificates. He also, however, owed a similar duty of care to the contractor arising out of their proximity . . . In *Sutcliffe v Thackrah* [1974] AC 727 the architect negligently certified more

12 See also *Clayton v Woodman & Son (Builders) Ltd* [1962] 1 WLR 585, CA.
13 (1984) 2 Con LR 43.
14 [1964] 1 QB 533, CA.
15 *Jackson and Powell on Profesional Negligence* (3rd edn, 1992) para 2.29.
16 [1977] AC 405, HL.

money was due than was in fact due, and he was successfully sued for the damage which this had caused his client. He might, however, have negligently certified that less money was payable than was in fact due and thereby starved the contractor of money. In a trade in which cash flow is especially important this might have caused the contractor serious damage for which the architect could have been successfully sued.'

Subsequently, however, there has been no reported case where a contractor succeeded in such a claim although in *Michael Salliss & Co Ltd v Calil and William F Newman & Associates*[17] Judge Fox Andrews QC held on the trial of a preliminary issue that a supervising officer did owe a duty of care to the contractor in certifying. He said:

'If the architect unfairly promotes the building employer's interest by low certification or merely fails properly to exercise reasonable care and skill in his certification it is reasonable that the contractor should not only have the right as against the owner to have the certificates reviewed in arbitration but also should have the right to recover damages against the unfair architect.'

Against this background the decision of the Court of Appeal in *Pacific Associates v Baxter and Halcrow*[18] was awaited eagerly. The plaintiffs, Pacific, contracted with the Ruler of Dubai to dredge a lagoon in the Gulf. The defendants Halcrow were appointed as engineer under the FIDIC conditions of contract. The contract included Particular Condition 86 which excluded liability on the part of the Ruler or those engaged by him. Pacific were delayed in carrying out the work and claimed extensions of time and additional expense. Their claim totalling £55m was rejected by Halcrow and they referred it to arbitration. Some time later, the Ruler of Dubai agreed to pay £10m in settlement of Pacific's claim. Pacific then issued a writ claiming the unrecovered balance of £45m from the engineer. The Court of Appeal held that the facts of the case, including Condition 86, did not give rise to a duty of care owed by the engineer to the contractor and that the engineer was not liable to the contractor for the balance claimed.

In fact the decision is something of a disappointment since it is so heavily dependent upon its particular facts. The basis of the decision was that because of Particular Condition 86 there could be no duty of care imposed or assumed. On the wider point of whether an engineer assumes a duty to a contractor to act with care, the court gave limited guidance. Ralph Gibson LJ appreciated that professional firms engaged in construction work as architects or engineers were

17 (1987) 13 Con LR 68.
18 (1988) 44 BLR 33, CA.

concerned to know whether the law imposes a duty of care upon the engineer to the contractor, not to cause economic loss to the contractor in the process of certifying and of accepting or rejecting claims under the contract. He went on to say that whether such a duty was owed depended upon the nature of the service he was asked to provide and by whom he was to provide it. Purchas LJ suggested that the existence of a duty of care may depend upon the presence or absence of an arbitration clause. He specifically stated that a question mark must reside over the decision of *Salliss*.[19] The different approach adopted by the three judges casts doubt on whether the decision resolves the question of liability of a certifier to a contractor but the decision was followed in *Leon Engineering & Construction Co Ltd v Ka Duk Investment Co Ltd.*[20] This was a Hong Kong case in which the judge refused to allow building contractors to join the architects as defendants to an action and allege that they owed a duty to the contractors to consider their claims promptly, impartially and properly.

It is hoped that there will be other cases on the point which will cast further light on the problem. In the meantime, *Pacific Associates*[1] is generally relied upon as authority for the proposition that a certifier does not owe a contractor a duty of care.

To third parties and subsequent purchasers

An architect may owe a duty of care to subsequent purchasers and tenants of a building constructed to his design or under his supervision. The retreat of the law of negligence referred to above culminating in the recent House of Lords decision in *Murphy v Brentwood District Council*[2] has rendered such a duty of so little protection to third parties, should the building prove defective, that the use of collateral or direct warranties, giving the building user a contractual relationship with its designer, has developed.

The exact scope of the duty owed by architects to building users has yet to be defined by the appellate courts, namely whether the duty is to keep building users safe from personal injury and damage to other property only or whether they should also be reimbursed for economic loss such as the cost of repair. An indication was given as to the likely development of the law by the decision of *Portsea Island Mutual Co-operative Society v Michael Brasier Associates*[3] where the court held that the architects were liable for the cost of making the building safe

19 *Michael Salliss & Co Ltd v Calil and William F Newman & Associates* (1987) 13 Con LR 68.
20 (1990) 47 BLR 139.
 1 *Pacific Associates v Baxter and Halcrow* (1988) 44 BLR 33, CA.
 2 [1991] 1 AC 398, [1990] 3 WLR 414, HL.
 3 (1989) CILL 520.

only and not for the cost of repairing it. It is doubted however, whether this judgment would have been the same had it been given after *Murphy*. It seems more likely that losses claimed against architects as a result of defects in a building, where they were involved in its construction, will be treated as economic loss and irrecoverable under the principles set out in *Murphy*. Architects may, however, be vulnerable to claims brought under one of the exceptions to the basic rule as described by Lord Bridge:

> '. . . if a building stands so close to the boundary of the building owner's land that after discovery of the dangerous defect it remains a potential source of injury to person or property on the neighbouring land or on the highway, the building owner ought, in principle, to be entitled to recover in tort . . . the cost of obviating the danger, whether by repair or demolition, so far as that cost is necessarily incurred in order to protect himself from potential liability to third parties.'[4]

If Lord Bridge's qualification is adopted, the owner of a building with defects that threaten injury to passers-by and adjacent property, may be able to claim, in tort, against those involved in its construction, the cost of repairing or demolishing the building so as to prevent such injury.

The question has arisen as to whether an architect owes a duty of care to every subsequent purchaser of the building. In *Perry v Tendring District Council* [5] Judge Newey QC found that a cause of action in tort accrues to the person who owns the building when the damage occurs. Thereafter, unless that cause of action is assigned, a subsequent purchaser can not bring a claim. The difficulties posed by this decision have been largely overcome by the Latent Damage Act 1986 which provides that in certain circumstances subsequent purchasers acquire a fresh cause of action in respect of any negligence to which the damage of the property is attributable.

The architect as agent

An architect may be engaged in a number of capacities. He may be asked to advise upon various aspects of a proposed development, or to prepare a design with schematic drawings for its construction, or he may be asked to act as architect under one of the standard forms of contract and administer the contract and supervise the construction works. In the initial stages of a project, therefore, the architect is

4 *Murphy v Brentwood District Council* [1991] 1 AC 398 at 475F, HL.
5 (1984) 3 Con LR 74.

employed to give advice or prepare a design and not to act on behalf of the employer or developer: thereafter the architect is engaged by the employer to act as his agent for the purpose of ensuring that the works are completed economically, efficiently and in accordance with the contract.

Agency

Agency is the relationship which exists between two persons, both of whom agree that one should act on behalf of the other.[6] The one who acts is known as the agent whereas the one on whose behalf the acts are done is the principal. The significance of the role of the agent arises from his capacity to bind his principal so long as the agent acts within the confines of his authority. The sources of an agent's authority and its scope are therefore of fundamental importance.

Agent's authority

The agent's authority to act on behalf of the principal can be actual or apparent. Actual authority results from an express agreement, whether in writing or made orally, or by implication from the particular circumstances. Usually an architect's engagement arises from a written agreement, the terms of which should be easily identified. If the architect has worked on a number of projects for one developer or employer, however, it is not uncommon for the terms of a particular engagement, and the extent of the architect's authority, to be implied by a course of dealing.

Apparent authority

Apparent or ostensible authority, is a legal concept devised to cover the situation where the principal represents to a third party, for example a supplier or contractor, that the agent has his authority to act on his behalf. The agent may have no actual authority at all but the third party will be entitled to assume that he has if it seems that the principal has consented to the agency. In such circumstances the principal can be bound to the third party by the act of the agent, although the agent may have no actual authority to so act. The case of *Richard Roberts Holdings v Douglas Smith Stimson Partnership (No 2)*[7] shows how the principle works in practice. Experts, engaged to give expert evidence in a trial as to the damages recoverable by the

6   *Bowstead on Agency* (15th edn, 1985) p 1, Art 1.
7   (1989) 47 BLR 113.

plaintiffs, met during the course of the trial to see whether they could narrow certain issues. The plaintiffs' expert was expressly told by the plaintiff not to reach agreement or sign anything but this was not communicated to the other parties. The experts left the meeting bearing a document entitled 'Basis of Costs from Experts Meeting'. The defendants contended that it recorded an agreement as to the sums to be recovered by the plaintiffs in the action. The plaintiffs disputed that they were bound by the agreement. The judge found that the parties had held out their experts as having their authority to make an agreement on their behalf, that the defendants were not notified of any limit to the authority of the plaintiffs' expert and that in the circumstances the document constituted an agreement binding on the plaintiffs. He said:

'. . . the parties representatives by their words and/or conduct encouraged the experts to consider other matters in issue, which all concerned money, and they proceeded to do so. In the late afternoon Mr Hayes effectively withdrew any authority which Mr Andrews had to commit [the plaintiffs] in writing without prior consultation on the following morning, but this was not brought to the attention of . . . anyone representing [the defendants] . . . I think that . . . both [the plaintiffs] and [the defendants] held out their respective experts as having legal authority to make an agreement on their behalf.'

Personal liability of agent

On the other hand the agent can be liable personally if he does not make it clear to the third party that he is acting on behalf of the principal. In the case of *Sika Contracts Ltd v B L Gill*,[8] Gill, a chartered civil engineer, invited Sika Contracts to submit a quotation for repairing concrete beams at premises owned by a property company. Gill accepted Sika's quotation but at no time did he inform Sika that he was acting on behalf of the property company or as their agent. After completing the works Sika invoiced Gill who, for the first time, stated that he was acting for the company. The property company went into liquidation before the sums due to Sika were paid and they brought proceedings against Gill. The court held that the contract had been signed by Gill in his own name without qualification and he was deemed to have contracted personally. The fact that he was qualified as a chartered civil engineer did not exclude his personal liability and he was liable to the contractors for the sums claimed by them. Gill could have avoided this unfortunate liability had he made clear to the contractors the capacity in which he invited their quotation. As Kerr J said:

8   (1978) 9 BLR 11.

> 'It would have been open to Mr Gill, though I accept that it is not usual, to have added to his signature words such as "as agent only" or even "acting for the building owner". I appreciate that this is not commonly done. But whether or not it is done may be crucial when the building owner unexpectedly goes into liquidation as here.'

As the editors of the *Building Law Reports* comment:

> 'The outcome of this little case brings home vividly the consequences to an engineer, architect or surveyor of less than punctilious observance of the laws of agency.'[9]

The employer will not be bound by any acts performed by the architect in excess of his authority, whether the authority is actual or apparent.[10] If he does exceed his brief the architect may be liable to the contractor for breach of an implied warranty of authority for any loss caused to the contractor, notwithstanding that the architect acted in good faith, for example under a mistaken belief that he had such authority.[11] This might happen, for instance, where his authority ceases by reason of the death of his principal or the dissolution of the company engaging him. Where the architect fraudulently professes authority, however, he will be liable additionally in the tort of deceit. He may also be liable in deceit if he acts fraudulently, for example, by dishonestly certifying the amount owing.[12] It is not a defence for the architect to prove that he merely acted on the instructions of his employer: all persons directly concerned in the commission of the fraud are treated as principals.[13] The architect cannot be liable, however, if the contractor was aware of the extent of his authority or lack of it.[14] In most cases involving a standard form of contract the architect is unlikely to be held liable to the contractor for breach of warranty of authority since the terms of the contract notify the contractor of the extent of the architect's authority.[15]

Duty to hold the balance fairly

The functions of an architect, broadly speaking, are two-fold. Firstly, to act on behalf of his client as his agent and protect his interests. In this respect he is bound to act on his client's instructions, whether or

9 9 BLR 11.
10 *Bowstead on Agency* (15th edn, 1985) p 308, Art 78.
11 Ibid, p 457, Art 112.
12 *Emden's Construction Law* (1990) Vol 1 IV, para 192.
13 *Cullen v Thomson's Trustees & Kerr* (1862) 4 Macq 424.
14 *Halbot v Lens* [1990] 1 CH 344.
15 *Keating on Building Contracts* (5th edn, 1991) p 203.

not he agrees with them. Secondly, duties requiring the architect to decide the value of work, whether it has been properly done, whether the contractor is entitled to extra payment and the time when the work ought reasonably to have been completed. Frequently such decisions will be reflected in the certificates issued by him and will have consequences for both the contractor and the employer. In performing this second function, while he remains the employer's agent throughout, he must act fairly in applying the terms of the building contract as well as exercising reasonable skill and care. At one time it was thought that in carrying out this double faceted function, of agent and independent professional, the architect was acting as a quasi arbitrator and was not therefore liable for negligence and could not be sued. The House of Lords decided in *Sutcliffe v Thackrah*[16] that an architect acting under a building contract is the employer's agent throughout. In his administration of the contract, however, he is under a duty to act fairly between the employer and the contractor. In so doing, he does not assume the role of an arbitrator and is not immune from suit.

This decision was considered in the later case of *Arenson v Casson Beckman Rutley & Co*[17] which involved auditors engaged to value shares. The House of Lords held that the essential pre-requisites for a claim to immunity were that, there is a dispute between the parties, that the dispute has been remitted to someone to resolve in such a manner that he is called upon to exercise a judicial function, and that the parties have agreed to accept his decision. From this it can be seen that when, for example, an interim certificate is issued, an architect will not enjoy immunity since there is no reference of any dispute, nor is there any agreement to abide by his decision as to the value of the work done; the architect is simply applying the terms of the contract.

The extent of the architect's authority is defined by the terms of his contract and the objects for which he was employed. In each case the courts have to consider the express terms of the contract, its implied terms and whether the authority is actual or apparent. Hard and fast rules can not therefore be set down. In respect of various matters the courts have considered the question of authority which arises by implication as a result of his engagement as an architect.

Variations

Unexpected problems can arise during the course of the work in relation to equipment, materials and the nature of the site arising from the stability and physical structure of the soil. The work as

16 (1974) 4 BLR 17, HL.
17 [1977] AC 405, HL.

originally specified may need to be modified to complete the project satisfactorily.   An architect has no implied authority to vary the works[18] although building contracts frequently give the employer or architect an express power to order variations in the works specified. If the architect does have express power to order variations, it must be exercised within the scope of the contract.   So he may not vary the whole scheme of the proposed works or allow the substitution of entirely different materials for those specified in the contract. Also he must comply with any requirements as to the time and manner in which the order for such variations may be given, such as the provisions of the standard forms of contract which require that all instructions issued by the architect shall be issued in writing. Equally the architect has no implied authority to order extra works[19] or to order as extras, works impliedly included in the work for which the contract sum is payable.[20] In ordinary circumstances, he cannot, without the employer's knowledge or consent, bind the employer by a promise that a condition of the contract will be waived or varied, or by authorising the contractor to deviate from plans he has prepared. Similarly an architect cannot, without express authority to do so, make, determine or vary a contract entered into by his client.

Tenders and contracts

Where an architect is instructed to do no more than prepare plans, his employment is not that of an agent and he has no implied authority to obtain tenders but if he is engaged 'to originate . . . design and . . . arrange the erection of buildings', he may have authority to invite tenders and employ a quantity surveyor to prepare bills of quantity.[1] Authority to obtain tenders does not, however, carry with it an implied authority to bind the employer by acceptance of a tender and he cannot pledge the employer's credit without prior agreement.[2] By contrast, an architect in salaried employment with, for example, a local authority or public corporation, may have ostensible authority to enter into a contract with the contractor depending on the extent of the powers given to him by his employer.   So where a borough surveyor purported to agree to a variation of the existing terms of the contract being negotiated and he was within the scope of his ostensible authority in so doing, the court ordered that the varied terms agreed by the surveyor applied.[3]

18 *Cooper v Langdon* (1841) 9 M&W 60.
19 Ibid.
20 *Sharpe v San Paulo Ry* (1873) 8 Ch App 597.
 1 *Keating on Building Contracts* (4th edn, 1978) p 201.
 2 *Vigers, Sons & Co Ltd v Swindell* [1939] 3 All ER 590.
 3 *Roberts & Co v Leicestershire CC* [1961] Ch 55 and *Carlton Contractors Ltd v Bexley Corp* (1962) 60 LGR 331.   Cf *North West Leicestershire*

Consultants

The architect may have express power to employ a quantity surveyor to prepare a bill of quantities. The employer will then be liable to the quantity surveyor for his fees.[4] An employer may expressly limit the authority of the architect to employ a quantity surveyor. It is unclear when or indeed whether an implied authority to employ a quantity surveyor exists.[5] In the past such authority has been implied where the employer authorised the architect to obtain tenders and such tenders could only be obtained if quantities were prepared and issued.[6] The existence or otherwise of this authority will depend on the circumstances of the particular case. Given modern contracting methods such an authority may be less readily inferred since tendering contractors employ their own quantity surveyors to price complicated work and the architect is not required to do the same. A court may also be reluctant to imply such authority where the employer's building plans are still inchoate and no definite order to proceed has been given to the architect.[7] Accordingly, the well advised architect should consult the employer before taking such a step. An architect has no implied authority to employ other consultants at the employer's expense. If other consultants are required, their appointment should be recommended to the employer and made by the employer.[8]

Misconduct, bribes and conflict

An architect who, whilst acting for an employer, receives money or property by way of bribe or secret commission from a person who seeks to deal with that employer, may be liable to criminal prosecution for conspiracy to offences under the Prevention of Corruption Act 1906.[9] In addition, the employer may have a number of remedies against the architect. He may dismiss the architect and the dismissal will still be justifiable, even if the bribery is not discovered until afterwards.[10] He may recover the money paid as a bribe or secret

District Council v East Midlands Ltd [1981] 1 WLR 1396, where if there is no evidence that the architect had authority to make contracts he will not have ostensible authority to bind his employers.

4 4 *Halsbury's Laws* (4th edn) para 554, n 2.
5 4 *Halsbury's Laws*, para 1323.
6 *Waghorn v Wimbledon Local Board* (1877) 2 HBC 52.
7 *Knox & Robb v The Scottish Garden Suburb Co Ltd* (1913) SC 872.
8 *Emden's Construction Law* (1990) Vol 1 (IV), para 974.
9 *Archbold on Pleading Evidence and Practice in Criminal Cases* (44th edn, 1992) vol 2, para 28ff.
10 *Bowstead on Agency* (15th edn, 1985) pp 187-188, Art 50.

commission[11] or bring an action for deceit for any loss suffered as a consequence of the architect entering into the transaction. This action will allow the recovery of a loss which exceeds the amount of the bribe but he can not recover both. An architect who takes a bribe may also forfeit his right to such commission or remuneration to which he would have otherwise have been entitled.[12] Further, the employer may rescind the contract between himself and the contractor or the other person concerned. The rule against an architect making secret profits also applies when he charges the builder for the cost of copies of drawings necessary to execute the works, for taking out quantities or the cost of measuring up variations if he does so without the knowledge of the employer.[13]

If the employer knows that such a profit will be received by the architect or that there is a conflict of interest between the architect and employer, but acquiesces in his continuing to act as agent, the employer may be treated as having waived the architect's breach of duty and the architect will still be entitled to his fees. In *Thornton Hall & Partners v Wembley Electrical Appliances Ltd*[14] the employers engaged a quantity surveyor to prepare a specification and supervise works carried out by building contractors. Before work commenced, the surveyor informed the employers that he had become managing director of the building company and he was allowed to continue. When the surveyor claimed his fees however, the employers contended that they were not liable for them because the surveyor's acceptance of the managing directorship of the building company conflicted with his duty to them as his principals and that he forfeited his rights against them. The court held that the surveyor's duties under the contract did conflict with his role of managing director of the building company but that the employers had acquiesced in his continuing to act as their agent, notwithstanding the conflict between his duty and interest and so had waived his breach of duty.

Equally, an architect may not, without the informed consent of the employer, use his employer's property or confidential information acquired whilst acting as architect, in order to acquire a benefit for himself.

11 *Grant v Gold Exploration* [1900] 1 QB 233.
12 *Bowstead*, p 242, Art 62.
13 *Emden's Construction Law* Vol 1 (IV), para 1161ff.
14 [1947] 2 All ER 630.

Statutory duty

The building regulations

The Building Act 1984, and the regulations made thereunder, impose duties on various parties involved in construction projects, including local authorities, builders, approved inspectors and developers. Breach of the building regulations may give rise to a claim for breach of statutory duty for damages suffered as a result of the breach. Section 38 of the 1984 Act provides that, except where the regulations otherwise provide, breach of a duty imposed by the building regulations, as far as it causes damage, is actionable.

Section 38, however, has yet to be brought into force. Until it is effective, the relevant case law suggests that breach of the building regulations does not of itself give rise to liability in damages for breach of statutory duty. In *Eames London Estates Ltd v North Hertfordshire District Council* [15] Judge Edgar Fay QC held that contractors were liable for breach of the relevant building by-laws irrespective of whether or not they had been negligent. The greater body of subsequent case law is contrary to this finding. In *Worlock v SAWS*[16] the court held that it would be wrong to regard the building regulations as giving rise to a statutory duty creating an absolute liability. This view was endorsed by the Court of Appeal in *Taylor Woodrow Construction v Charcon Structures Ltd*,[17] where Waller LJ doubted whether breach of a building regulation would by itself give rise to an action for damages without proof of negligence, since he was of the view that a regulation of that kind would be difficult to construe as a regulation imposing an absolute duty in an action for damages. Subsequently, Judge Newey QC considered a breach of the building by-laws in *Perry v Tendring District Council*.[18] He held that a breach did not give rise to liability in damages. More recently Judge Esyr Lewis QC expressly held in *Kijowksi v New Capital Properties Ltd*[19] that breach of the Building Regulations (SI 1985/1065) did not give rise to liability in damages.

It seems therefore that until s 38 of the 1984 Act is brought into force, a breach of the building regulations will not give rise to a claim for damages in the absence of negligence. The cases referred to above were all decided before the dramatic changes in the law of negligence effected by the decision of the House of Lords in *Murphy v Brentwood District Council*[20] and all concern claims made against contractors or

15 (1980) 18 BLR 23.
16 (1982) 20 BLR 94.
17 (1980) 30 BLR 76, CA.
18 (1984) 30 BLR 118.
19 (1988) unreported.
20 [1991] 1 AC 398, [1990] 3 WLR 414, HL.

local authorities.   Can a claim be brought against a designer or
building professional for breach of the building regulations?

There is little guidance on this point and the fact that very few
claims of this nature have been made suggests that the building
regulations do not provide fertile ground for claims against
construction professionals.   The relatively early case of *Townsend
(Builders) Ltd v Cinema News and Property Management Ltd*[1] is
worthy of note however.   Townsend carried out conversion works to a
dwelling for a director of the defendant company, one Harris.   The
works were designed and supervised by a firm of architects, Wilkie.
Wilkie designed and Townsend constructed two bathrooms that did
not accord with the water closet by-laws.   Also it was agreed between
Townsend and Wilkie that the architects would serve necessary
notices before work started.   These notices were not served.   The
standard form of RIBA building contract provided that Townsend
were obliged to carry out the works in accordance with the building
byelaws and serve necessary notices upon the local authority, but
Townsend's evidence was to the effect that it was clearly established
practice in the building industry for builders to rely upon architects to
prepare designs which complied with the by-laws and to serve notices.
Townsend claimed from Wilkie an indemnity in respect of any liability
to Harris as a result of their carrying out works in contravention of
the building regulations.   The Court of Appeal held that Harris was
entitled to recover damages from Townsend for breach of the building
contract.   He was also entitled to claim against Wilkie for professional
negligence for designing bathrooms which failed to comply with the
regulations.   The total claim against both was the cost of the work
required to put both bathrooms into a state which complied with the
regulations.   For their part, however, Townsend were entitled to be
indemnified by Wilkie in respect of their liability to Harris for breach
of contract.   The net result was that Wilkie was held liable for the
total cost of remedying the breach of the building regulations.

The Court of Appeal's decision was based on their finding that
Wilkie were professional architects whose relationship with Townsend
was such that they owed them a duty.   The circumstances of the case
were such as to give rise to a duty which 'pervaded the whole
relationship from first to last'.

It seems, however, that, although it was not expressly stated in the
judgment of Lord Evershed MR,[2] the court relied heavily on the fact
that Wilkie had informed Townsend that, as architects, they would be
responsible for the service of notices and that as professional men
acting gratuitously in this respect they owed Townsend a duty.   The
other breach found against Townsend, that of building the bathrooms

1   (1958) 20 BLR 118, CA.
2   See the commentary on this case in (1958) 20 BLR 118 at 118 and 126.

in contravention of the regulations, was not considered by Lord Evershed in relation to the indemnity question.

The architects' liability to the builder in this case can be better understood if it is seen as a forerunner of that established by the House of Lords in *Hedley Byrne & Co Ltd v Heller & Partners Ltd*,[3] in that the duty was found to arise out of the builders reliance upon the architect, rather than simply as a liability arising for breach of the building regulations. Thus in similar circumstances where an architect has undertaken a duty to the contractor he may be liable to the builder for its negligent performance.[4]

Defective Premises Act 1972

The Defective Premises Act was brought into force in 1974. Shortly thereafter the tide of negligence began to rise in the wake of decisions such as *Dutton v Bognor Regis Urban District Council*[5] and *Anns v Merton London Borough Council*.[6] Little recourse was made to the 1972 Act since the law of tort provided the owner or occupier of a defective building with a remedy which had a more favourable limitation period. With the retreat of the law of negligence however, the Defective Premises Act 1972 has enjoyed a new prominence.

The Act imposes a duty as defined by s 1(1) which provides that:

> 'A person taking on work for or in connection with the provision of a dwelling (whether the dwelling is provided by the erection or by the conversion or enlargement of the building) owes a duty
>
> > (a) if the dwelling is provided to the order of any person, to that person and
> > (b) ... to every person who acquires an interest (whether legal or equitable) in the dwelling
>
> to see that the work which he takes on is done in a workmanlike or, as the case may be, professional manner, with proper materials and so that as regards that work the dwelling will be fit for habitation when completed.'

Several points are worthy of note in relation to s 1. The duty set out in s 1 applies only to work taken on after the commencement date of the Act which was 1 January 1974. The 1972 Act applies to those who 'take on work', including both contractors and designers alike. The duty imposed by the Act relates only to the provision of dwellings,

3   [1964] AC 465, HL.
4   See *Keating on Building Contracts* (5th edn, 1991) p 180.
5   [1972] 1 QB 373.
6   [1978] AC 728.

including those that are created by conversion or enlargement of buildings. It does not therefore apply to commercial construction. The duty is, however, owed, not only to the person for whom the work is carried out but also to every other person who acquires an interest in the dwelling, that is to all subsequent purchasers.

It used to be thought that the Defective Premises Act 1972 imposed a two-pronged duty upon designers, namely to see that the work taken on is done in a professional manner with proper materials *and* to design a dwelling which, upon completion, would be fit for human habitation. The recent decision of *Thompson v Clive Alexander & Partners*[7] has cast doubt upon this reasoning. Three house owners brought proceedings against the architects and engineers whom they alleged designed and supervised the construction of their house. The action was based exclusively upon the provisions of the s 1(1) of the 1972 Act. The designers argued that it was an essential ingredient of the house owners' claim that any breach of the Act rendered their homes unfit for habitation. They said that the words 'and so that as regards that work the dwelling would be fit for habitation' did not impose a separate duty on them but was simply part of the standard required in carrying out the duty 'to see that the work which he takes on was done in a workmanlike or professional manner'.

The house owners claimed in respect of many defects which did not make their homes uninhabitable. Thus if the designers were successful in their argument, the home owners' claim would fail in respect of a large number of defects. Judge Esyr Lewis QC held that the duty imposed by s 1(1) was limited to the kind of defect in the work done and the materials used which makes the dwelling unfit for habitation upon completion. It was not enough for a plaintiff to prove that the defects arose because of the architects' failure to carry out their work in a professional manner with proper materials.

With the demise of the law of tort it is thought that the wording of the Act will be subjected to a lot more judicial scrutiny: the *Thompson* case may be taken to the Court of Appeal. The meaning of the term 'fit for habitation' has yet to be considered, for example, although no doubt the comparatively generous standard applied in cases under the law relating to landlord and tenant will be contended for by house owners.

Section 2 of the 1972 Act creates an exception to the imposition of the duty, in cases where an 'approved scheme' applies to the dwelling. The National House Building Council (NHBC) operate a 10-year protection scheme which covers many of the new houses constructed in this country and which was at one time approved by the Secretary of State.

It was originally envisaged that the Act would provide a remedy for house owners who did not have the benefit of an NHBC certificate. Central to the NHBC scheme is the House Purchaser's Agreement (MBA), form HB5. This forms a contract between the builder and the

7   (1992) CILL 755.

purchaser and contains a warranty from the builder 'to build in an efficient and workmanlike manner and of proper materials and so as to be fit for habitation'.

The NHBC require that builders registered with them construct dwellings in accordance with their 'Technical Requirements'. These requirements were revised and amended from time to time and the NHBC were obliged to obtain approval from the Secretary of State for each new revision. The last scheme to be approved was the 1979 scheme. No application has been made for approval of subsequent schemes. As a result, those who own properties to which a subsequent NHBC scheme applies also have a remedy under the Defective Premises Act 1972, s 1.

The Act provides its own rules for limitation of actions brought for breach of s 1. Any cause of action becomes statute barred six years from the date when the dwelling was completed, or if remedial works were carried out thereafter, from the date when those works were completed. Thus there would be a limitation defence to any action commenced after six years from the date of completion or completion of remedial works.

The Supply of Goods and Services Act 1982

The Supply of Goods and Services Act 1982 applies, inter alia, to contracts for the supply of services which are defined as contracts 'under which a person, the supplier, agrees to carry out a service'. This is the case irrespective of whether goods are also supplied or transferred under the contract.

The sections of the 1982 Act relating to the supply of services apply, therefore, to architects, other building professionals, nominated sub-contractors and other suppliers carrying out design functions.

The 1982 Act provides for the implication of a term that the services provided in the course of a business will be carried out with reasonable skill and care.[8] In the case of an architect therefore, or other construction designer, the Act imposes a duty analogous to that imposed by common law. Where there is already an express term in the contract between the supplier and his client that services will be carried out with reasonable skill and care, the express term will not modify the implied term unless inconsistent with it. More importantly the Act does not limit any express provision which calls for an obligation higher than that of reasonable skill and care. If, for example, it is a term of an architect's engagement that his design will be fit for its purpose, he will not be able to rely upon the provisions of the Act to reduce his obligation to the use of reasonable skill and care only. Further, the parties to a contract for services can restrict or

8   Section 13.

vary the effect of the Act by express agreement or by a course of dealing, subject to the provisions of the Unfair Contracts Terms Act 1977.

The 1982 Act also provides that where goods are transferred in the course of business and the buyer or transferee, makes known to the transferor, or seller, a particular purpose for which the goods are required, there is an implied term that the goods are reasonably fit for their purpose. No such term will be implied, however, where the buyer does not rely upon the expertise of the seller. Thus the Act codifies the common law position that where, for example, an architect selects particular materials and instructs a contractor to use them, the architect is not relying upon the contractor's skill and judgment in the choice of materials. In the circumstances it is unlikely that there would be an implication that the goods would be fit for their purpose.

Interrelation of contract and tort

As explained elsewhere, under the present law an architect owes duties to his client arising both under the contract between them (contractual duties) and also under the general law (duties in tort), whereas to any third party, the architect only owes duties in tort. This distinction is of great significance in the two areas of limitation of actions and the amount of damages recoverable from the architect if he is in breach of any of these duties. The position of the architect in relation to his client and in relation to any third party will be considered generally at first and then specifically from the standpoint of limitation of actions and measure of damages.

Liability of the architect in relation to his client

Concurrency of duties in contract and in tort

Before 1976 the better view seemed to be that an architect's duties to his client were founded in contract alone as held by Diplock LJ in *Bagot v Stevens Scanlan*.[9] However, in *Esso Petroleum v Mardon*[10] Lord Denning MR suggested that 'in the case of a professional man, a duty to use reasonable care arises not only in contract, but is also imposed by the law apart from the contract, and is therefore actionable in tort'. Since then, this principle has been generally accepted and was applied in the case of a developer,[11] a solicitor,[12] and

9 [1966] 1 QB 197, CA.
10 [1976] QB 801, CA.
11 *Batty v Metropolitan Property Realisations* [1978] QB 554.
12 *Ross v Caunters* [1980] Ch 297.

an engineer.[13] One of the main reasons why the law developed in this direction was that an action against a professional man for breach of contract would often be barred by limitation before the client became aware that he had suffered any loss whereas this result would often not ensue if the claim could be brought in tort.

However, more recently, with the retreat of the law of negligence and the corresponding advance of the law of contract, this position has been reconsidered on a number of occasions. In *Great Nottingham Co-op v Cementation*[14] the Court of Appeal held that a nominated sub-contractor who had entered into a direct contract with the employer owed no duty of care in tort to the employer to protect him from economic loss caused by the sub-contractor's negligence. This was because the direct contract gave the employer no remedy in such circumstances and the law of tort would not supply a remedy which the parties could have stipulated for but did not.

In the light of these recent developments in the law of negligence and the apparent policy of the law to give primacy to any contractual relations between the parties[15] it is likely that the question of principle, ie whether or not a professional man owes any duties in tort to his client and, if so, what is the extent of those duties, will receive consideration by the appellate courts in the not too distant future. If so, it is thought likely that, just as the decision of *Murphy v Brentwood District Council*[16] has returned the law of negligence to where it stood before 1970 so it will be held that generally a professional man does not owe duties in tort to his client in parallel to existing contractual duties.

The present position

Until this aspect of the law is reviewed by an appellate court, the present position would appear to be as follows:

Liabilities in contract The architect will be liable for any breach of contract which will commonly be breach of the implied term as to the exercise of the degree of skill and care to be expected of an ordinarily competent architect. The limitation period applicable will be six years from the date of breach in the case of a simple contract or 12 years in the case of a contract made as a deed.[17] The measure of damages recoverable against the architect will be the usual measure in the law of the contract, namely the first and second limbs in *Hadley*

13 *Pirelli General Castle Works v Oscar Faber & Partners* [1983] 2 AC 1.
14 [1989] QB 71, CA.
15 *Tai Hing Cotton Mill v Liu Chong Haing Bank* [1986] AC 80.
16 [1991] 1 AC 398, [1990] 3 WLR 414, HL.
17 Limitation Act 1980, ss 5 and 8.

v Baxendale,[18] ie in respect of losses arising naturally in the ordinary course of things from the breach and/or losses arising due to special circumstances known to the defendant at the time the contract was made.[19]

In tort   The architect may also be sued by his client for the tort of negligence for breach of the ordinary duty of care which, to all intents and purposes, is identical to the duty owed in contract. The limitation period in respect of such cause of action expires six years after the physical damage, caused by the breach of duty, first occurs, whether or not it was then discovered. This is a far more favourable limitation period than that which exists for a breach of contract. Even this longer period may itself be extended in certain circumstances under the provisions of the Latent Damage Act 1986. The amount of damages recoverable for such breach of duty will, subject to proof of causation, be those which were reasonably foreseeable at the time of the breach of duty. These will include economic loss since the relationship between client and architect is sufficiently close to give rise to an assumption of responsibility by the architect to compensate his client for economic loss suffered by his negligence. The working of these principles is illustrated in the case of *Pirelli General Cable Works v Oscar Faber & Partners*[20] which, it is thought, remains good law even after *Murphy v Brentwood District Council*.[1] The *Pirelli* case is considered further in the section on damages (see p 70, below).

Liability of the architect in relation to third parties

The architect will owe a duty of care to third parties with whom he has no contractual relations provided that he could have reasonably contemplated that the third party would be likely to suffer loss or damage on account of any carelessness by the architect. Not everyone will come within the reasonable contemplation of the architect but workmen on the building site[2] and adjoining owners are likely to. But even if a duty of care is found to exist in any given case and the architect is held to have been in breach of that duty, it does not follow that he will be liable to pay substantial damages to the plaintiff. In particular, in ordinary circumstances, it is unlikely that the architect will be responsible for any 'economic loss' suffered by the third party. If, as seems likely, the principles laid down by the House of Lords in *Murphy v Brentwood District Council*[3] apply to architects as well as to

18 (1854) 9 Ex 341.
19 See the section on damages at p 70 ff, post.
20 [1983] 2 AC 1, HL.
 1 [1990] 3 WLR 414, HL.
 2 *Clay v AC Crump & Sons Ltd* [1964] 1 QB 533.
 3 [1991] 1 AC 398, [1990] 3 WLR 414, HL.

contractors, the architect will only be liable for personal injury or damage to the property of the third party other than the very thing itself which is the subject of the architect's activities. For example, if a structure carelessly designed by an architect collapses during the course of construction and falls outside the building site, then the architect will be liable to third parties in respect of any personal injuries suffered or damage caused to adjoining property. But he will not be liable in tort to any third party for the cost of repairing the collapsed structure itself since that would be pure 'economic loss' This will bring the architect's liability into line with that of the contractor or sub-contractor and any other result would seem to be anomalous and unfair to the architect. So far as limitation is concerned, the cause of action in favour of the third party arises when the physical damage caused by the architect's negligence first occurs. In this context 'physical damage' means such damage as is sufficient to give rise to the cause of action in tort, ie damage to the person or to property of the third party other than the very thing itself.[4]

Breach of duty

Advice relating to legal matters

An architect is not expected to have an in-depth knowledge of the law. He is, however, expected to have a grasp of those legal matters which relate to his engagement, so that he can perform his functions under the contract with reasonable skill and care.

In two cases[5] an architect was held liable for failing to obtain licences and serve notices necessary before the commencement of building works, as it was accepted by the court that it was the universal practice for the architect to deal with this aspect of the contract rather than the contractor.

In *B L Holdings Ltd v Robert J Wood and Partners*[6] the judge at first instance considered the knowledge of the law required by an architect. He said that an architect could discharge his duty by advising his client that he knows little or nothing of the relevant principles of law and suggesting that the client seek legal advice before incurring any expense. On the facts, however, the judge found that the architects had taken upon themselves the obligation of knowing enough of the principles of planning law relating to commercial office development to be able to give proper advice. In

---

4 *Nitrigin Eireann Teoranta v Inco Alloys Ltd* [1992] 1 WLR 498.
5 *Strongman v Sincock* [1955] 2 QB 525 and *Townsends (Builders) Ltd v Cinema News* (1958) 20 BLR 118.
6 (1978) 10 BLR 48 and (1979) 12 BLR 1, CA.

giving that advice, the architects had relied upon discussions with an officer of the local planning authority who had told them that the authority would not take areas designated for car-parking into account in determining whether a Office Development Permit was necessary. The architects designed and constructed a building which exceeded the permitted areas but did not obtain a permit. A prospective tenant spotted the need for a permit. Thereafter the owners were unable to let the building until the permit levels were raised.

The Court of Appeal agreed with the judge's statements of principle, that an architect should know enough about the law to give proper advice. They found, however, that the architects were not negligent in taking the view that the question of whether car parking should be taken into account when determining the need for a permit was for the discretion of the local authority. Because the issue was a difficult one they were entitled to rely upon the advice of the planning authority and were not in breach for failing to advise their clients to take legal advice.

In *St Thomas a Becket Framfield*,[7] architects prepared a specification of works of internal repair and redecoration for a church which dated from the 16th century. Notwithstanding that the Diocesan Advisory Committee recommended that the use of a lime wash application should be investigated, the redecoration was completed, under the architects' direction, using emulsion paint. The judge, sitting as a Judge of Consistory Court, held that architects who accepted commissions for the execution of works to consecrated buildings over which a consistory court had jurisdiction, had a duty to satisfy themselves that there was due ecclesiastical authority for the execution of those works before they were begun.

Examination of site

A prudent architect will examine the site of the proposed development in order to ascertain whether there are any factors which may restrict the use of the site and the nature of the ground upon which the project is to be constructed.

Restrictions on use of site

The obvious source of information as to whether there are any restrictions on the use to which the site may be put is the owner of the land. Thus the architect ought to make reasonable enquiries concerning the rights of neighbouring landowners, rights of way, easements, restrictive covenants and planning restrictions. The architect should also use his own initiative and watch out for any evidence of such rights or restrictions that are apparent on a visual inspection.

7   [1989] 1 WLR 689.

The architect's design must not infringe adjoining owners' rights. This is particularly important in view of the remedies that are available to aggrieved neighbours who may apply for an injunction requiring the offending building to be removed or at least its construction halted, or may bring an action for trespass.

In *Armitage v Palmer*[8] neighbours complained that the architects' scheme infringed their rights of light. In the course of his judgment the judge said:

> 'If by reason of the manner in which an architect sited a building it infringed an easement enjoyed by a neighbouring owner of which the architect had actual or constructive notice, he had not exercised reasonable skill and care.'

In that case however, the neighbours were unable to establish that their rights had been infringed and the architects were not found to be negligent.

Nature of soil

Architects and engineers have been found to be negligent for failing to examine the nature of the soil before designing foundations and for failing to measure and survey the site.[9] The courts are consistent in their findings that it is the duty of designers to ascertain the relevant information for themselves. Equally, if, for example, determining the nature of sub-soil or its composition is beyond the expertise of the designer, he should advise the employer that specialists should be engaged to carry out the necessary examinations.

In *Eames London Estates Ltd v North Hertfordshire District Council*,[10] an architect designed foundations for an industrial building to be constructed on made up ground without making an examination of the soil, assuming that it was an old railway embankment. He was found to be negligent for two reasons. He specified pier loadings without ascertaining the grounds bearing capacity. He also failed to act upon a query as to the adequacy of the depth of foundations which was made by a practical man on the spot. The judge was critical of the architect's approach to his design function which seemed to be limited to finding out what would 'get by the local authority'.

In *Investors in Industry Commercial Properties v South Bedfordshire District Council*[11] the developers engaged architects to design warehouses to be constructed on an in-filled site. The

8 (1959) 173 EG 91.
9 *Moneypenny v Hartland* (1824) 1 Car & P 351 and *Columbus v Clowes* [1903] 1 KB 244.
10 18 BLR 50.
11 [1986] 1 All ER 787, CA.

architects advised that the foundations should be designed by structural engineers. Inadequate trial holes were dug instead of investigating the ground by means of bore holes and analysing the samples obtained. The Court of Appeal affirmed the judge's findings that the architects were entitled to rely upon the engineers' advice as to what foundations were suitable and that they had discharged their duty arising out of the difficult ground conditions by ensuring that engineers were appointed to deal with it.

An architect should be aware not only of obvious hazards such as those presented by a made up site but also the less obvious such as the recent removal from the site of trees and shrubs. In *Balcombe v Wards Construction (Medway) Ltd*,[12] an engineer was found to be negligent for failing to make enquiries as to whether there had been trees on the site before it was cleared for development. The judge said:

> 'I find the conclusion inescapable that in 1971 a competent engineer encountering London clay, as in this case, would have made enquiries whether there had been trees on the site, and finding that there had been would have caused moisture content and plastic limit tests to be carried out. Had that course been taken there can be no doubt that the defendant would have advised that the proposed foundations were inadequate.'

It is submitted that the same test would apply to an architect designing foundations in similar circumstances.

Inaccurate estimates

An architect may be asked by his client for an estimate of the likely building costs of the proposed project. In providing an estimate the architect is under a duty to give a figure that is reasonably close to the ultimate cost, that takes into account the effect of inflation or is expressed to be current cost only. The estimate should also fall within any budget limit imposed by the client. An architect should therefore ascertain whether the client has any costs limit and prepare a scheme that is capable of being carried out within that limit. In any event the architect should ensure that his proposals can be executed for a reasonable cost having regard to the scope and function of the works.

In *Gordon Shaw Concrete Products Ltd v Design Collaborative Ltd*[13] Canadian architects were asked to investigate the possibility of constructing a house for C\$60,000. They designed a scheme that would cost over C\$100,000 to build. The plaintiffs sued for negligence and claimed repayment of fees paid on the grounds that the work

12 (1981) 259 EG 765.
13 (1986) 35 CCLT 100.

carried out was useless. The architects were found to be negligent
and to have failed to provide any consideration for the fees paid to
them. The judge said:

> 'The architect was under a duty to submit an estimate of
> construction costs that was reasonably cost to the ultimate cost and
> if there was a wide discrepancy between the two then to explain the
> reason for that discrepancy. There was no reasonable explanation
> of the great discrepancy between the estimated and ultimate
> construction figure.'

In the light of the case of *Nye Saunders v Bristow*[14] it seems
unlikely that the effects of inflation can amount to a reasonable
explanation for a sizeable discrepancy between forecast and ultimate
cost. In that case Bristow commissioned architects to renovate his
Elizabethan mansion in Surrey. He gave a budget figure of £250,000
and the original estimate of £238,000 was given in February 1974. By
the time the works were costed in September of the same year the
likely completion costs were £440,000 and still rising. The defendant
refused to continue with the project or pay the architects their fees on
the grounds that had he been warned as to the effect inflation might
have upon the original estimate he would not have commenced the
project. The Court of Appeal upheld the judge's decision that the
architects had been negligent in failing to make it clear the extent to
which they had taken inflation into account.

In *Flannagan v Mate*[15] Australian architects were found to be
negligent for failing to warn their client that the client's limit of
Aust$4,000 was likely to be exceeded and that it was unlikely that the
project would be completed for that sum.

Design

Designing a structure, including preparing the necessary plans and
drawings and selecting the appropriate materials for its construction,
may be viewed as one of the architect's main functions. Whether an
architect has been negligent in implementing his design will depend
upon the facts of the case in question and, in particular, upon the
terms of his engagement. The following principals can be determined
from the various authorities:

(a) An architect can not escape liability for a design he has
undertaken to carry out by delegating it to another.
(b) If a design is innovative or experimental, the architect is under a
duty continually to check the design as it develops.

14 (1987) 37 BLR 92, CA.
15 [1876] 2 Vict LR 157.

(c) The more novel the design, or the more serious the consequences of failure, the greater the obligation on the architect to ensure that his design is workable.

(d) If new or untried materials are selected the architect should research their suitability.

(e) If the architect's design relates to part only of the building, he should take into account the design and construction of the whole.

Delegation

In *Moresk Cleaners Ltd v Hick*[16] the defendant architect delegated the design of a building's reinforced concrete frame to a structural engineer. The court held that the architect was negligent in so doing since it was not ordinary practice for an architect to delegate his work on design and then disown responsibility for it. This view was supported by the Court of Appeal in *Nye Saunders v Bristow*.[17] Although the court accepted that it was prudent for an architect to consult a quantity surveyor on the ultimate cost of the project, he could not avoid responsibility for failing to draw to the client's attention the fact that inflation had not been taken into account.

If, however, a particular part of the design work requires specialist knowledge or skills beyond that which the architect possesses then he is at liberty to recommend to his client that an independent consultant with the necessary skills be appointed by the client. This is illustrated by the case of *Investors in Industry Commercial Properties v Bedfordshire District Council*[18] where the claim against the architects in respect of defective foundations failed because they had ensured that engineers were appointed to deal with the problems presented by nature of the ground.

Continuing duty to check design

An architect is under a continuing obligation to review his design and to correct any errors that emerge.[19] This is particularly so where the design is experimental or in need of amplification as the project progresses. If the design pushes at the frontiers of recognised building techniques, then its failure may not be indicative of negligence. If the consequences of failure are a threat to safety then the designer's obligation to ensure that his design is workable is increased accordingly. This is illustrated by the decision of the Court of Appeal in *Eckersley v Binnie*[20] which concerned the Abbeystead disaster,

16 [1966] 2 Lloyd's Rep 338.
17 (1987) 37 BLR 92, CA.
18 [1986] 1 All ER 787, CA.
19 *Brickfield Properties Ltd v Newton* [1971] 1 WLR 862.
20 (1988) 18 Con LR 1, CA.

where an accumulation of methane in the tunnel and valve house caused an explosion killing 16 people. The majority of the Court of Appeal held that the defendant engineers ought to have foreseen, at the design stage, that sufficient quantities of the gas could accumulate so as to give rise to the risk of explosion.

Untried materials

Most construction projects involve the use of materials that are familiar to all involved and there is no need to investigate their suitability. If, however, new or untried materials are to be incorporated the prudent architect should carry out sufficient research so as to be satisfied that they are appropriate for the job.

In *University of Manchester v Hugh Wilson*[1] the defendant architects designed a large group of buildings known as the Precinct Centre for the University. Their design called for a reinforced concrete structure clad partly in brick and partly in ceramic tiles. The design proved to be defective in that the tiles subsequently fell off. Judge Newey QC found that the architects were negligent for producing a design that was defective in many respects. In particular, it failed to protect the tiles from rain and gave insufficient attention to the building problems of fixing the tiles. Further, the architects had not inspected the fixing adequately. The judge did not find the architects to be in breach of duty for adopting a relatively innovative design. He said:

> 'It was not wrong in itself to use the relatively untried method of cladding with ceramic tiles but it did call for special caution. The architects should have warned the plaintiffs of the dangers inherent in using a new method.'[2]

In *Richard Roberts Holdings Ltd v Douglas Smith Stimson*[3] the defendant architects designed an effluent tank for the plaintiffs' dyeworks in Leicestershire. Unlike the plaintiffs' previous projects, no consultant engineer was involved with the design. Two quotations were received for different methods of the lining of the tank. The lower quotation was accepted by the plaintiffs after the architects had indicated their approval. The plaintiffs entered into a direct contract for the tank lining works and the architect did not charge any fee in respect of those works. The tank lining failed shortly after installation. The architects denied liability in respect of the tank, maintaining that they were not responsible for the design of the lining. Judge Newey QC held that the architects had been engaged to design the tanks and that had they wanted to limit their role they

1   (1984) 2 Con LR 43.
2   Ibid, p 74.
3   (1988) 46 BLR 50.

should have done so expressly in writing. They were negligent in that they had failed to investigate the lining proposed by the contractors or to advise the plaintiffs adequately before the contractors' quotation was accepted.

Design of part of building

In the case of *Carosella v Ginos and Gilbert*[4] engineers designed foundations without reference to the superstructure of the building. An Australian court held such a course to be negligent. In the more recent case of *Holland Hannen & Cubitts (Northern) Ltd v Welsh Health Technical Services Organisation*,[5] the Court of Appeal held that designers are not required to 'exercise due care and skill' beyond the limits of their own discipline. The case concerned the design of concrete floors for a hospital which were out of level. The majority of the Court of Appeal held that the engineers' design functions did not extend to the visual appearance of the floors. Dillon LJ said:

'. . . matters of visual appearance or aesthetic effect are matters for the architect and are not within the province of the structural engineer. It is for the structural engineer to work out what the deflections of a floor will be; it is for the architect to decide whether a floor with those deflections will be visually or aesthetically satisfactory when the finishes chosen by the architect have been applied.'

In a dissenting judgment, however, Robert Goff LJ expressed the view that the engineers should have ensured that the floor would have been acceptable.

Selection of contractors

Where the architect is responsible for recommending contractors, he may be under a duty to make reasonable enquiries as to their solvency and suitability for the work. In *Equitable Debenture Assets Corp Ltd v William Moss Group Ltd,*[6] the architects were found liable for failing to make sufficient enquiries about the sub-contractors who provided the curtain walling. In *Pratt v George Hill and Associates*[7] the defendant architects obtained tenders from two contractors for the construction of a bungalow for Pratt. The architects described the contractors as 'very

4   (1981) 27 SASR 515.
5   (1985) 35 BLR 1, CA.
6   (1984) 2 Con LR 1.
7   (1987) 38 BLR 25, CA.

reliable' and as a result Pratt entered into a building contract with one of them. In fact they turned out to be wholly unreliable: the Court of Appeal remarked that 'they appear to have done almost everything wrong'. The builders failed to complete the works and were required to leave the site. They commenced arbitration proceedings against Pratt and subsequently went into liquidation. Pratt claimed damages against the architects for negligently recommending the builders. The claim included sums paid to the builders upon certificates and the costs incurred in the arbitration proceedings.

At trial, the judge held that the architects were in breach of their duty to recommend a suitable, reliable builder and that the builders' lack of suitability led to the disastrous execution of the works. The Court of Appeal held that losses claimed by Pratt arose directly from the misrepresentation given by the architects which caused Pratt to make a contract with highly unreliable builders.

As this case illustrates, the consequences of contracting with inappropriate contractors are seldom limited to, for example, bad workmanship or incomplete work. In order to avoid liability for the cost of a contract that goes badly wrong, the architect should investigate whether the contractors have the resources and skills necessary to execute the proposed works.

Architects should also take care at the tender stage of the contract. In *Hutchinson v Harris*[8] the architects were found to be negligent for failing to put house conversion works out to competitive tender. If the architect is considering and advising upon the tenders submitted by contractors, he should watch out for excessive quantities and inflated prices, and not recommend their acceptance.[9]

Selection and administration of building contract

With the increase in the number of standard forms of building contract available, the architect's client may look to him for guidance when selecting the appropriate form. This is more likely to be the case if the client has little experience of contracting. Although there are cases where the employer has failed to complete the contractual formalities to his cost, for example in *Temloc v Errill Properties*[10] where the insertion of '£nil' against the provisions of liquidated damages, was held by the Court of Appeal to mean that the employer was not entitled to any damages at all for late completion, there is little authority upon what is expected from an architect at this stage of the project.

8 (1978) 10 BLR 19.
9 *Tyrer v District Auditor of Monmouthshire* (1973) 230 EG 973.
10 (1987) 39 BLR 30, CA.

The editors of *Keating on Building Contracts*[11] suggest that the architect should give general advice including practical guidance on the advantages and disadvantages of particular forms and their pitfalls. He should ensure that the appendices and all blanks in the standard form are completed and the requirements complied with. They suggest that the architect should advise that the contract be entered into as a deed so as to give the employer additional protection of a 12-year limitation period. Where, however, the architect's recommendations are of a legal nature, particularly with regard to amending the standard form or drafting particular terms, the architect should either seek legal advise himself or, better still, ensure that the client does so.

Once the contract has been let, the terms of most standard forms empower the architect to administer the contract by issuing certificates, notices or opinions in writing. The architect's duties include the issuing of instructions requiring variations, extending time for completion of the works, ascertaining any loss and expense payable to the contractor for prolongation or disruption and issuing certificates for payment. The architect is obliged to take care when exercising these various functions.

In *Croudace Limited v London Borough of Lambeth*[12] Judge Newey QC held that an architect, in that case the defendant borough's chief architect, was obliged to consider the plaintiffs' claim for loss and expense. Since the architect had retired before the contractor's claim had been determined, and had not been replaced, the architect had failed to comply with that obligation and since he was acting as the defendant's agent, the defendants were liable for breach of contract.

In *Fairclough Building Ltd v Rhuddlan Borough Council*[13] the Court of Appeal suggested that an architect should renominate a replacement sub-contractor's contract, within a reasonable time. If the time taken to make such a renomination was not unreasonable then the main contractor would normally have no remedy for any delay caused as a result.

In *London Borough of Merton v Stanley Hugh Leach Limited*[14] Vinelott J held that the architect owed a duty to the employer and the contractor to estimate the amount of delay and grant an extension as soon as he is aware of any delaying factors, irrespective of whether the contractor has applied for an extension of time. In that case the parties entered into a JCT 63 Standard Form of Contract. The wording of the relevant clause, now clause 25, has been changed in JCT 80. It is a matter of some debate, whether the architect is obliged to consider the giving of an extension of time whether or not the

11　5th edn, 1991, p 322.
12　(1986) 2 Construction LJ 98.
13　(1983) 30 BLR 26, CA.
14　(1985) 32 BLR 51.

contractor has applied for one.[15] Contractors tend not to be slow off the mark in giving notice that they have been delayed. Seldom, however do they give the sort of detail required by clause 25 as to the effect of the relevant event and the likely delay caused thereby. The usual response from the architect is to ask the contractor for this detail together with supporting information and to do nothing further until it is received. It seems from *Leach* that the architect ought to consider the contractors application whether or not it is supported by detail and substantiation and to give an extension of time if it is reasonable to do so.

It is not clear when an extension of time ought to be granted. The authorities vary depending upon the nature and cause of the delay. In *Miller v London County Council*[16] the court held that an extension should be granted within a reasonable time after the delay had occurred and before completion of the work. In *Anderson v Tuapeka County Council*,[17] the court held that an extension of time should be granted at the same time as extra works were required. In *Amalgamated Building Contractors Ltd v Waltham Holy Cross Urban District Council*,[18] delay was caused by the shortage of labour and materials. The court held that the architect was entitled to grant an extension of time after the delay had ceased and if necessary after the original completion date.

The authorities were reviewed in *Fernbrook Trading Company v Taggart*[19] and can be summarised in this way. If the delay is caused by events for which the employer is responsible and the effect of which is easily ascertainable then an extension should be awarded at the time. If the delay is caused by events over which the employer has no control, or its duration is uncertain, then the extension should be given a reasonable time after the relevant factors have been established. Where there are multiple causes of delay there may be no alternative but to leave the final decision until just before the issue of the final certificate. In any event, the contractor should be informed of his new completion date as soon as it is reasonably practicable.

In *West Faulkner & Associates v London Borough of Newham*[20] the defendants met the plaintiff architects' claim for fees with counter allegations of negligence. They said that the architects had failed to issue a notice under JCT 63, clause 25 stating that the contractors had failed to proceed regularly and diligently with the works. The contractors' performance was very poor and although they generally had sufficient men and materials on site, they were so disorganised and inefficient that their progress was extremely slow. Had the architects issued a notice under clause 25, Newham would have been

15 See Keating (5th edn) p 570.
16 (1934) 151 LT 425.
17 (1900) 19 NZLR 1.
18 [1952] 2 All ER 452.
19 [1979] 1 NZLR 556.
20 (1992) 9 Constr LJ 232.

able to determine the contractors' contract. Without a notice they had to negotiate an agreement with the contractors that they would leave the site. Judge Newey QC held that since the contractors' failures were so very extreme, the architects ought to have realised that they were not proceeding regularly and diligently and were in breach of contract for failing to give a notice to that effect.

When considering the architect's functions under the building contract the guiding principle is that he exercise his discretion fairly, holding the balance between his client and the contractor.[1] Further, the architect is obliged to issue instructions and information required for the execution of works within a reasonable time.[2]

Supervision

An architect owes his client a duty to supervise or inspect the works with a view to ensuring that they are carried out to the standard contracted for.   The number and frequency of the architect's inspections will depend upon the circumstances of each case and the terms of the particular contract.   Reasonable supervision has been defined as such supervision as would enable the architect to give an honest certificate that the work had been executed according to the contract.[3] In that case the court held that the architect should inspect principal parts of the work before they are covered up and require the contractor to notify him before an operation is carried out which would prevent inspection of an important part of the works.

An architect is not required, however, to examine every detail on site and failing to discover a defect which reasonable examination may have disclosed is not necessarily negligent. In *Cotton v Wallis*[4] the Court of Appeal held that a certain degree of tolerance must be allowed for in determining the quality of work supervised although this did not necessarily give the architect a general dispensing power. It is well established that an architect is not obliged to stand over the contractor whilst he carries out the work or to instruct him how to go about it. The case of *Clayton v Woodman and Son (Builders) Ltd*[5] shows that an architect is generally under no duty to tell the contractor the manner of performance of his work or what safety precautions to take. If, however, he sees that the contractor is failing to take special precautions which would be necessary to reduce the risk of personal injury or damage to property he may owe a duty to warn the contractors of the consequences.[6]

1   *Sutcliffe v Thackrah* [1974] AC 727.
2   See generally, *Hudson's Building and Engineering Contracts* (10th edn, 1970, supp 1979).
3   *Jameson v Simon* (1899) 1 F(Ct of Sess) 1211.
4   [1955] 1 WLR 1176, CA.
5   [1962] 1 WLR 585.
6   See generally, *Jackson and Powell on Professional Negligence* (3rd edn, 1992) para 2.102.

The relationship between the architect and the quantity surveyor in the preparation of interim valuations and inspections was considered in detail by Judge Stabb QC in *Sutcliffe v Chippendale and Edmondson*.[7] In particular he was concerned with the question: to what extent, if any, is a quantity surveyor obliged to take into account the fact that the work is defective in certain respects when he comes to prepare a valuation of it? The trial judge had the benefit of a considerable body of expert opinion as to what in practice was required of an architect and quantity surveyor. He concluded:

> 'I readily acknowledge and accept that any prolonged or detailed inspection or measurement at an interim stage is impracticable and not to be expected. On the other hand, . . . the issuing of certificates is a continuing process, leaving each time a limited amount of work to be inspected and I should have thought that more than a glance around was to be expected. Furthermore, since everyone agreed that the quality of the work was always the responsibility of the architect and never that of the quantity surveyor and since work properly executed is the work for which a progress payment is being recommended, I think that the architect is in duty bound to notify the quantity surveyor in advance of any work which he, the architect classifies as not properly executed so as to give the quantity surveyor the opportunity of excluding it.'[8]

Sutcliffe can be relied upon as authority for the following two propositions, namely first that the quality of the contractors work is the responsibility of the architect and not of the quantity surveyor and second that the architect should inform the quantity surveyor of defective work before the latter prepares his valuation.

Certification

An architect owes a duty to his client to take care when issuing certificates. That duty was considered by the House of Lords in *Sutcliffe v Thackrah*.[9] They held that the architect owed a duty to act in a fair and unbiased manner and to reach decisions fairly, holding the balance between the client and the contractor. They reiterated the point, however, that an error in certification may not necessarily be negligent.

In *Lubenham v South Pembrokeshire District Council*,[10] architects were found to have been negligent for issuing incorrectly calculated

7 (1971) 18 BLR 149. This case was subsequently appealed to the Court of Appeal and the House of Lords under the name of *Sutcliffe v Thackrah* [1973] 1 WLR 888 and [1974] AC 727, HL.
8 (1971) 18 BLR 149 at 165. See also the commentary at 151 ff.
9 [1974] AC 727, HL.
10 (1986) 33 BLR 39, CA.

interim certificates. The architects had certified in respect of the total value of work carried out, irrespective of whether it had been done properly and had subsequently sought to make a deduction for defective work. It was accepted that the defective work ought to have been taken into account when computing the total value of work properly executed. Further the architects had made deductions in respect of liquidated damages even though, at the date of the certificates, the contractual date for completion had not passed. The Court of Appeal upheld the judge's decision that the architects' breaches had not caused the losses claimed. The judge had found that the partner in the architects' firm had honestly believed that liquidated damages could be deducted and had acted in what he believed to be the best interests of his client. The Court of Appeal were of the view that, had the architect deliberately misapplied the contractual provisions and sought to make such deductions in order to penalise the contractor, the contractor may have a claim against the architect for interfering with the performance of the building contract. Whether such a claim could still be made in the light of their subsequent decision in *Pacific Associates v Baxter*[11] is open to question.

If the contract provides that the quality of materials and standards of workmanship for some of the works is a matter for the architect's opinion, as opposed to being specified in the contract, the case of *Colbart v H Kumar*[12] suggests that a final certificate may be conclusive evidence of the architect's satisfaction of all materials and workmanship where approval is inherently something for the opinion of the architect.[13]

Damages

The general principle governing the award of damages is that they are *compensatory*, ie the award of damages is to compensate the plaintiff for the loss which he has suffered. The thrust of the enquiry here is to determine what loss the plaintiff has suffered which has been caused by the actionable wrong on the part of the defendant. If, notwithstanding a breach of contract on the part of the defendant, the plaintiff has suffered no loss, then the law awards him *nominal* damages conventionally assessed at £2 or £5. On the other hand, with a few rare exceptions, the law does not award *punitive* or *exemplary* damages in order to punish the defendant: this is properly the province of the criminal and not the civil law.[14]

11 [1990] 1 QB 993.
12 (1992) 59 BLR 89.
13 But see the commentary at 59 BLR 90 for a contrary view.
14 *Broome v Cassell* [1972] AC 1027.

But not all losses suffered by the plaintiff and caused by wrong on the part of the defendant will be recoverable by way of damages. Detailed rules have developed which limit the losses recoverable in any given case. In particular two principle factors determine what losses are compensated for by an award of damages. First, the nature of the cause of action and second, the surrounding facts as known to the parties. It is only when these two matters have been established that it is possible to determine whether any particular loss will result in an award of damages.

There is a further principle which limits the recovery of damages, namely the *mitigation of loss*. This principle provides that a plaintiff may not recover any part of his loss which could have been avoided by taking reasonable steps to do so. But provided that the plaintiff acts reasonably and prudently in the circumstances in which he finds himself, he will be able to recover all of his losses, even additional losses which have been caused inspite of his own reasonable actions.[15]

Damages recoverable in contract and in tort

The rules regarding the recovery of damages differ according to whether the cause of action arises for breach of contract or in tort, for example negligence. In general, the rules applying to a breach of contract are more favourable to a plaintiff than those applying to tort. This is one of the reasons why, if he has a choice, a plaintiff will often prefer to bring his action in contract rather than in tort.

Contract

This branch of the law is still governed by the old case of *Hadley v Baxendale*.[16] The rule there stated by Alderson B divides the relevant test into two limbs:

'Where two parties have made a contract which one of them has broken the damages which the other ought to receive in respect of such breach of contract should be such as may fairly and reasonably be considered either arising naturally, ie according to the usual course of things from such breach of contract itself or such as may reasonably be supposed to have been in the contemplation of both parties at the time they made the contract, as the probable result of it.'

Under the first limb damages are recoverable for any loss which arises naturally, that is according to the usual course of things, from

15 *British Westinghouse v Underground Railways Co* [1912] AC 673.
16 (1854) 9 Ex 341.

the breach of contract. It is not necessary that the defendant actually contemplated that the particular loss would result from his breach of contract so long as a reasonable man situated as the defendant was would have considered that the loss was liable to result. Thus, under the first limb, knowledge of certain basic facts surrounding the transaction in question is imputed to the parties but not any special or particular knowledge. In *Hadley v Baxendale* itself the court held that loss of profits from being unable to perform contracts caused by the late delivery of a mill wheel shaft arose under the first limb.

Damages under the second limb are recoverable, even if the losses do not arise naturally and according to the usual course of things, provided that they arise from circumstances communicated to the defendant at the time the contract was made. Thus, in *Hadley v Baxendale*, it was held that the loss of profits on especially lucrative contracts were not recoverable by way of damages since it was not established that, at the time of the making of the contract, the defendant knew about these particular contracts.

The principles derived from *Hadley v Baxendale* have been reasserted by the courts on countless occasions and can be regarded as firmly established in the law.[17]

Limitation By virtue of the Limitation Act 1980, ss 5 and 8, a claim in respect of a breach of contract becomes statute barred at the expiry of six years or 12 years respectively from the date of breach, according to whether the contract was a simple contract or one executed as a deed. The cause of action arises at the date of the breach whether or not any loss is then caused or whether the plaintiff knows about the breach. This rule is unfavourable to the plaintiff for it can lead to the unjust situation where the plaintiff's claim becomes statute barred before he was aware that a breach of contract had been committed or that it had caused him any loss. Contrast the position in tort which is more favourable to the plaintiff (see next section).

Tort

The general principle in tort is that damages are recoverable in respect of losses which were reasonably foreseeable by a reasonable man in the position of the defendant at the time the tort was committed. But this general principle has been restricted in the case of the tort of negligence so that generally damages are only recoverable in respect of *physical* damage either to the person or to' the property of the plaintiff caused by the act of negligence.[18] Recently the House of Lords had affirmed that the principle of *Donoghue v*

17 See, for example, *Koufos v Czarnikow* [1969] 1 AC 350, HL.
18 *Donoghue v Stevenson* [1932] AC 562.

Stevenson applies to negligence in relation to the construction of buildings. In particular, it has been held that as regards the plaintiff's property, damages are only recoverable in respect of damage caused to 'other property' of the plaintiff, ie not including the building itself which was negligently constructed.[19] This area of law is bedevilled by confusing terminology but, save where special circumstances exist leading to a particularly close relationship between plaintiff and defendant, where an act of negligence causes damage to a building the following classes of loss are recoverable as damages in tort:

(a) Physical damage to property of the plaintiff other than the building itself;
(b) Personal injury to the plaintiff;
(c) Economic loss, for example repair costs or loss of earnings, consequential upon the physical damage in the first two categories.

The following categories of loss are *not* recoverable in such circumstances:

(a) Economic loss arising from physical damage caused to the very property which was the subject matter of the act of negligence;
(b) *Pure economic loss*, ie economic loss unrelated to any physical damage to person or property.

Before damages in respect of *pure economic loss* to be recoverable in negligence it is necessary to show a special relationship of proximity existing between the plaintiff and the defendant which may exist, for example, where the plaintiff has relied upon the defendant's advice or where the defendant has voluntarily assumed responsibility to the plaintiff. It is thought that, in a normal contractual relationship between client and architect, a special relationship of proximity will exist, leading to recovery of pure economic loss should the plaintiff bring his claim in negligence.

Limitation In negligence the cause of action arises, not when the wrongful act takes place, but when the damage caused by that act occurs. This rule was confirmed by the House of Lords in *Pirelli General Cable Works v Oscar Faber & Partners*.[20] In that case the defendants, a firm of consulting engineers, advised the plaintiffs on the design of a factory including the provision of a chimney. The chimney was built in June/July 1969. The defendants' design of the chimney was negligent with the result that, in April 1970, cracks developed at the top of the chimney. This physical damage was

19 *Murphy v Brentwood District Council* [1991] 1 AC 398, [1990] 3 WLR 414, HL.
20 [1983] 2 AC 1, HL.

actually discovered by the plaintiffs in November 1977 and they issued their writ against the defendants (thereby stopping the limitation period from running) in October 1978. The cause of action for breach of contract was plainly statute barred since more than six years had passed between the date of the breach of contract in 1969 and the issue of the writ in 1978. The House of Lords held that the cause of action in negligence was also statute barred because that cause of action arose in April 1970 when physical damage caused by the negligence first occurred, ie over six years before the issue of the writ.

In this area of the law the critical enquiry concerns the date when the physical damage which triggers the cause of action first occurs. The facts of the recent case of *Nitrigin Eireann Teoranta v Inco Alloys Limited*[1] illustrate this point well.   In June 1981 the defendants manufactured and supplied to the plaintiffs alloy tubing to be used in a chemical plant producing various chemicals.   In July 1983 the plaintiffs discovered cracks in a section of the works made from the alloy tubing.   The plaintiffs, without discovering the cause of the cracking, repaired the tube by grinding out the crack. On 27 June 1984 the tube burst causing a methane gas explosion which disabled the plant.   On 21 June 1990 (just under six years from the date of the explosion) the plaintiffs issued their writ claiming damages on account of the defendant's negligence in the manufacture of the alloy tubing.   May J held that the plaintiff's cause of action in negligence did not arise in 1983 when the cracking occurred since the cracking was simply damage to the pipe itself constituting a defect of quality resulting in economic loss irrecoverable in negligence.   The plaintiff's cause of action in negligence arose when the tube burst in 1984 causing the explosion and accordingly it was not statue barred.

The injustice of the operation of the rule in negligence whereby a plaintiff's claim can be statute barred before he is even aware that he has suffered any loss, has been greatly attenuated by the passage of the Latent Damage Act 1986. Under this Act the limitation period in tort (but not in contract) becomes three years starting from the date when the plaintiff had both the knowledge required for bringing an action in respect of the relevant damage and had the right to bring such an action.   But the Act also provides a 'long stop' period of 15 years from the date of the act of negligence beyond which no action may be brought whatever the plaintiff's injuries. Curiously, were the facts of the *Pirelli*[2] case to occur today, the plaintiffs would still fail, not now on the ground of limitation, but on the basis of *Murphy v Brentwood District Council*[3], namely that the plaintiffs have no claim in negligence in respect of the pure economic loss. Indeed the House of Lords' decision in *Murphy*'s case has removed the main anomaly which the Latent Damage Act 1986 was intended to correct.

1   [1992] 1 WLR 498.
2   *Pirelli General Cable Works v Oscar Faber & Partners* [1983] 2 AC 1, HL.
3   *Murphy & Brentwood District Council* [1991] AC 398, [1990] 3 WLR 414, HL.

Measure of damages

Once it has been established that a particular head of loss is recoverable in principle, the enquiry turns to the assessment of the damages to be awarded. This assessment is known as the *measure of damages*. There are a number of typical heads of loss which frequently arise in the field of construction: they will be considered in turn.

Defective building work or design

Where building work has been designed or carried out defectively, the usual measure of damages is the cost of remedial works, ie the cost of reinstatement.[4] Thus provided that it is reasonable to carry out remedial works and the plaintiff proves that he has already done so or that he intends to do so, the cost of appropriate remedial works would be the measure of damages. Less commonly, the proper measure will be the diminution in value of the building, ie the difference between its value were there no defects and its value in its defective condition. This will be the proper measure where the plaintiff has no intention of carrying out works of reinstatement or where it would be unreasonable for him to do so because, for example, the cost of such works would be disproportionate to the extent of the defect.[5]

Betterment Three quite distinct situations must be contrasted under this head. First, where, for example, the design was defective but, had it been sufficient at the outset, the plaintiff would have had to pay additional costs in having the proper design executed. In such a case the plaintiff will usually have to give credit against the damages recoverable for such notional additional cost.[6] The second situation arises where appropriate remedial works can only reasonably be carried out in one way but the finished result produces a better building than previously existed, for example by replacing old with new. In such a case the plaintiff does not have to give any credit, for the advantageous position in which he finds himself has been caused by his acting reasonably as a result of the defendant's breach.[7] The third situation arises where the plaintiff has a choice in the nature or extent of remedial works carried out and he chooses a more expensive or extensive method. In such a case the plaintiff must give credit for the ensuing *betterment*, ie the damages will usually be assessed on the basis of the less expensive but reasonable repair costs.

4 *East Ham Borough Council v Bernard Sunley & Sons Limited* [1966] AC 406.
5 *CR Taylor v Hepworths* [1977] 1 WLR 659.
6 *Bevan Investments v Blackhall and Struthers* (1977) 11 BLR 78.
7 *Harbutt's Plasticine Limited v Wayne Tank & Pump Co Limited* [1970] 1 QB 447.

Loss of profit / wasted expenditure

Provided that the loss falls within either the first or second limb of the rule in *Hadley v Baxendale* [8] loss of profit incurred by the plaintiff in being unable to use the building will be recoverable from the defendant. But the plaintiff must prove that the use to which he intended to put the building would have been profitable to him. Alternatively, the plaintiff may claim the recovery of his expenditure wasted as a result of the defendant's breach of contract. But the wasted expenditure may only be recovered from the defendant if the plaintiff would have been able to recover it as profit if the contract had been performed This is an example of the principle of damages being intended to put the plaintiff in the same position that he would have been in had the contract been performed. The plaintiff may elect between claiming loss of profit or wasted expenditure, but he cannot recover both.

Contractor's claims for delay or disruption

If an architect, in breach of contract, fails to give to the contractor the necessary drawings or details in good time or gives instructions or orders variations late so that the contractor is caused delay and disruption, then, in principle, the client can recover from the architect the amount of such claims payable to the contractor. The assessment of such claims is usually difficult in practice particularly where there are concurrent or competing causes for the delay or disruption in question.

Inconvenience

Generally damages in respect of inconvenience or annoyance caused by the defendant's breach of contract are not recoverable in law on policy grounds[9] exceptionally however, where the contract in question concerned the plaintiff's own home, damages can be awarded to compensate the plaintiff for the distress and inconvenience of being kept out of his home or having to live in distressing conditions. But, conventionally, the measure of such damages is low.[10]

Date of assessment

Two different situations should be contrasted. First where, at the date of trial, the plaintiff has carried out the necessary remedial

8 (1854) 9 Ex 341. See above at pp 71-72.
9 *Hayes v James & Charles Dodd*, (1988) Times, 14 July.
10 *Hutchinson v Harris* 1978) 10 BLR 19.

works and second, where he has not done so. In the first case, the plaintiff will recover the costs of remedial works actually incurred provided that the plaintiff did not delay unreasonably in having them carried out. In the latter case, the court will enquire as to when it would be reasonable for the plaintiff to carry out remedial works and assess damages as of that date. That date may be in the past or in the future, depending on the circumstances, but the actions of the defendant, particularly in denying liability, will be relevant.[11] Where, at the date of trial, the plaintiff has already expended money on remedial costs, then, in addition to the award of damages, the plaintiff will usually be awarded interest at a commercial rate under the Supreme Court Act 1981 from the date when the expenditure was incurred until the date of judgment.

Apportionment of damages

The plaintiff may have his damages reduced if he has contributed to his loss by his own fault. Under the Law Reform (Contributory Negligence) Act 1945 the court may reduce the plaintiff's damages as it considers 'just and reasonable' if the necessary conditions are met. But the Act may only be relied upon by a defendant where the plaintiff claims in tort or, although the claim is in contract, the defendant's contractual liability is the same as his liability would be in tort independently of the contract.[12] In this context the term *contributory negligence* merely refers to the fault of the plaintiff and not breach of a duty of care owed by him to the defendant. Thus the rules applying to the tort of negligence are irrelevant here.

Another means by which the defendant may reduce his liability to pay damages is pursuant to the Civil Liability (Contribution) Act 1978. Under this statute a defendant who is liable to the plaintiff may seek a contribution towards the damages payable from any other person also liable to the plaintiff in respect of the same damage whether that liability arises in contract, tort or otherwise. If the party against whom a contribution is sought is not already a party to the action, the defendant may join him as a third party and, at the trial, the court may make an apportionment between the defendant and the third party according to what it considers to be just and equitable in all the circumstances of the case. This Act does not affect any express or implied rights to contribution or indemnity which may exist in the contracts between the various parties to a development. But the 1978 Act is a powerful weapon available to a defendant who is the only person from whom the plaintiff seeks to recover damages, in circumstances where there are other persons also liable to the plaintiff.

11 *Dodd Properties v Canterbury City Council* [1980] 1 WLR 433.
12 *Vesta v Butcher* [1989] AC 852, [1986] 2 All ER 488, CA.

Chapter 3

The practising architect

Hugh Cawdron

Background

The work of practising architects is as varied as the buildings that they are called upon to create. Post war reconstruction created a period of intense building activity, particularly in the fields of industrial development and local authority housing. The Festival of Britain in 1951 is seen by many as having been a benchmark which opened the eyes of professionals and laymen alike to the importance of design in everyday life.

Yet with this innovative spirit also came something of a curb on the relative freedom that the architect in private practice had previously enjoyed. Traditional methods of building continued but active encouragement was given to the use of prefabrication which had a profound effect on the building industry as a whole. Not only was the architect required to design within the technological constraints laid down by specialist manufacturers of structural components, but also to adopt unfamiliar techniques and to use materials that were often new and untried.

The architect, therefore, even if it was thought necessary to employ one, became secondary, often doing little more than advising on the integration of buildings, predominately made from scheduled components, within an environmental framework laid down by the now well established and powerful town planning authorities. Now, 30 years on, we are all too familiar with the failings of this unfortunate era.

In recent years, a dramatic rise and fall in speculative commercial developments has placed additional and at times almost unbearable strains on the building industry. It has been a period in which substantial attempts to change if not overthrow the traditional professional teamwork in favour of contractor led design management, with the architect pushed even further into the background.

Competition for work is now intense, contractors often bidding at cost or even below in order to secure a contract in the expectation that they will be able to exploit any failings or omissions in the tender documentation and subsequent production information.

For a contractor to prepare a design and build submission is a costly process and invariably leaves much to be assumed, any shortcomings are hoped to be passed on to the client or back to the sub-contractors. There is an increasing tendency for contractors to withhold payments due to their sub-contractors who, in turn, seek to make maximum economies in their performance.

Clients also find themselves in considerable difficulty on realising that their development is not proceeding as quickly as intended or is running over cost or that their investment, conceived in boom years, is now worth only a fraction of the anticipated return.

Architects therefore are placed under severe pressure from both parties, often having to cope with contractual demands for additional payments and extensions of time, and client requests to delay practical and final certification of building in order to offset interest charges on a development that is slow to let. If that is not enough, the architect can become the fulcrum of dispute particularly if it is considered that there may be grounds for complaint of inadequate performance.

Running parallel to all this is the marked change in the way in which architects receive their training. Long gone is the highly practical but physically wearing combination of working in the day and studying at night and weekends. Practising architects are not predominant among the tutorial staffs in colleges and universities. Students receive very little practical training prior to graduation and few, if any, will have had any experience other than that gained from the obligatory 'year out' during which, at best all they can hope for is to scratch the surface, of the complexity of modern working practice, before arriving after a further two years at the point where they are legally entitled to call themselves architects and assume their full responsibilities.

The appointment of an architect

The Royal Institute of British Architects has published guidance for members and their clients in respect of conditions of engagement for many years. The early editions were simple documents and presumably adequate for the purpose at the time. A more comprehensive version appeared in 1966 and, in July 1982, the Architect's Appointment, often referred to as the 'Blue Book', appeared as a 24-page edition.

This was a considerable improvement on its predecessors and, for the first time, drew attention to the need for architects not only to agree with their clients the nature and extent of their involvement but to formally record their appointment.

By February 1990, this document had been amended seven times in attempts to meet the challenging requirements of professional services and an increasing litigious environment for all those involved in the building industry.

It had become apparent that architects cannot afford to act without clarity of instruction and that they must take the lead in describing with precision the professional services they can offer for the price they seek when providing that service. It is not only common sense for this to be recorded in a properly formulated agreement, it is also a requirement of the RIBA Code of Professional Conduct.

A new form of agreement was required which would be flexible enough to meet the needs of practices ranging from the smallest to the largest and which would be capable of being customised to fit any particular requirement arising within that range.

In the autumn of 1989, by reason of presidential initiative involving the Royal Institute of British Architects, the Royal Institute of Architects in Scotland, the Royal Society of Ulster Architects and the Association of Consulting Architects, a review group was formally set up and given the task of formulating a new set of documents which would allow architects to set out clearly, precisely and comprehensively the range of services which clients are demanding in today's competitive market.

The group conducted a lengthy process of consultation and referral to ensure that the consensus for, and therefore the authority of, the new document was as comprehensive as possible. A considerable amount of feedback about content and format was incorporated into a series of draft documents, each an important improvement or refinement of the last. After detailed scrutiny by legal experts, the document was submitted for general approval to the four Institutes and, after further modification, was passed to RIBA Publications for publication.

The 1982 Architect's Appointment

It should not be thought that the 1982 Blue Book, as it has come to be known, is now discontinued, for the intention is for this to be published until at least 1995 and reference to it will be made for many years to come, as parties in conflict look within its pages for justification for their grievances or defences.

I have always regarded the Blue Book, like the curate's egg – 'excellent in parts.' Unfortunately, in my experience, impending litigants search for the parts which are vague and therefore best suited to their case and I make mention of these not to denigrate the publication, which was essentially a compendium of good advice, ways and means with methods of charging, but to expose the weaknesses which I have encountered time and time again when instructed to advise either architect or client.

The foreword

This states the intention of the publication as being to help achieve a clear understanding of the client's requirements, the nature of the service to be provided and the responsibilities of all involved.

The role of the client is described as an important one: to provide adequate information on the project, site and budget and to understand fully and approve the architect's proposals at the various stages of the work as it proceeds.

The introduction

This states that the RIBA requires of its members that, when making an engagement for professional services, they shall define and record the terms of the engagement including the scope of the service, the allocation of responsibilities and any limitation of liability, the method of calculation and remuneration and provision for termination.

It then explains the structuring of the *Architect's Appointment* into four parts.

Part One, Architect Services comprises preliminary and basic provisions by the architect divided into eleven work stages, A-L (omitting I to avoid possible numerical confusion).

Part Two is concerned with augmenting services which may be provided and which are subject to a separate appointment, usually charged on a time or lump sum basis.

Part Three sets out the conditions which apply to an architect's appointment.

Part Four deals with recommended fees and expenses, the method of calculation and apportioning between work stages. This part also includes a sample Memorandum of Agreement and Schedule of Fees. A concluding paragraph recommends that client and architect should discuss the appointment and agree in writing the services, conditions and fee basis which should be stated in the memorandum or, alternatively, be the subject of a formal letter of appointment.

Before entering into a more detailed appraisal of the Blue Book, I would draw particular attention to a paragraph in the introduction which refers to the *RIBA Plan of Work*, upon which the work stages are based.

I have always though it unfortunate that the Plan of Work is not given greater prominence for, had it been, many recent cases involving disputes between client and architect might have been avoided. I have often wondered how many clients have been made sufficiently aware of this booklet to have requested a copy and read it. For that matter, how many architects have offered copies to their clients or, indeed, studied and applied the suggested procedures themselves to any meaningful extent? My experience would suggest very few.

Because of the significance of the Plan of Work, a brief description of it will not waste the reader's time and I shall make detailed reference to some of the contents later.

The *RIBA Plan of Work* was originally published in the first edition of the *RIBA Architect's Handbook* in 1965. Its intention was to provide a model procedure for methodical working of the design team and also to serve as a framework for other sections of the handbook and to be applicable to projects which have sufficient common factors to make it widely relevant.

Reference is made to another RIBA publication, *The Architect's Job Book*, which provides detailed means of ensuring relevant actions are not overlooked.

Part 1

Part One of the Blue Book sets out to describe preliminary and basic services which an architect would normally provides divided into a serious of work stages.

Work stage A

This describes the inception of a commission; the brief; information to be provided by the client; site appraisal by the architect who will advise on the need for other consultants' services, design work by specialist firms and the need for site staff, and who will prepare, where required, an outline timetable and fee basis for further services, all for the client's approval. In other words, the architect sets up a client liaison arrangement for briefing in order to prepare a general outline of requirements and plan future action.

This work stage provides little more than an aide memoir to the obvious discussion and activity to be expected during the preliminary stages of architect and client introduction and involvement.

Work stage B

This is concerned with feasibility and I have come to regard this as an inadequate, unsatisfactory paragraph which in five short lines requires of the architect such studies as may be necessary to determine the feasibility of the client's needs; to review with the client alternative design and construction approaches and cost implications; and to advise on the need to obtain planning permission, approvals under building acts or regulations and other similar statutory requirements. This is intended to provide the client with an appraisal and recommendation in order that he may determine the form in which the project is to proceed, ensuring that it is feasible functionally, technically and financially.

This can, and often does, constitute a very considerable amount of work and expense by the architect, who will probably be required to carry out studies of user needs, site conditions, planning, design and cost, etc, as necessary, to reach a decision. The study could involve client, architect, engineers, quantity surveyors and accountants, according to the nature of the project, a fact which is not always recognised by the client. It is unlikely that any formal arrangement for payment for such work has been agreed at this time, particularly concerning the time to be spent on such activity and therefore the first seeds of dispute are sown.

Work stage C

This is the first section of the Blue Book to be accorded the status of a Basic Service (whatever that might mean) and to be charged on a percentage basis: 15% of the total fee. It consists of three lines and states that the architect, with other consultants where appointed, should analyse the client's requirements and prepare outline proposals and an approximation of the construction cost for the client's preliminary approval.

According to the *Plan of Work*, the purpose of this stage is for the architect to determine the general approach to layout, design and construction which entails developing the brief further – carrying out studies on user needs, technical problems, planning, design and costs as necessary to reach decisions – in order to obtain authoritative approval of the client on the outline proposals and accompanying report.

Work stage D

Work stage D, scheme design, is even more unsatisfactory for it is only a little less vague than its predecessor and yet more than doubles the proportion of the total percentage fee to 35%. I have on several occasions been involved in cases in which serious disagreement has arisen between architect and client as to the interpretation and worth of the three paragraphs which make up this stage.

Briefly, stage D states that, with other consultants where appointed, the architect is to develop upon work stage C, taking into account amendments requested by the client to prepare a cost estimate and where applicable give an indication of possible start and completion dates for a building contract. This scheme is to indicate the size and character of the project in sufficient detail to enable the client to agree the spatial arrangements, materials and appearance. The client is entitled to receive advice on the implication of any subsequent changes on the cost of the project and the overall programme and where required, the architect will make application for planning permission although sensibly, as this is beyond the architect's control, there can be no guarantee this will be granted.

The *Plan of Work* is somewhat more forthcoming and states that the purpose of work stage D is for the architect to compete the brief and decide on particular proposals including planning arrangement, appearance, constructional methods, outline specification and cost, and to obtain all approvals. All this could entail the final development of the brief, full design of the project by the architect, preliminary design by the engineers, preparation of cost plan and full explanatory report and submission proposals for all approvals.

I find some difficulty in separating the requirements and expectations of work stages C and D. Unless the client is familiar with the *Plan of Work*, he can be excused from enquiring what exactly has been done in order to qualify for a third of the total fee, particularly as this is based on an assessment of overall cost by the architect.

I was recently asked to advise in a case where an architect, with minimal brief and who had not clearly set out his terms and conditions other than to refer loosely to the Blue Book, had prepared, over the course of a few weeks, drawings showing various configurations of housing on a large inner city site to which he had put a construction cost of £10.5m. The client, whilst acknowledging that work had been done on his behalf, not unnaturally refused to pay the requested fee of £220.500 on the grounds that the scheme did not illustrate the character of the project in sufficient detail for him to agree a special arrangement, materials and appearance, and in the belief that, because the architect had not consulted him properly throughout the preparation stages, and had not negotiated with the local authority and other statutory bodies (including British Rail and the highways authority in respect of a major motorway) the likelihood of obtaining planning consent was minimal.

This may be an extreme instance, but I have known many more, albeit of lesser financial import, which have caused a great deal of worry and expense to the parties concerned.

Work stage E

This is concerned with detailed design where an architect, with other consultants where appointed, will develop the scheme design, obtain client's approval of the type of construction, quality of materials and standard of workmanship; co-ordinate any design work done by consultants, specialist contractors, sub-contractors and suppliers; and obtain quotations and other information in connection with specialist work. The architect will also carry out cost checks as necessary; advise the client on the consequences of any subsequent change in the cost and programme: and make and negotiate, where required, applications for approvals under building Acts, regulations or other statutory requirements.

In my experience, a conscientious architect will thoroughly earn the cumulative 55% of the total fee during this stage, where the scene is set for the proposed development. If the work has been competently done, there should be little difficulty in obtaining the necessary consents and proceedings without undue problem.

According to the *Plan of Work*, the architect will have obtained a final decision on every part and component of the building by collaboration with all concerned, on every matter related to design, specification, construction and cost, and all cost checking will have been completed.

I am bound to observe that it is unlikely that an architect will find it possible to achieve this idealistic state of affairs at this stage. I know from my own experience that it is often quite impractical to design every part and component of a building at this time and it is unlikely that those entrusted with specialist roles will be in a position, even if they agree, to bring their design work to a stage of completion as suggested here.

It should be realised that work stage E precedes application for approvals under building Acts, regulations and other statutory requirements and that it is likely that tenders will not have been sought at this time. These items alone are capable of causing major changes in the detailed design of a building. It is therefore unwise to progress the state of drawn and described information on the overall project, only to have to reconsider and possibly waste some of it in the process of complying with requirements which, more often than not, are impossible to avoid.

Work stages F and G

These are given one title in the Blue Book, 'Production Information and, Bills of Quantities'. I do not understand why this should be so and, in my experience, this can be the cause of further misunderstanding. The paragraph requires the architect, with other consultants where appointed, to prepare production information including drawings, schedules and specifications of materials and workmanship; provide information for bills of quantities, if any, to be prepared; and to present all information complete in sufficient detail to enable a contractor to prepare a tender.

The *Plan of Work* does not assist very much in defining this activity, merely stating that it is to prepare production information and make final detailed decisions to carry out the works. One could be forgiven for querying why a work stage F is necessary when it is so akin to its predecessor, E.

The ideal and, I believe, the intention of this paragraph is to prepare at this time all the drawings and specifications which will be required throughout the course of the works. In fact this is rarely achieved, because of the near certainty of changes occurring as a result of amended requirements, and subsequent input of specialist information obtained by the contractor and, as often happens, the need to design to accommodate reductions in costs.

It has been my experience that some architects interpret this paragraph as being little more than tidying up the drawings they had prepared for work stage E, supplementing them by specification notes, usually in response to questionnaires, and passing the package over to the quantity surveyor for preparation of a bill of quantities. This can lead to serious problems, both at the onset and throughout the course of the works.

Quantity surveyors are usually careful and disciplined people, capable of describing and measuring the material and work content of a building in great detail, but they are not designers. Nor should they be expected to work out construction techniques which are the entire responsibility of the architect or other technical specialists.

Time and time again, when researching cases concerned with professional negligence, I have found that the architect has failed to specify materials and workmanship properly, if he has done at all, leaving this for the quantity surveyor to include somewhere in the bills.

The quantity surveyor and the contractor are entitled to know precisely what the architect requires and, if this information is not forthcoming at the appropriate time, assumptions will be made and misunderstandings will arise as a result. The architect will undoubtedly find the need to issue confirmatory or new instructions during the course of the works and these will be eagerly seized upon by a contractor who is out to exploit just such a situation, either financially or as an excuse for poor performance, or both.

The same applies to inadequate drawings. I can understand up to a point but cannot excuse the attitude of some architects that, provided the contractor has enough to make a start, the remainder of drawings and schedules can be made and issued during the progress of the works.

Clearly, if the contractor is made aware initially that, say, certain walls and doors are to be painted in the final decoration stage of the building, the details of the colour scheme will not be required until shortly beforehand, which will give the architect an opportunity of assessing the spatial and lighting conditions of the interior and allowing the reflectivity and weight of colours to be selected accordingly in order to achieve the desired effect.

Conversely, if the architect does not, very early on in the contract, supply adequate information on, for example, services which may include long delivery, such as radiators, special lighting fittings or selected sanitary ware, or establish the requirement to run drains and ducts throughout the building, thereby affecting the structure, late detailing can be the cause of serious delays and avoidable extra cost to the contract.

I have been involved in a number of cases where the architect's appointment was limited to the completion of work stages F & G. Invariably there have been problems in that the contractor finds the production information is insufficient or incomplete or contradicting, particularly when there is no mechanism for continuing consultation between the parties. It is not unusual for an architect to seek, by way of particular clauses in the specification, or notes on the drawings, to pass full responsibility for the implementation of the production information on to the contractor, with the intention of limiting the responsibility of the practice, if not totally exonerating it.

In my opinion, this is at best wishful thinking and exposes the architect to a claim of negligence in respect of any work done which is subsequently found to be incorrect or impractical. Likewise, the termination of an architect's engagement at the completion of work stage E leaves the contractor a relatively free hand and total responsibility to detail, programme and construct within the disciplines imposed by the overall design of the project. Passing the baton from architect to contractor at or around work stages H and J is almost bound to result in some mishandling and upset, and so prevent what would have been a smooth continuity of the run to the finish.

I believe that it is the duty of architects to make sure their clients understand the continuity problems involved and, if still insisted upon by the client, reach a proper and sensible agreement as to how the transition is to be made and to clarify the precise terms of respective responsibility.

Work stages H and J

These are concerned with the action required by the architect in respect of obtaining tenders for the project works; assisting the successful contractor to programme the work in accordance with the contract conditions; and making arrangements for it to commence on site. These are all operations which are relatively straightforward and, where appointed, the quantity surveyor and other consultants will take an active role.

In respect of programming. I am becoming increasingly aware of the real problems which can and do arise because the architect has not included in the tender documents a requirement for the contractor to supply a considered master and trade programme in respect of the project works, before a start is made or, where this a stated requirement, such as clause 5.3.1.2 of the JCT Standard Form, 1980 edition, to insist that it is complied with before a contractual commitment is made.

I cannot stress too highly the need for the architect to make time to examine such programmes carefully, together with the contractor, and to make sure they are realistic in terms of trade sequence, duration, availability of services and materials, and that they are set out in such a way as to enable the almost inevitable claim for an extension of time on the contract to be capable of accurate assessment.

Although an architect is not required to, and should not, agree the sequential trade operations forming a construction programme, (which is entirely the responsibility of the contractor) it should be considered carefully and questions should be asked, particularly if the individual operations appear to be unrealistic in duration or conflicting with others. The architect should also be satisfied that any contingency requirements have been included and shown as such. For example, if an existing drain is known to cross the area of building excavation or is believed to be in a condition which may require reconstruction, this should be assessed and included in the programme as a contingency operation, even if it means that the contract completion date may be set back as a consequence. It is far better to be realistic about these things than to invite disagreements about extension of time later on.

Because of the high level of liquidated and ascertained damages often now required by employers, claims of this sort are taking up an increasing amount of court and arbitration time, for they are potentially lucrative to one party or the other.

Work stage K

This relates to operations on site and is set out in three short sentences which require the architect to administer the terms of the building contract; visit the site as appropriate to inspect generally the progress and quality of the work; and, with other consultants where appointed, make where required periodic financial reports to the client including the effect of any variations on the construction cost.

I sometimes wonder whether the person or committee responsible for drafting this section of the Blue Book had ever been closely associated with a building in the course of construction or had any real understanding of the amount of technical, financial or contractual work and responsibility which is often entailed, not to mention the duration of such a process.

I doubt whether anybody with such experience would have written such bland lines and awarded such a low proportion of the overall fee, 25% only and this also includes stages H J and L.

The *Plan of Work* is even more matter of fact in stating that the purpose of the work and decisions to be reached is 'to follow plans through to practical completion of the building'. Really!

It has been my experience over the years that stage K as described in the Blue Book, has led to the highest incidence of claims against architects for professional negligence.

For six years following the publication of the 1982 Architect's Appointment, the companion reference was *The Architect's Job Book* (4th revised edition). This is probably still retained and consulted in many professional offices, because it sets out the activities required of an architect clearly, progressively and concisely. It is also referred to quite often during the course of litigation concerned with professional negligence claims, where the architect was appointed prior to 1988, the year of publication of the fifth edition, which should now be regarded as current reading.

In Section K: Operations on Site, the action checklist provides the following advice, with particular reminders given in bold print:

'Job administration
  – Keep client regularly updated on progress and financial position as works proceed; adopt client's procedure/format if required.
  – Make sure that client confirms in writing any instructions for varying the works; advise about related fees.
  – Provide client with estimates of cost variations arising from changes.
  – Obtain from client supplementary financial approvals as required.
  – Establish scope of maintenance manual and related fees.
  – **Initiate and maintain relevant Job Record.**
  – Record of defective work.
  – Record of site delays observed.
  – Schedule of claims by contractor.

Design team and reports:
  – Maintain liaison through architect's meetings.
  – Coordinate work required to implement client's changes into instructions to the contractor.
  – Maintain regular progress and financial reports to client.
  – **Maintain relevant Job Record.**

Contract:
- Regularly monitor the contractor's progress reviewing it fully at each progress meeting.
- Regularly check with clerk of works and consultants that full records for building owner's manual are being kept.
- Hold regular architect's progress meetings and regulate inspection visits.
- Maintain formal minutes and distribute without delay.
- Meet contractor on site to note setting out, including boundaries, location of the works, temporary units etc, spoil heaps.
- Attend contractor's production meetings, if asked.
- Nominate any outstanding suppliers and sub-contractors.
- Provide drawings, specifications instructions etc in accordance with contractor's "information required programme". Review regularly.
- Visit site as necessary to meet contractor and clerk of works and to inspect the site; issue instructions as necessary. Occasionally make unannounced visits.
- Liaise with clerk of works and with consultants.
- Liaise with quantity surveyor to maintain cost control against variations and for cost forecasting for monthly report.
- Notify quantity surveyor of any work against which monies must be withheld or where an 'appropriate deduction' from the contract sum is to be made.
- Respond quickly to contractor's requests for information.
- Adjudicate claims fairly and promptly. Liaise with consultants as necessary. Issue notifications under relevant clauses stating events which have been covered. Inform client.
- Authorise dayworks where justified.
- In the event of the contractor being in default, advise the employer of his rights to determine the employment of the contractor.
- Maintain general inspection and liaise with consultants to initiate programme for commissioning and performance testing.
- Remind employer of the need to appoint maintenance staff in time to attend commissioning.
- At the appropriate time compile list of outstanding items for internal use to prepare for handing over the works to the employer. (These must not be sent to the contractor.)
- Maintain architect's records for as-built drawings etc for building owner's manual.
- Should the employer require partial possession, advise him of the contractual implications and proceed as instructed.

- **Initiate/maintain relevant Job Record forms eg:**
  Architect's Instructions issued.
  Record of defective work.
  Schedule of claims by contractor.

Watchpoints:
Acquire a good understanding of the contract. Not only does the architect have many duties and responsibilities under it but he must be able to interpret it fairly between the contractor and client without fear or favour.

All instructions to the contractor should be in writing on an Architect's Instruction Form. Establish an invariable rule in your office about this.

Keep instructions up-to-date to avoid difficulties with the contract and to ensure that cost appraisals are realistic. **Never instruct the contractor how to carry out his work.**

Progress meetings are for management, site meetings for technical matters. Site inspections must be methodical; it helps to devise checklists related to the stage of work. Allow adequate time on site to examine each item properly.

All meetings, visits, discussions should be recorded and copied to interested parties. In assessing contractor's subsequent claims (or even threats of litigation) these records will prove invaluable and more than justify the effort required to maintain them. Use site visit memorandum form and keep up-to-date the relevant Job Record forms.

Be punctilious about valuations and payment of certificates. Ensure that any work not properly carried out is notified to the contractor in writing and copied to the quantity surveyor so that he can deduct its value from valuation.

Do not let contractor's claims fester, deal with them at once.

The client depends upon the architect to report progress and events. **Provide regular financial reports and agree any changes proposed to the works.**

The contractor should supervise his own works in order to conform with the contract requirements. **The architect's duty is to inspect the works.**

Make sure that the contractor and consultants are aware that any commissioning must be completed and

operating manuals available before the building is handed over.

Start a system for listing outstanding items (for office use) to monitor progress towards completion. **Finishing a contract needs special effort and this must be pursued with vigour.**

Variations may attract claims for extensions of time. This risk is particularly high when claims occur near the completion date.

The client will want to be given basic as-built drawings. Get these together in good time; the clerk of works can help.

Remember to maintain Job Record forms:
>   Enter information as soon as it becomes available; do not delay.
>   Remember to date each action and note the source/authority as appropriate.
>   Check that all contributors supply the required information, or the value of the Job Record will be lost.'

Work stage L

Again, three short sentences enjoin the architect to administer the terms of the building contract related to completion of the works; to give general guidance on maintenance and to provide the client with a set of drawings showing the building, main lines of drainage; and to arrange for record drawings of building services.

The Architect's Job Book lists the following activities under the sectional heading 'Completion':

'Job administration:
  – Inform client of proposed handover date and procedures.
  – If necessary, advise client about his own contractor and staff operations for occupation in relation to the building contract.
  – Remind client of his need to insure the building and contents before occupation.
  – Advise client about the release of retention monies.
  – Advise client on availability of maintenance contracts following the period of maintenance covered by the contract.

  – **Initiate project completion and assessment forms.**
  – Record of completed project.
  – Assessment of project.

Design team and reports:
- Review requirements to enable handover at practical completion (for part or all of the works) including arrangements for client's own contractor's access and facilities within the building.
- Establish with the client the scope of any additional works now required and agree the appropriate contractual procedures to follow practical completion.

Contract:
- Ensure that the works generally and commissioning of all engineerings systems is proceeding to own and consultant's satisfaction.
- Obtain contractor's forecast date for practical completion.
- Initiate pre-completion checks on the works with the clerk of works.
- Check that contractor maintains his programme for commissioning and liaise with consultants.
- Arrange for client's maintenance staff to attend commissioning tests.
- Ensure that contractor arranges for all maintenance staff to be properly instructed on operation M & E and other specialist installations provided for in the contract.
- Remind contractor that M & E and other operating manuals are to be checked, completed and handed over at practical completion.
- Check that the works will be ready for handover meeting and that works programme is realistic.
- Hold handover meeting.
- Provide client with building maintenance M & E and other operating manuals and as-built drawings as agreed.
- Issue Certificates of Practical Completion with schedule of defective items and work still to be satisfactorily completed, referring to and maintaining relevant Job Record forms.
- Ensure consultant's own schedules of defective works are issued within 14 days.
- Issue certificate (if relevant) to release part of retention monies etc.
- If necessary, review procedures concerning non-completion under the contract, issue certificates and notices if relevant.

- **Refer to relevant Job Record forms, eg:**
  Architects Instructions issued.
  Record of defective work.
  Record of site delays observed.
  Schedule of claims by contractor.

- Advise client of his right to deduct liquidated damages from architect's certificate if contractor defaults on completion.
- Agree programme with contractor and client for remedial works to the occupied building.
- Check that any making good required under the contract is completed.
- Prepare drawings, programme, instructions for client's additional works, cost check with quantity surveyor and/or contractor and obtain client's agreement.
- Inspection of additional and remedial works as necessary; notify contractor of defects within period stated in the contract.
- Receive contractor's notice that remedial works are complete.
- Carry out final inspection of the works (in phrases or total) and **only if completely satisfied** issue Certificate of Completion of Making Good Defects and certificate to release retention monies where applicable.
- Help to resolve any outstanding financial and other differences.
- Complete final account and send to contractor for agreement, then send to client with explanatory notes as necessary.
- Issue Final Certificate when all outstanding contractual issues are resolved.

- **Complete relevant Job Record Forms eg:**
  Defects reported under practical completion.
  Record of completed project. Assessment of completed project.

Watchpoints
It is the architect's duty to assess practical completion. **Be careful to avoid conflict arising from the client pressing to occupy a building before it is completed.** It may be necessary to negotiate partial possession or occupation before completion but remember that principals do not give up their rights easily.

Remind the client of his responsibility for the building as soon as it is handed over in terms of insurance, security, maintenance.

Make sure that operating manuals have been properly checked and are ready by the time of the handover meeting. If they are not, retention monies may be considered or, in particular circumstances, the handover delayed.

The architect's own manual should also be ready. Check the accuracy of it. Basic drawings are essential and may have to be supplemented with information on structural performance, provisions for extension or changes, or for alternative occupancy.

Do not issue a Certificate of Practical Completion or of Completion of Making Good Defects of the Final Certificate until you are sure that there are no associated issues still outstanding.

Complete Job Record forms.'

It has been suggested to me that these lists are idealistic. This is possibly so, overall, and some of the checks may never arise to be dealt with, but there is always the possibility and the prudent architect will be prepared for them.

The problems that can and do arise during the construction stages of a building can be varied, numerous and far reaching. H B Creswell in his book *The Honeywood File* managed to describe the situation in a light-hearted manner but I found very little humour in the cases which have come to my attention over the years. I refer the reader to my comments on site inspection later on in the chapter.

Part 2

Part Two of the Blue Book describes services which may be provided by the architect to augment those of Part 1, or which may be the subject of a separate appointment.

This part is divided into six sections which, briefly, are these:

Surveys and investigations

These involve advice on the selection and suitability of sites, negotiations in respect of them, measured surveys, preparation of plans, soil investigations, inspections of condition of property, preparation of schedules of dilapidations, structural surveys, investigation and advice on building failures, restoration work, advice on the performance of buildings and valuations.

Development services

These entail the preparation of special drawings, models or technical information, negotiation with ground landlords, adjoining owners, public and licensing authorities, development of estate plans, details of roads and sewers, advice on demolitions and environmental studies.

Design services

Design services in respect of furniture and fittings, shop fittings and exhibition works, selection and/or commissioning of works of art, acoustic investigations, special constructional research and building system and component advice and evaluation.

Cost estimating and financial advisory services

These include cost plans and cash flow requests, schedules of rates and quantities, cost of replacement and grant applications.

Negotiations

Conduct exceptional negotiations with planning and other statutory authorities, prepare for, advise and submit planning appeals, make other submissions, submit building plans for agreement of landlords, mortgagors, freeholders and others and advise on the rights and responsibilities of owners and lessees in various respects including party wall negotiation. Prepare and give evidence in litigation and arbitration.

Administration and management of building projects

Provide site staff for frequent or constant inspection of the works, project management, services to client whether employer or contractor, or in connection with separate trade contracts, supervise client direct labour arrangements, provide as built drawings, maintenance and operational manuals and contracts etc.

These cover a very wide ranging port folio of activities, some of which, I suggest, are beyond the usual training and expertise of many architects who would be well advised to consider very carefully their ability to undertake such commissions, if offered, in case they find themselves involved in matters for which they are neither trained nor familiar.

Since the publication of the Blue Book in 1982, the requirement of the architect to provide 'other services' has lengthened particularly to embrace new forms of contracts and other contemporary needs which extend even further the scope of activity with might be pertinent to the practising architect.

Part 3

Part Three describes the conditions which normally apply to an architect's appointment and lays down important ground rules to be observed by client and architect alike.

Authority

This establishes that the architect will act on behalf of the client whose authority will be obtained before initiating any service or work stage. This is an important proviso, because the proportion of fee charged can jump quite substantially from one stage to another over a short period of time and, unless the client is kept informed and understands the situation, objections may well be raised and requests for payments disputed.

Another important discipline is the obligation of the architect not to make material alterations, additions or omissions from a client's approved design without his knowledge or consent, except if this is found necessary during the course of construction, in which case the architect shall inform the client without delay.

Similarly, the architect must keep his client fully appraised of the total expenditure on the works and any variation in the likely duration of the contract.

These matters are often of intense interest to a client who may well be budgeting both time and money to fine limits in order to justify his investment. I have known cases where an employer has remained unaware of these matters, even after honouring intermediate certificates of payment to the contractor, only to be faced with an impossible *fait accompli* when architects' intermediate certificates exceed the contract figure.

In my experience, there are few clients who do not appreciate their architects keeping them in very close touch with day to day events. An architect who does not do so, by means of regular written appraisals, is denying his client the opportunity of stating his concern and giving appropriate instruction on how he wishes to proceed within the terms of the contract.

Consultants

Consultants may be nominated by either the client or the architect, subject to acceptance by each party. Where the client employs a consultant, either directly or through the agency of the architect, the client will hold each consultant, and not the architect, responsible for the competence, general inspection and performance of the work entrusted to that consultant. However, it is made clear that such arrangements shall not affect the responsibility of the architect for issuing instructions or for other functions ascribed to the architect under the contract.

The architect maintains the authority to co-ordinate and integrate into the overall design the services provided by any consultant, however employed.

This is an important proviso for even a simple building embracing, say, a reinforced concrete frame and traditional brick cladding will have many interfaces between the two, each of which require to be detailed properly. For instance, where a structural beam projects as a feature on an elevation, the engineer's drawings should incorporate a weathered top surface with an underside drip recess. Some engineers, in my experience, object to incorporating what they regard as 'architectural features' on their drawings. In all probability, the contractor will erect the frame using the engineer's drawings only and the shuttering carpenter will follow the profiles shown thereon. If these do not include weatherings and drips, they will not be provided and it will then be left to the architect to settle a time-wasting and costly dispute as to how these may now be incorporated, even if that is possible.

As well as professional consultants, the architect may find himself in a design relationship with specialist sub-contractors. In essence, the same rules apply. He has a duty to co-ordinate, within the extent of his expertise, what is reasonably to be expected of a competent architect.

For example, an architect should not be expected to know precisely the intricate mechanical detailing of joints and fittings of a large window walling system, but he would be expected to be aware that such an area of metal and glass would be subject to considerable thermal movement and that perimeter abutments with, say, solid masonry, would require to be designed to accept such movement without compromising the weather resisting seals, by reason of over stretching or over compression. He may not himself feel competent to design such a movement joint, but he would know where suitable advice was to be found. It would be his responsibility to ensure that the joint be detailed, either on the drawings of the window sub-contractor, or on his own.

The architect assumes a fair degree of responsibility in respect of such co-ordination and should be aware of this from the commencement of design work. It is essential that, as leader of the team, the architect discusses, agrees and records the precise framework into which each consultant fits and maintains regular checks by way of minuted project meetings to ensure that everybody is complying with the overall plan of work and that the interfaces between the work of one consultant and another are clearly defined.

Part 4

This covers recommended fees and expenses which are relatively straightforward and understandable. The Blue Book ends with the all important Memorandum of Agreement and Schedule of Services and Fees.

Memorandum of Agreement and Schedule of Services and Fees

Recent research has found that many architects appear to be afraid of referring to their appointment as a contract and obtaining anything in writing at all. However, it is very important that their appointment should be confirmed sufficiently to establish, without doubt, the scope of the work for which they have been engaged and the basis of remuneration.

I would urge those who intend to continue the use of the Blue Book, in respect of new commissions, to ensure that the memorandum document, a specimen of which is shown in the final pages, is completed, signed and exchanged with the client. The act of so doing will certainly concentrate the mind as to the full extent of the architectural services being offered and accepted, the remuneration for them and, importantly, the specific exclusions which are also just as necessary to record. It should be borne in mind that, by a peculiarity of English law, if a service is not excluded from a contract document, a professional can be considered to have included it within those others which have been perceived as the normal range of activity.

Contractor, sub-contractors and suppliers

This provides for specialist involvement of such parties in respect of design input to any part of the works, provided both client and architect agree. This is an obvious but important proviso. I have known a number of instances where a client has imposed a specialist, against the advice of an architect, and thus caused real problems.

In particular, I recall a case where an architect designed a large, fully centrally-heated house and where, shortly before completion was due, the client introduced an interior designer who promptly proposed the installation of a coal effect gas fire in the living room, where no flue had been constructed. As part of his decor, it was agreed that the fire should be placed on an inside wall, the beaten copper hood being connected to a duct consisting of asbestos board lining above ceiling level and running between two first floor joists to the external wall where an electric fan, wired to a thermostat, would start up when the fire was lit.

The initial testing of the arrangement appeared successful but on a cold night, when the ceramic Derby Brights were ablaze and the housewarming party in full swing, guests became aware of suffocating fumes and, shortly thereafter, fire broke out in the bedroom above, requiring the hasty summoning of the fire brigade and the even more hasty retreat of the revellers.

The cause of the conflagration was established as being due to the melting of the plastics fan blades from heat, which reduced the flue extract to almost nothing. The client sued the architect whose defence was that the responsibility lay with the interior decorator who had, in the meantime, returned to his home in Spain. A pyrogenic expert was called, who gave evidence to the effect that the fire was caused by reason of heat transmittance through the clout nailed fixings of the lining to the timber joists; an unlikely theory in my view but one which persuaded the plaintiff to discontinue his action.

This somewhat unusual and bizarre case was not so amusing at the time, particularly for the architect who, if still practising, will no doubt be keen to ensure that condition 3.9 is fully complied with on each new commission.

Site inspection

I think it is now becoming recognised that the architect does not provide 'site supervision', although some lawyers continue to prefer this to be the case and incorporate the words into their pleadings. It is the contractor's responsibility to supervise the works in accordance with the drawings and specification and subsequent instructions, and to provide sufficient plant, materials and labour under his control so to do.

Published architects' conditions of engagement prior to 1971 referred to an architect obligation to provide 'site supervision'. Later editions required the making of 'such periodic visits to the site to inspect generally the progress and quality of the work and to determine if the work is proceeding in accordance with the contract documents'.

It seems to me quite remarkable that, although two decades have elapsed since the term 'supervision' was expunged from the conditions, it is still referred to in the context of an architect's duties during the construction works – usually by lawyers but on occasions by architects themselves – rather in the way that some still refer to the defects liability period as the 'maintenance period' which, of course, it is not.

Nevertheless, it is my experience that in actions against architects, plaintiffs or claimants rely heavily on the duty of inspection to prosecute cases of poor construction, and I suspect as long as architects employ the Blue Book and the particular wording of condition 3.10, this will remain the case, for who can define what are 'intervals appropriate to the stage of construction'?

This is an involved subject and one which undoubtedly occupies an excessive amount of court and arbitration time. I have given my opinion on work stage K earlier in this chapter and space does not allow me here to pursue the subject, other than to give a few pointers which, in my experience, frequently emerge in litigation.

Architects, knowing that a full inspection is virtually impossible, should concentrate on making maximum use of the limited time available by checking up on the more obvious and repetitive failures of builders, such as: mortar and debris in cavities; lack of wall ties; badly made cavity wall damp course trays with improperly made joints and absence of stopped ends and weepholes; inadequately formed chases at the top of asphalt skirtings and undersized fillets at the base of them; poor stacking and lack of protection to joinery and windows and doors; thin priming; inadequate bedding to glass in frames; inadequately supported service pipes; and many such items which can often be seen at a glance during a walk around a building and which are not easily covered up by the operative during such inspection.

Other elements of construction, often taken for granted but frequently in the forefront of complaint, not surprisingly relate to weathering and waterproofing and are more difficult to assess on a visit. Here the architect needs to rely to some extent on intuition.

For example, British Standard Code of Practice 144, Part 4, 1970: Roof Coverings states that on horizontal roof surfaces, asphalt should be laid in two coats to a total thickness of not less than 20mm.

On a recent investigation of a prestigious civic building roof, I found that of the total of 39 samples taken, thickness varied from 9mm to 18mm with an average of 14mm. Spreading of asphalt on a large roof takes several days and I submit that it would be 'an appropriate stage of construction' for an architect to pay an unannounced site visit to observe the depth of laying battens, to see bay edges and, if necessary, to instruct the asphalter to warm up and cut out a small sample of mid bay asphalt for measurement and, incidentally, to check whether it had been laid on the essential isolating felt.

If all is in order, no reasonable client would object to the small expense involved in making good the sample area but, should a defect be found, the opportunity presents itself immediately to take positive action to effect a full and proper remedy.

Condition 3.11 refers to the employment of a clerk of works, where frequent or constant inspection is required. Although he will usually be under the control of the architect, his presence does not excuse the architect from complying with the duty of inspection, although it will enable more of the work to be checked and in greater detail.

I have found, in a number of cases, that the employment of a clerk of works is regarded as an extension of the architect's involvement particularly if the clerk was engaged and paid by the architect. My advice, generally, would be for architects to insist that the appointment, employment and payment is a direct responsibility of the client. In this way there can be no dispute as to where loyalties lie, although a clerk of works should be regarded – and, in my experience, usually acts – as an independent and impartial inspector.

Similarly, an architect should consider carefully the requirement of condition 3.12 and the wisdom of appointing a member of his own staff to take residence on site during the course of the works. Although there can be considerable benefit from this, particularly if the contract is one of a intricate or high quality nature, such action can be claimed to extend the limits of work stages K and L enormously and the architect might find himself being considered as taking on the function of works supervisor. This should be resisted strongly, it being made plain that the description applies only to the contractor.

I am aware of a recent case where the architect, no doubt in the best interest of the development, set up a small office on site for the daily use of the job assistant who otherwise would have operated from the main office some distance away. Because of his presence on site, albeit without the formal designation of site architect, this was considered to have extended the architect's duty from periodic inspection to a full time role. It also encouraged the contractor to take the easy way out and use the architect as a means of obtaining ready answers to queries and problems, well within their ability and responsibility to solve for themselves.

Almost without exception, in my experience, contractors seek to require the architect to make pre-finishing inspections and issue lists of 'snags' to enable the work to be completed and I am constantly amazed at the willingness of architects to agree to such imposition on their time. It is the contractor's responsibility to bring the work to a state of complete finish before seeking the acceptance of the architect.

The 1992 Standard Forms of Agreement for the Appointment of an Architect, 'The Black Book'

The Blue Book, which I have described and commented upon in this chapter, has lasted, with revisions, for approximately a decade but does not now meet the requirements of a changing society which demands far more from those providing professional services. Times have changed, not only in respect of the nature of clients as patrons but in the style and type of commission and in the climate in which those commissions are offered. Nor has life stood still for architects, other members of the building industry, professions or general contractors.

The effect of the abolition of mandatory scales, the growth of consumerism and the recessionary nature of current economics have all led to pressures upon performance which lead inexorably towards litigation in many cases. It is therefore essential that architects organise their administration well. There is no comfort to be obtained from the courts or from arbitration, or from searching enquiries by expert witness if there is no formal agreement or contract relating to the services to be provided.

Architects, in my experience, are not renowned for their business acumen when it comes to their own appointment and often rely on agreements in various forms of their own whether by introductory

STANDARD FORM OF AGREEMENT FOR THE APPOINTMENT OF AN ARCHITECT

SFA/92

THE MEMORANDUM OF AGREEMENT
identifies the parties: states intentions,
defines nature, scope and cost of services
alternative form available if executed as a deed

definitions

**CONDITION
Part One**

common to all
commissions:
law of
contract;
obligation of
parties;
assignment;
sub-
contracting;
payment;
suspension;
resumption;
termination;
copyright;
dispute
resolution.

**CONDITION
Part Two**

specifically
related   to
matters con-
cerning design
of   building
p r o j e c t s
during work
stages A-H of
RIBA Plan of
Work

(pre-contract)

**CONDITION
Part Three**

specifically
related to mat-
ters concern-
ing   admin-
istration   of
building cont-
racts: inspect-
ion of works
during stages
J-L of RIBA
Plan of Work.

(post-contract)

**CONDITION
Part Four**

specifically
related to ap-
pointment of
c o n s u l t a n t s
and specialists
where archi-
tect is lead
consultant.

SCHEDULE 1

information to
be supplied by
the client.

SCHEDULE 2

sets out ser-
vices to be
supplied by
the architect.

SCHEDULE 3

sets out the
way payment
for service is
c a l c u l a t e d ,
charged and
paid.

SCHEDULE 4

client accept-
ance of ap-
pointment of
consultants,
specialists and
site staff.

letters or adaptations of the Blue Book which, although perhaps better than nothing, are not sufficient.

Increasingly, architects are being required to accept conditions laid upon them by their clients, some of which include terms which, while the architect may not fully understand them, can be extremely onerous. No one can stop a client from producing a bespoke form of appointment but, equally, there is nothing to prevent a prudent practitioner from examining such a document, with the example of SFA/92 alongside it, to highlight matters of concern.

The creators of SFA/92 have endeavoured to produce a fair but tough document between architect and client, who should both feel confident in the capacity of the other to bring the requisite skills to the meeting table and, having agreed upon their respective roles, incorporate them in a signed agreement. If it is has been completed thoroughly, the need should never arise to refer to it again.

They have covered much, if not all, of the ground which an architect is likely to traverse in the course of an engagement, by producing two main versions of SFA/92: those being for general practice use, which embrace supplements to meet specific needs of historic buildings, repairs and conservation; and the Design and Build documents, intended to meet the method of building procurement which is becoming increasingly adopted in the UK construction industry.

It is not my purpose to enter into detailed consideration of each document but simply to give a brief résumé of the contents, sufficient to enable the reader to understand in some measure what is now available for use and assess the advantages to be gained in practice by using the new forms on which so much effort has been expended on behalf of the profession.

General Practice Edition (with supplementary Schedules of Services)

Format

This is published in two editions: the 'RIBA Edition', and the 'RIAS Edition' for use in Scotland. For easy identification, the cover of the RIBA Edition is black with red and white lettering whereas the RIAS is black with yellow and white lettering. The only difference in the documents themselves is that in the RIAS Edition the alternative version of the Memorandum of Agreement (for execution as a Deed) has been specially drafted to conform with Scots law.

Complementary to these is the separately published SFA Guide to the Standard Form of Agreement for the Appointment of an Architect, resplendent in a bright red cover, the primary purpose of which is to provide architects with information and advice about the 1992 Standard Form for their appointment. The content of the Guide, however, is essentially factual and clients can be advised to refer to it where architects think this might be appropriate. Clients who are considering the appointment of an architect and wish to inform themselves about architects' services and conditions of appointment will also find the Guide helpful and as generally relevant to their own concerns as to those of architects.

In my view, the Guide is essential reading, not only to assist in the full understanding of the Agreement but in its own right. For example, the Guide sets out four indicative letters from architect to client, covering the subjects of preliminary appointment, a holding confirmation of preliminary agreement until the full agreement can be properly completed and signed, confirmation of amendment in respect of changes made following the signing and another example letter in the event of the architect's appointment being activated in stages, as site or other determinants are cleared.

Another section of the Guide offers advice on the method of charging, calculating percentage fees, time charges, lump sum fees and unit price fees, as well as the more unusual but apparently incoming method of obtaining payment by means of betterment fees, equity shares and incentives. Expenses, disbursements and other costs are set out in some detail.

In order to maintain a healthy cash flow and to enable the client to know his financial commitment at regular defined intervals, the Guide sets out two example programmes of charging.

The Guide provides five appendices as follows:

1   The SFA/92 documents: worked samples
   -   preliminary appointment for feasibility study
   -   the Memorandum of Agreement related to it
   -   the Conditions of Appointment and Schedules.
2   Alternative/supplementary Schedules of Services:
   -   in respect of community architecture
   -   historic buildings, repairs and renovation work, etc.
3   Summary of actions arising from the Conditions of Appointment
   -   defining in brief terms those required from both architect and client.
4   Notes for Architect negotiating an Appointment:
   -   collaboration: the client, the architect, the resources
   -   communication: speculative work, the briefing process, terminology, the timetable, written records, avoiding disputes
   -   negotiation: selecting services, consultants and specialists; fees

- agreement: use of SFA/92, warranties, varying the service, working in stages, client forms of appointment
- follow up: further information sources and feedback.

5 Survey of Fees:

As recommended fees are no longer published by the professional bodies, information obtained from a survey of the architectural profession in respect of jobs undertaken between 1985 and 1990 is given in relation to classified building types and the calibre of service provided by the architect. The results of fees charged as a percentage of construction cost are set down in table form.

In my opinion, this is particularly welcome information, for it is all too easy for an architect, negotiating for a project of a type which is unfamiliar or for which he has no current experience, to miscalculate the likely cost in terms of time and therefore fee value, without some reliable guidance. It is to be hoped that the RIBA will, from time to time, publish amendments to Appendix 5 which is, unavoidably, already out of date by five years or more.

Although I consider the Guide to be a valuable reference, SFA/92 comes with its own notes on use and completion. These explain that the Standard Form of Agreement consists of a set of documents which, taken together, should enable architect and client to express formally and unequivocally the agreement reached between them; the completed memorandum will signify common understanding and acceptance. It is in the interests of both parties that the agreement fully reflects their intentions and requirements.

These notes briefly describe the function and format of the documents and indicate the way they are best completed. In all cases, the schedules will be used as a basis for discussion and, in most instances, the architect will complete the documents to record the agreement reached with the client. Wherever possible, the details of appointment should be agreed sufficiently for the memorandum to be signed at the outset by both parties.

In the event of professional services requiring to be revised subsequently, the advice given is to record the variation in a formal amending letter which will then become part of the agreement. Attempts by the parties to amend the agreement itself could lead to confusion and misunderstanding.

Memorandum of Agreement

This appears at the front of the agreement although it cannot be completed and signed until the services and costs have been agreed and the details set out in the following schedules which, together with the conditions, must be attached to the Memorandum and clearly identified on each page as belonging to it. They are then incorporated into the agreement by reference.

The Memorandum identifies the project and the parties and states their intentions and agreement concerning the nature, scope and the cost of the professional services to be provided. The Memorandum will usually be signed as a simple contract but some clients may require it to be executed as a deed. An alternative version of the Memorandum is included for this purpose.

Of particular interest and significance are the following clauses:

> '5   No action or proceedings for any breach of this Agreement shall be commenced against the Architect after the expiry of . . . years from completion of the Architects Services, or, where the Services specific to building projects Stages K-L are provided by the Architect, from the date of practical completion of the Project.
>
> 6.1 The Architect's liability for loss or damage shall be limited to such sum as the Architect ought reasonably to pay having regard to his responsibility for the same on the basis that all other consultants, specialists, and the contractor, shall where appointed, be deemed to have proved to the Client contractual undertakings in respect of their services and shall be deemed to have paid to the Client such contribution as may be appropriate having regard to the extent of their responsibility for such loss or damage.
>
> 6.2 The liability of the Architect for any loss or damage arising out of any action or proceedings referred to in clause 5 shall, notwithstanding the provisions of clause 6.1, in any event be limited to a sum not exceeding £.....
>
> 6.3 For the avoidance of doubt the Architect's liability shall never exceed the lower of the sum calculated in accordance with clause 6.1 above and the sum provided for in clause 6.2.'

The Guide explains that Points of Agreement 5 and 6 provide an opportunity to limit the liability of the architect to the client in period of time, in maximum amount of damages payable and to a fair contribution depending on responsibility. The Limitation Act 1980 refers to periods of six years and twelve years from the date of a breach of contract, simple or deed respectively. In Scotland, the Proscription and Limitation Act 1973 refers to a period of five years from the date of discovery of damage.

Where architects provide a service which includes for work stages J-L as described in Part 3 of the conditions, practical completion under the building contract may not be achieved until a number of years after the date of the signed memorandum, and this should be borne in mind in discussions about a suitable limitation period.

Damages for breach of contract are unlimited in law and may include consequential losses. In no circumstances should a figure be entered under 6.2 which exceeds the insurance cover taken out.

Enquiries I have made with leading professional indemnity brokers indicate support for the Memorandum as a good development because it sets out at the beginning the intention of the parties who are contracting with each other.

In respect of clause B5, since the Memorandum of Agreement is a simple contract, the period of six years should be inserted. There may well be attempts from time to time to insert 12 years but, if that happens, obviously the form of the memorandum will have to be changed because it will require to be executed as a deed.

Clause B6 is regarded as a positive development which has come about to some extent from the insistence of some insurers that they wish a net contribution clause to appear in all appointments and therefore recommend that the architects' profession should insist on this clause or something similar being incorporated into all contract documents.

Concerning clause B6.2, the brokers' advice is that the figure to be shown in the Memorandum should be capped at the level of fees being charged by the architect and should certainly not be greater than the limit of indemnity under the architect's professional indemnity policy but this latter figure should not be taken as the norm because clearly there is much room for negotiating a sum in between the two amounts.

The advice I have to offer is simple: if in doubt, the architect should consult his PI insurance broker, constantly bearing in mind that the amount of cover available at the time of signing the Memorandum may not necessarily apply at the time a claim is made on it, which may be several years ahead.

Definitions

Two pages of useful definitions and explanations are provided.

The Conditions of Appointment

These have been conceived as an entity. They are in four parts, printed on one side of a spread sheet. Not all the conditions will necessarily apply to every commission. Part 1 applies to all, but Parts 2 and 3 only apply where the service entails design and/or administration of the building contract and site inspection. Part 4 only applies where the consultants and specialists are to be appointed.

Part One

Part One is common to all commissions and relates to the law of the contract; the obligations of the parties; assignment and sub-contracting; payment; suspension, resumption and termination; copyright; and dispute resolution.

It commences with the clear statement that the application of the appointment shall be governed by the laws of England and Wales, Northern Ireland or Scotland, whichever is appropriate.

The obligations of the parties are as follows:

'Duty of care: The Architect **shall** in providing the Services exercise reasonable skill and care in conformity with the normal standards of the Architect's profession.

Architect's authority: The Architect **shall** act on behalf of the Client in the matters set out or necessarily implied in the appointment.

The Architect **shall** at those points and/or dates referred to in the Timetable obtain the authority of the Client before proceedings with the Services.

No alteration: The Architect **shall** make no material
to service: alteration or addition to or omission from the Services without the knowledge and consent of the Client except in the case of emergency when the Architect shall inform the Client without delay.

Variations: The Architect **shall** inform the Client upon its becoming apparent that there is any incompatibility between any of the Client's Requirements; or between the Client's Requirements, the Budget and the Timetable; or any need to vary any part of them.

The Architect **shall** inform the Client on its becoming apparent that the Services and/or the fees and/or any other part of the Appointment and/or any information or approvals need to be varied. The Architect **shall** confirm in writing any agreement reached.

Client's representative: The Client **shall** name the person who shall exercise the powers of the Client under the Appointment and through whom all instructions to the Architect shall be given.

Information:	The Client **shall** provide to the Architect the information specified in Schedule One.
	The Client **shall** provide to the Architect such further information as the Architect shall reasonably and necessarily request for the performance of the Services: all such information to be provided free of charge and at such times as shall permit the Architect to comply with the Timetable.
	The Client **accepts** that the Architect will rely on the accuracy, sufficiency and consistency of the information supplied by the Client.
	The Client **shall** advise the Architect of the relative priorities of the Client's Requirements, the Budget and the Timetable and shall inform the Architect of any variations to any of them.
Decisions and approvals:	The Client **shall** give such decisions and approvals as are necessary for the performance of the Services and at such times as to enable the Architect to comply with the Timetable.
Architect does not warrant:	The Client **acknowledges** that the Architect does not warrant the work or products of others nor warrants that the Services will or can be completed in accordance with the Timetable.'

Assignment and sub-contracting Part One continues by setting out in two clauses the restriction that neither architect nor client shall assign the whole or any part of the benefit or in any way transfer the obligation of the appointment without the consent in writing of the other and that the architect shall not sub-contract any of the services without the consent in writing of the client, which consent shall not be unreasonably withheld.

Payment Payment for the architect's services shall be calculated, charged for and paid as set out at Schedule Three. This should be completed with great care. Where these are stated to be on a percentage basis then, unless any other arrangement has been agreed between architect and client and confirmed in writing, the fee shall be based on the total construction cost of the works. On the issue of the final certificate under the building contract, fees and/or expenses shall be recalculated but until that time, they should be worked out on the pre-tender cost estimate, or the lowest acceptable tender thereafter, or the contract sum.

There is provision for time and mileage rates for vehicles, agreed in Schedule Three, to be revised annually.

In the event of any change made to architect's services, client's requirements, the budget or timetable, or where the architect consents to enter into any collateral agreement, the form or beneficiary of which had not been agreed by the architect at the date of the appointment, the fees specified in Schedule Three shall be varied.

Similarly, lump sum fees and expenses may be varied.

Where the architect is involved in extra work and/or expenses which are not otherwise remunerated and caused by client variations to completed work or services, the examination and/or negotiation of notices, applications or claims under a building contract, delay for any other reason beyond the architect's control, then the architect shall be entitled to additional fees calculated on a time basis.

Other clauses continue in respect of the procedure to be followed where the architect carries out any part of specified services, expenses and disbursements.

The architect is under an obligation to maintain records of expenses and disbursements, to be made available to the client on reasonable request.

The timing of payment is set down and the client undertakes not to withhold or reduce any sum payable to the architect under the appointment by reason of claims or alleged claims against the architect other than of rights of set-off which the client may otherwise exercise in common law. In addition, the client undertakes not to withhold payment of the remainder of an account in the event of any item or part subject to dispute or question.

There is provision for the architect to receive interest on accounts unpaid at the expiry of 28 days from the date of submission.

Other clauses deal with the payment of the architect on suspension or termination of the appointment.

The client assumes responsibility for payment of value added tax on all fees, expenses and disbursements.

Suspension, resumption and termination The rights of both architect and client are covered in a further seven clauses in respect of inability of the architect to carry out the services in accordance with the timetable, suspension and/or resumption of performance by either party or termination of the appointment.

Copyright Copyright in all documents and drawings prepared by the architect and in any work executed from those documents and drawings shall remain the property of the architect.

Dispute resolution The final section of Part One requires, in England and Wales, that any difference or dispute arising out of the appointment to be referred by either architect or client to arbitration. The arbitrator shall be appointed by mutual consent of the parties or failing this, be nominated by the President of the Chartered Institute of Arbitrators. Variations of this requirement occur in Scotland and in Northern Ireland.

In Northern Ireland or Scotland but not, surprisingly, in England, it is a requirement of this appointment that the parties shall attempt to settle any dispute by negotiation and that no procedure shall be commenced until the expiry of 28 days after the notification has been given in writing by one to the other, of a difference in dispute.

The final paragraph makes the admirable suggestion that nothing contained in the appointment shall prevent the parties agreeing to settle any difference or dispute arising out of it without recourse to arbitration.

I am bound to observe that it has been my experience that there have been occasions where the parties in dispute have not been best served by resorting to arbitration as required by their agreements and their costs have certainly been considerably greater in this respect than they would otherwise have been by obtaining judgment in a court. I would advise that careful consideration be given to alternative means of dispute resolution and any decisions or alternative requirements be recognised and recorded as such at the time the appointment is made.

Part Two

Part Two relates specifically to matters concerning the design of building projects during work stages A to H of the *RIBA Model Plan of Work*.

The obligations of the parts are as follows.

'Architect's authority:	The Architect **shall**, where specified in the Timetable, obtain the authority of the Client before initiating any Work Stage and shall confirm that authority in writing.
Procurement for the Project:	The Architect **shall** advise on the options for the Procurement Method
No alteration to design:	The Architect **shall** make no material alteration, addition to or omission from the approved design without the knowledge and consent of the client and shall confirm such consent in writing.

Statutory requirements:The Client **shall** instruct the making of applications for planning permission and approval under Building Acts, Regulations and other statutory requirements and applications for consents by freeholders and all others having an interest in the Project and shall pay any statutory charges and any fees, expenses and disbursements in respect of such applications.

The Client **shall** have informed the Architect prior to the date of the Appointment whether any third party will acquire or is likely to acquire an interest in the whole or any part of the Project.

Collateral Agreements: The Client **shall not** require the Architect to enter into any Collateral Agreement with a third party which imposes greater obligations or liabilities on the Architect than does the Appointment.

Procurement Method: The Client **shall** confirm the Procurement Method for the Project.'

Copyright Part Two concludes with four clauses dealing with various conditions of copyright.

Notwithstanding the right of the architect to own the copyright of all documents and drawings prepared and any work executed therefrom, the client shall be entitled to reproduce the architect's design by proceeding to execute the project provided that:
– the entitlement applies only to the site or part of it to which the design relates;
– the architect has completed a scheme design or has provided detailed design and production information;
– any fees, expenses and disbursements due to the architect have been paid;
– this entitlement shall also apply to the maintenance, repair and/ or renewal of the works.
Where the architect has not completed a scheme design, the client shall not reproduce or execute it without the consent of the architect. Where the services of an architect have been limited to negotiating and making planning applications, the client may not reproduce the design without the consent of the architect, which shall not be reasonably withheld and after payment of any additional fees which may be incurred.

The architect shall not be held liable for the consequences of any use of such information except for the purpose for which it was provided. This is to safeguard the architect whose work may be applied beyond the intended purpose.

Part Three

Part Three relates specifically to matters concerning the administration of the building contract and inspection of the works.
The obligations of the parties are as follows.

'Visits to the Works:	The Architect **shall** in providing the Services specified in stages K and L of Schedule Two make such visits to the Works as the Architect at the date of the Appointment reasonably expected to be necessary. The Architect shall confirm such expectation in writing.
Variations to visits to the Works:	The Architect **shall**, on its becoming apparent that the expectation of the visits to the Works needs to be varied, inform the Client in writing of his recommendations and any consequential variation in fees.
More frequent visits to the Works:	The Architect **shall**, where the Client requires more frequent visits to the Works than that specified by the Architect in condition 3.1.1, inform the Client of any consequential variation in fees. The Architect shall confirm in writing any agreement reached.
Alteration to design only in emergency:	The Architect **may** in an emergency make an alteration, addition or omission without the Client's knowledge and consent but shall inform the Client without delay and shall confirm that in writing. Otherwise the Architect shall make no material alteration or addition to or omission from the approved design during construction without the knowledge and consent of the Client, and the Architect shall confirm such consent in writing.
Contractor:	The Client **shall** employ a contractor under a separate agreement to

	undertake construction or other works relating to the Project.
Responsibilities of contractor:	The Client **shall** hold the contractor and not the Architect responsible for the contractor's management and operational methods and for the proper carrying out and completion of the Works and for health and safety provisions on the Site.
Products and and materials	The Client **shall** hold the contractor not the Architect responsible for the proper installation and incorporation of all products and materials into the Works.
Collateral Agreements:	The Client **shall**, where the Architect consents to enter into a Collateral Agreement with a third party in respect of the Project, procure that the contractor is equally bound.
Instructions:	The Client **shall** only issue instructions to the contractor through the Architect, and the Client shall not hold the Architect responsible for any instructions issued other than through the Architect.
Site staff:	The Architect assumes the responsibility for recommending the appointment of site staff needed to carry out appropriate specified services and to confirm in writing to the Client their descriptions and the expected duration of their employment, and clarify who shall appoint them and the arrangements for doing so. Such site staff **shall** be under the direction of the Architect. [I would suggest that the Architect should, in addition, clarify in writing to the Client how the on site presence of such architectural staff will affect the operations described under Schedule Two K-L, particularly 08.]'

Part Four

Part Four relates specifically to the appointment of consultants and specialists where the architect is the lead consultant.

The obligations of the parties are as follows:

'Nomination

The Architect **shall** identify professional services which may require the appointment of consultants. Such consultants may be nominated at any time by either the Client of the Architect subject to acceptance by each party.

Appointment:

The Client **shall** appoint and pay the nominated consultants.

The consultants to be appointed at the date of the Appointment and the services to be provided by them shall be confirmed in writing by the Architect to the Client.

Collateral Agreements:

The Client **shall** where the Architect consents to enter into a Collateral Agreement with a third party in respect of the Project, procure that all consultants are equally bound.

Lead Consultant:

The Client **shall** appoint and give authority to the Architect as Lead Consultant in relation to all consultants however employed. The Architect shall be the medium of all communication and instruction between the Client and the consultants, co-ordinate and integrate into the overall design the services of the consultants, require reports from the consultants.

The Client **shall** procure that the provision of this condition will be incorporated into the conditions of appointment of all consultants however employed and shall provide a copy of such conditions of appointment to the Architect.

Responsibilities of consultants:

The Client **shall** hold each consultant however appointed and not the Architect responsible for the competence and performance of the services to be performed by the consultants and for the general inspection of the execution of the work designed by the consultant.

Responsibilities of Architect:

Nothing in this Part **shall** affect any responsibility of the Architect for issuing instructions under the building contract or for other functions ascribed to the Architect under the building contract in relation to work designed by a consultant.

Nomination:	A Specialist who is employed directly by the Client or indirectly through the contractor to design any part of the Works **may** be nominated by either the Architect or the Client subject to acceptance by each party.
Appointment:	Specialists to be appointed at the date of the Appointment and the services to be provided by them **shall** be those confirmed in writing by the Architect to the Client.
Collateral agreements:	The Client **shall**, where the Architect consents to enter into a collateral agreement with a third party in respect of the Project, procure that all specialists are equally bound.
Co-ordination and integration:	The Client **shall** give the authority to the Architect to co-ordinate and integrate the services of all Specialists into the overall design and the Architect shall be responsible for such co-ordination and integration.
Responsibilities of Specialists:	The Client **shall** hold any Specialist and not the Architect responsible for the products and materials supplied by the Specialist and for the competence, proper execution and performance of the work with which such Specialists are entrusted.'

The schedules

The schedules are intended to be used to help identify the client's requirements and match these with the professional services to be provided by the architect. They will form the basis for discussion and will be completed by the architect to record agreement on the information to be supplied by the client (Schedule 1), the complement of professional services to be provided by the architect (Schedule 2) and the anticipated fees and charges arising and their method of payment (Schedule 3). Where consultants, specialists and site staff are to be appointed, Schedule 4 will also be used.

Schedule 1: Information to be supplied by the client

This is a single page and the schedule is separated into three parts.

Part One applies to all commissions and the standard items which the client is to supply, namely requirements, budget and timetable, are pre-printed. This information is essential for the proper application of the conditions and it will be for the parties to agree on the extent and detail of what is needed. Space is allocated for any other matters which may require to be entered.

Part Two relates to services for the design of building projects, as described under RIBA Plan of Work, stages A-H. Again, the items on which information is most commonly required are pre-printed and there is room for other matters.

Part Three relates to services connected with contract administration and inspection of the works. This part is needed only when appointment includes these services. It should be specified in the space provided which items of information relating to contract administration and site inspection are to be supplied by the client. Although architects are entitled to rely on the accuracy and adequacy of information provided by the client, they will still be vulnerable to allegations of negligence for overlooking something that a competent architect should have noticed.

Schedule 2: Services to be provided by the architect

This schedule is printed on the reverse side of the conditions spread sheet and identifies the wide range of architectural services available, itemised under 12 headings. In the paraphrasing of the full text, I have not specifically differentiated between the items which are highlighted as being the basic service and other items which are an extension to the basic service, if the architect and client so require. There is no reason why the parties may not add to the list of items in the event of some special activity to be incorporated and this is anticipated in the printed text.

To quote the words of Ian Thornton, chairman of the Architects' Appointment Review Group:

> 'Every project is individual and each will attract its own special conditions and requirements. Some contracts may therefore take a generalist's view, others a more specific view of the terms and details.
>
> There will be many contracts of a small nature not requiring the full implementation of all the documents and their side issues and for this purpose care has been taken to spell out the basic service which it is assumed will be offered in those situations.

It must not be taken, however, that those basic conditions can just be assumed without careful examination of each situation to ensure that both parties are sufficiently protected.

Even the simplest and smallest contract is likely to attract the same complexity of problems albeit on a smaller scale as the larger contract and it is for this purpose that the framework and structure of the document has been presented, so that both Client and Architect can feel assured that if they have properly discussed the appointment and terms, and details of that appointment have been confirmed between them, they have a workable basis of proceedings firstly to work together and secondly to procure from the industry a project satisfying the need of the original enquiry.'

1 *Design skills*

– These range from providing interior design services, advice on the design or the selection of furniture and fittings and advice, information and inspection of works of special quality, to advice on commissioning or selection of works of art.
– The provision of industrial design services; development of building systems or components for mass production; examination and advice on existing building systems; and the monitoring and testing of prototypes.
– Provision of town planning and urban, landscape, graphic and exhibition design services.
– Provision of perspective and other illustrations; model making and photographic record services, etc.

2 *Consultancy services*

– Provision of services as a consultant architect on a regular or intermittent basis.
– Consultations; provision of information in connection with local authority, government and other grants; and making submissions to other non statutory or advisory bodies.
– Advice, negotiation and provision of information in respect of rights including easements, responsibilities of owners and lessees.
– Advice on party wall matters; services in connection with planning appeals and/or enquiries.
– Advice on the use of energy in new or existing buildings; undertaking life cycle analyses to determine likely costs.
– Provision of services in connection with environmental studies; health and safety matters.
– Preparation of proofs; attendance at conferences to give evidence.
– Acting as expert witness or witness as to fact.
– Acting as an arbitrator.
– Provision of project management services, etc.

3 *Buildings and sites*
– Advice on the suitability and selection of sites; making measured surveys including levels and preparing plans; arranging for investigations of soil conditions.
– Advice on the suitability and selection of buildings; making measured surveys; preparing drawings, inspection reports and schedules of condition and dilapidation of existing buildings.
– Preparing estimates for the replacement and reinstatement of buildings and plant.
– Preparation submission and negotiation of claims following damage by fire and other causes.
– Investigation and advice on the means of escape; change of use in existing buildings.
– Investigation and reporting on building failures; arranging for exploratory work by contractors and specialists in connection with building failures.
– Preparation of site development layouts for large building complexes; preparation of drawings and specifications for the construction of estate roads and sewers.
– Making structural surveys and reports; investigating and advising on floor loadings and sound insulation in connection with existing buildings.
– Investigation and advice on fire protection; security systems for existing buildings.
– Inspection and preparation of valuation reports for mortgage and other purposes, etc.

I cannot but feel that some of these services are beyond the normal expertise of an architect to perform, as they cater for the specialist skills provided by only a minority of the profession. An architect should be careful not to be carried away by the extent of services listed and to enter into situations which may be beyond his or her ability to achieve fully and competently.

4 *All commissions*
– Obtain client's requirements, budget and timetable.
– Advise on the need for and the scope of consultants services and arrange for and assist in the selection of consultants.

Schedule 2 continues with services specific to building projects which comprise eight stages as follows:

Stage A-B: Inception and Feasibility
– Obtain information about the site from the client; visit the site and carry out an initial appraisal.
– Assist in preparation of client's requirements.

- Advise client on method of procuring construction, the need for specialist contractors, sub-contractors and suppliers to design and execute parts of the works.
- Prepare proposals and make application for outline planning permission.
- Carry out such studies as may be necessary to determine the feasibility of the client's requirements.
- Review with the client alternative design and construction approaches and cost implications.
- Advise on the need to obtain planning permission, approvals under Building Acts and/or Regulations and other statutory requirements.
- Advise on environmental matters, etc.

Stage C: Outline Proposals
- Analyse the client's requirements; prepare outline proposals.
- Liaise with other consultants where appointed; prepare approximate construction costs, advise on and implement cost planning and control procedures.
- Prepare special presentation drawings, brochures models or technical information for the use of the client or others.
- Carry out negotiation with tenants or others identified by the client, etc.

Stage D: Scheme Design
- Develop scheme design from approved outline proposals.
- Provide information to and negotiate with other consultants; prepare cost estimate and construction timetable.
- Consult with all statutory, fire, environmental and licensing authorities; prepare and apply for full planning permission.
- Conduct negotiations generally.
- Make any necessary revisions and re-submissions.
- Carry out special constructional research, etc.

Stage E: Detail Design
- Develop detail design from approved scheme design.
- Provide information to and negotiate with other consultants to prepare detailed design and revised cost estimates.
- Prepare applications for approvals under Building Acts and/or Regulations and other statutory requirements.
- Agree the form of building contract and explain the client's obligations thereunder.
- Obtain client approval of the type of construction, quality of materials and standard of workmanship.
- Apply for and conduct negotiations in respect of Building Acts and/or Regulations and other statutory requirements and revise production information, etc.

Stages F-G: Production Information and Bills of Quantities
–   Prepare production drawings, specifications and information for the preparation of bills of quantities and/or schedules or works.
–   Negotiate with and co-ordinate the work of other consultants.
–   Revise cost estimate and review timetable for construction.
–   Prepare other production information.
–   Submit plans for proposed building works for approval of landlords, funders, freeholders, tenants or others as requested by the client, etc.

Stage H: Tender Action
–   Advise on and obtain client's approval to a list of tenders for the building contract; invite tenders and, together with other consultants, report on them.
–   Together with other consultants, negotiate a price with contractors.
–   Revise production information to adjust tender sum.
–   Arrange for other contracts to be let prior to the main building contract, etc.

Stage J: Project Planning
–   Advise client on the appointment of the contractor and on the responsibilities of the parties and the architect under the building contract.
–   Prepare the building contract and arrange for it to be signed.
–   Provide production information as required by the building contract.
–   Provide services in connection with demolitions.
–   Arrange for other contracts to be let subsequent to the commencement of the building contract, etc.

Stage K-L: Operations on Site and Completion
–   Administer the terms of the building contract.
–   Conduct meetings with the contractor to review progress.
–   Provide information to other consultants for the preparation of financial reports to the client.
–   Prepare financial reports to the client.
–   Generally inspect materials delivered to the site.
–   As appropriate, instruct sample taking and carrying out tests of materials, components, techniques and workmanship and examine the conduct and results of such tests whether on or off site.
–   As appropriate, instruct the opening up of completed work to determine that it is generally in accordance with the contract documents.
–   As appropriate, visit the sites of the extraction and fabrication and assembly of materials and components, to inspect such materials and workmanship before delivery to site.

- At intervals appropriate to the stage of construction, visit the works to inspect the progress and quality of the works and to determine that they are being executed generally in accordance with the contract documents.
- Direct and control the activities of site staff.
- Provide drawings showing the building and the main lines of drainage.
- Arrange for drawings of building services installations to be provided.
- Give general advice on maintenance.

In this final stage, which I have reproduced in full from the SFA/92 Form, it will be seen that the basic services to be provided by the architect are set out in useful detail. This is not the case in respect of the 1982 Architect's Appointment which dismisses this most important stage of the building development in three short sentences which leave the client and, I suspect, many architects who have not studied the *RIBA Plan of Work*, with an incomplete understanding of what is expected and required.

It is not surprising, therefore, that the inadequately defined duties and responsibilities of the architect as contained in the Blue Book in respect of post contract activity all too frequently become the subject of dispute between the parties and, in my experience, accounts for a high percentage of issues which become the subject of litigation between the client and architect.

I therefore welcome the spelling out of the architect's duties in SFA/92 which substantially cover the more usual activities associated with work on site and will undoubtedly assist both architect and client in their understanding of what is offered and expected.

I particularly applaud the introduction into the terms of SFA/92 the positive requirement for architects to adopt a more positive approach to construction and quality assessment of materials and components, important subjects overlooked in the Blue Book.

The actions stated above form part of the basic services described in the new Black Book.

The following additional services are given and the list below may be expanded to incorporate further services which might be agreed between architect and client.

- Administer the terms of other contracts.
- Monitor the progress of the works against the contractor's programme and report to the client.
- Prepare valuations of work carried out and completed.
- Provide specially prepared drawings of a building as built.
- Prepare drawings for conveyancing purposes.
- Compile maintenance and operation manuals.
- Incorporate information prepared by others in maintenance manuals.

– Prepare a programme for the maintenance of a building.
– Arrange maintenance contracts, etc.

Schedule 3: Fees and Expenses

This sets out on one page the manner in which payment for the agreed services is calculated, charged and paid.

The seven sections of Schedule 3 leave space for the appropriate information to be inserted under the sub-headings of: Fees, Time Rates, Expenses, Disbursements, Instalments, Site Staff and Interest on Overdue Accounts

Schedule 4: Appointment of Consultants, Specialists and Site Staff

This is used to record the details of appointment of other consultants and specialists where the architect is lead consultant and, as far as is possible, of any site staff envisaged.

Under Part Four of the conditions, the architect is required to identify and confirm in writing to the client the professional services for which the consultants need to be appointed. They may be nominated by the client or the architect, subject to mutual acceptance, but the client appoints and pays them direct.

It should be noted that Schedule 4 applies only where the architect is appointed as lead consultant with authority over all other appointed consultants and responsibility for co-ordinating and integrating their work with the overall design.

The client holds the consultants responsible for the competence and performance of their work and for general inspection of the execution of it. I refer readers to the cautioning advice given earlier concerning the Blue Book, Part Three, in respect of the continuing responsibility of architects to co-ordinate the work of sub-contractors.

The client holds the specialist responsible for the products and materials they supply and for the competence, proper execution and performance of their work.

Final certificate

The architect's responsibility for issuing this is a heavy one, for it is not merely the last certificate but, subject to certain qualifications, represents 'conclusive evidence that where the quality of materials or the standard workmanship are to be to the reasonable satisfaction of the architect the same are to such satisfaction'.

Architects should also be aware of the judgment in the recent case, *Colbalt Ltd v H Kumar*[1] where it was ruled that an architect was not only responsible for approving such materials and workmanship as were expressly reserved by the contract but also in respect of all materials and workmanship where approval is inherently a matter for the opinion of the architect.

It is fortuitous therefore that SFA/92 includes in Schedule 2, stages K-L, the requirement for an architect generally to inspect materials delivered to site, instruct sample taking and tests as appropriate and to instruct where considered necessary the opening up of completed work to determine that it is in general accordance with the contract documents. The architect should be fully satisfied, therefore, that the contract documents are properly compiled and technically competent.

Alternative Schedule of Services

The Standard Form of Agreement, which I have, albeit briefly, described above, is applicable generally to all aspects of the normal work of an architect. In recognition of the need and increasing opportunity for an architect to become involved in the more specialist aspects of practice, however, two alternative Schedules of Services are available as follows.

Historic buildings: repairs and conservation work

This alternative schedule is intended for use where the architect's services are provided in connection with the repair or conservation of a historic building. The task may involve alterations to the building as well as repair of the fabric and its degree of complexity can vary considerably. The work typically requires more decision making on site than is normal for other types of building work; therefore it is the nature of the activity, rather then the class of building that will determine the scope of the architect's services.

For the purpose of this document, a historic building is defined as a building, monument or structure of architectural, historical or archaeological interest. Some are protected by legislation and are categorised by various descriptions such as 'Listed Building', 'Scheduled Monument', 'Ancient Monument' and as buildings in 'conservation areas'. Others may warrant the same special care and attention because of their inherent artistic character or age.

The definition of conservation is given as 'the action taken to prevent decay, embracing all acts that prolong the life of our cultural and natural heritage, the object being to present to those who use and

1   (1992) 59 BLR 89, QBD.

look at historic buildings with wonder, the artistic and human messages that such buildings possess'.

Schedule Two in the standard set of SFA/92 documents is replaced by an alternative, but the conditions printed on the reverse side remain the same.

The lists of service are significantly different from those set out in the standard Schedule 2 in order to reflect the nature and complexity of conservation work and the need for expert knowledge and skills in many aspects of it. In particular, the arrangement of work stages A-D differs from the arrangement under the *RIBA Plan of Work.*

Community architecture projects

Community architecture services apply where the intended user (or users) is able to play a full part as user/client in the design process and, sometimes, in the building process. The user/client may or may not be the client who is financing the project. The architect may be employed to act as the 'enabler' in matters of organisation, promotion and fund raising. The user/client is frequently a group of people and the architect may be employed to co-ordinate input from the group into the design of building processes.

The scope and extent of community architecture services can seldom be defined precisely at the outset and for this reason services will normally be charged on a time basis, although for some services an agreed lump sum will be appropriate. While most services will concern the inception and feasibility stages, some will relate to design and construction.

Some of the services set out in this supplementary schedule will be relevant to spheres of work other than those under a community architecture banner, particularly in the housing field.

This Supplementary Schedule reminds architects that it is essential to distinguish between 'the client' as defined in the Standard Form of Agreement for the appointment of an architect, and the 'user/ client', ie the intended user of the project who plays a critical role throughout its design and construction and who may or may not be the client. To clarify this distinction, there are additional conditions of appointment which apply where the user/client is not the client. These are intended to overcome any problems arising in connection with lines of communication and/or authority.

Because the nature of community architecture work makes it difficult to predict with certainty at the outset the scope and cost of the services to be provided, it is essential for the parties to maintain systematic administrative procedures and confirm agreed additions/ amendments to the services promptly and accurately.

Negotiating the appointment

Some architects find the essential process of formally and properly agreeing their conditions of engagement and remuneration to be difficult, if not distasteful.

SFA/92 should be of considerable assistance to them in that a great deal of the ground to be covered is already mapped out.

I have already briefly referred to Appendix 4 of the SFA Guide which provides very good advice to the architect when negotiating an appointment. This booklet must be read and studied in order to obtain full benefit of such advice but I give here a precis of selected extracts which are particularly important in my view.

When architect and client sign the Standard Form of Agreement for the appointment of an architect, they enter into a business and legal relationship which is, one hopes, backed by a considerable degree of personal rapport, trust and mutual support.

It is important to start off the negotiation on the right foot; the first meeting can set the tone for what is to follow.

The client

The first person the architect meets is not necessarily the 'client'. There are user/clients, paymaster clients and others, all with differing roles, powers and needs. It is essential to be certain who the real client is. In the case of the married couple, a committee, an association, a partnership or a body corporate, it is important to identify a single authorised contact with clearly described powers.

Some clients know clearly what they want and what will be involved, but others do not. An architect's duty of care relates to the client's known level of experience; it is wise not to make assumptions. The architect should explain his role and responsibilities and outline the professional services that can be offered.

The architect should clarify the client's financial authority in relation to the project and if possible check credit worthiness and whether there are or will be available resources sufficient for the project needs.

The architect

The RIBA Code of Professional Conduct obliges architects to carry out faithfully the services they undertake to provide and ensure that their own resources are adequate and properly directed. It also requires them to declare to the client any potential conflict of interest in undertaking the work.

A professional relationship can only flourish if it is based on trust and a willing exchange of information. The client will want to explore the architect's attitude to design, professional competence, working arrangements and resources. The architect should be careful not to exaggerate practice experience and capability.

To preserve peace of mind and to avoid future difficulty, the architect should be satisfied that the project will fit into the practice's work schedule, that there is available time to carry it out, that the work involved will return a profit, that the cash flow situation will allow the proper servicing of the work involved and that the right staff with the right skills are available when needed.

The architect should ensure that an adequate level of professional indemnity insurance is available, not only for self protection but also for the protection of the client.

When negotiating an appointment for services, the architect should bear the following points closely in mind, remembering always that the commitment will probably be long term and any mistakes, omissions or shortcomings will be equally long term.

– Identify and assess any problems looming and balance these out against possible trade-offs and benefits to the practice overall. Be realistic.

– If disputes do arise, a well documented project based on the SFA/92 with evidence that the client has been kept informed will not only be useful to insurers but invaluable in the event of arbitration proceedings.

– A good negotiator knows when to stop. The aim should never to be to land a commission at any price; the kind of project where the fee is not going to cover the costs and where unacceptable risks are imposed on the practice is never not worth having.

– If a client insists on amending the wording of SFA/92 or presents specially drafted conditions, always be prepared to refer these to a lawyer, preferably one who is experienced in architectural or construction contracts, and always notify your insurers of any changes proposed.

– It is all too easy to get dragged into providing services as a matter of goodwill after the project has been completed. Remember that architects are not obliged to provide their professional services free.

Design and Build Edition (Employer Client and Contractor Client versions)

The concept of design and build is not new. Indeed, I recall becoming involved in something similar over 30 years ago, when the prospect of

STANDARD FORM OF AGREEMENT FOR THE APPOINTMENT OF AN ARCHITECT

DESIGN AND BUILD

THE MEMORANDUM OF AGREEMENT
identifies the parties: states intentions
defines nature, scope and cost of services
alternative form available if executed as a deed
(Employer Client edition)

definitions

CONDITION Part One	CONDITION Part Two	CONDITION Part Three	CONDITION Part Four
common to all commissions: law of contract; obligation of parties; assignment; sub-contracting; payment; suspension; resumption; termination; copyright; dispute resolution.	relates to matters concerning conditions specific to architects' services. (pre-contract)	relates to matters concerning conditions specific to architects' services. (post-contract)	specifically related to appointment of consultants and specialists.

SCHEDULE 1	SCHEDULE 2	SCHEDULE 3	SCHEDULE 4
information to be supplied by the client.	sets out services to be supplied by the architect.	sets out the way payment for service is calculated, charged and paid.	client acceptance of appointment of consultants, specialists and site staff.

bringing together architects, structural and services' consultants and quantity surveyors to work in close liaison with contractors seemed to make good sense. The liaison resulted in the design and construction of one of the first commercial nuclear power stations commissioned in this country.

Development projects such as these, however, are to be regarded as special cases where it may be argued that such a meeting of design and construction skills is the only practical way of obtaining the objective.

The traditional means of creating and achieving a building or other project – where the client employs consultants to design and then to ensure proper implementation of that design by providing a contractual administration and inspection discipline on the contractor – has, particularly in recent years, faced criticisms by some clients who consider that the established system, is too cumbersome and costly to meet modern commercial pressures. Additionally, some contractors prefer not to have to work under the control of the professional, who may be perceived as being semi-literate in the common-sense approach to construction, programming and costing.

In a recent survey carried out on behalf of the RIBA South East Region, questionnaires were sent out to 4,000 regular users of construction professionals. The result showed that over the past five years the traditional procurement options had fallen dramatically from grace, whereas the design and build alternative had increased to near equity, with the prospect of further gains in the future.

One of the theoretical attractions of design and build, for the employer, is that, once the requirements of the development have been established, all the intricacies involved thereafter in the creation and implementation of the building, or whatever, will be undertaken by the appointed contractor, leaving the employer with little to do other than to meet stage payments and, in due course, take possession of the completed development.

In my experience, such a concept is seldom achieved: the ideal can become an ordeal, not only for the employer but for those who form the team put together by the contractor. The employer may find that the attractions of design and build fade somewhat when it is realised that the contract does not provide for consultation or approval for the completion of the design and that there may be financial penalties if changes are required during the course of the works.

Contractors are not usually designers and may therefore seek to select the professional team more on the basis of its willingness to work within financial and time constraints set by the contractor, which might not be to ultimate advantage or to the particular interest of the employer. Conflicts in respect of ethics, responsibility and co-ordination can arise within the consortium, particularly if leadership is lacking or misconceived.

These and associated problems are regularly brought before the courts and to arbitration. For every such case known, there must be many more which are settled beforehand and therefore do not come to public notice.

My purpose in this chapter is not to discuss the merits of the design and build contract – and even less to enter into description of the various alternatives on offer such as management fee, construction management, management contracting, fast track and other working arrangements – but to draw attention to the need for architects to cover themselves against becoming involved, perhaps unwittingly, in situations for which they are not prepared either professionally or in respect of liability.

The JCT Standard Form of Building Contract with Contractors Design, (1981 edn) has become the recognised form to use with design and build contracts.

The conditions of engagement between architect and client then available were those to be found in the RIBA publication of 1971, which, being linked with the traditional method of procedure, did not cover this new situation. Although the need to provide for this new procurement method was recognised when the SFA/92 was in preparation, it proved impossible to provide for all methods within the same structure of documents, and the SFA/92 Design and Build was therefore issued separately. It comprises two separate and complete sets of documents, one for use when the client of the architect is the employer (the employer/client version), the other where the architect is appointed by the contractor (the contractor/client version).

These documents have been produced with specific reference to the JCT WCD 81 form of contract. The format of each is similar to that of the standard form which I have already described, although the subject matter differs considerably in specific detail.

As previously, there is an accompanying Guide which, although similar in layout and containing complementary general advice, sets out to clarify these particular forms of appointment and take the architect and the client through the intricacies of the new arrangement which, briefly is as follows. Although the employer/client and contractor/client forms of agreement appear to be similar, careful scrutiny, particularly of the Conditions of Appointment and Schedule 2, reveal important differences, as might be expected. It is for this reason that the Guide deals with each form separately.

Memorandum of Agreement

This will usually be signed as a simple contract, but in the event of an employer client requiring it to be executed as a deed, an alternative memorandum is included for that purpose.

It is my advice to architects that they should read carefully the explanatory paragraphs given in the accompanying Guide, which inform on some of the vital matters relating to liability and provides useful general reference on the execution and signing of the document.

Conditions of Appointment

Part 1: Conditions common to all commissions these include architect's obligations, client obligations, payment and dispute resolution.

Part 2: Conditions specific to the architect's services pre-contract the employer client version includes architect's obligations, client obligations and copyright.   The contractor client version carries additional paragraphs on collateral agreements.

Part 3: Conditions specific to the architect's services post-contract both versions comprise architect's obligations, employer obligations and provide for site staffing arrangements.

Part 4: Conditions specific to the appointment of consultants and specialists.

Schedule 1: concerns information to be supplied by the employer or contractor client and is in three parts:
Part 1:   applies to all commissions and the standard items which the client is to supply, information which is essential for the proper application of the conditions.
Part 2:   relates to services specific to the designing of the projects. These services will be limited to the extent required for the preparation of client's requirements.
Part 3:   relates to post-contract services.

Schedule 2: is used to identify the services to be provided by the architect.

Schedule 3: is for setting out the way payment for the agreed services is calculated, charged and made.

Schedule 4: is used to record the details of appointment of other consultants and specialists where the architect is lead consultant and, if relevant, of any site staff envisaged.

The Guide continues with advice on the application of the SFA/92 Design and Build Form in various situations.   It then provides a useful checklist relating to JCT WCD 81 Form of Building Contract

and concludes with an appendix in respect of a particular situation
known as 'The Consultant Switch' which is not adequately covered by
the SFA/92 Design and Build documents and requires an additional
'tri-partite' agreement, for which specimen heads of agreement are
offered.

Further advice is given to the vulnerability of the architect's
position in this situation and some practical suggestions are offered to
help formulate the required contractual arrangements. Architects
are cautioned not to attempt to do this themselves but to obtain
appropriate legal advice as drafting expertise is essential. Although
specimen clauses are set out, they are intended purely as a starting
point for discussion with legal advisers.

The switch, in essence, works on the principle that the employer
client appoints the professional team to progress the design up to the
stage where tenders are sought after which the successful contractor
assumes full responsibility for the project but takes over the continued
employment of that team. This can present particular problems and
dangers for the architect member who may be torn between decisions
made initially in the best interests of the employer client and the need
to serve the particular requirements of the new contractor master. It
is essential, therefore, that special contractual arrangements are
made to safeguard the position.

Conclusion

I am conscious that within the confines of one section of this book, it
has only been possible to touch briefly upon some of the complexities
which face the architect in practice at this time.

I am aware that some architects find it difficult, if not distasteful,
to invite potential clients to enter into a formal contractual
understanding or even to require any written confirmation of their
appointment. I know of some practices who have never used the Blue
Book, let alone the memorandum contained within it. They are,
presumably, content to place their skills, time and livelihood at risk,
particularly if the project fails or client relationships do not develop as
hoped.

I have met architects who consider that they have such a close
relationship with their clients as not to warrant a formal agreement, a
handshake being all that is required.

Perhaps some practices, particularly those with private individual
or small company clients, will regard SFA/92 as an over complicated
document, more likely to deter than attract. Certainly, I have not
found it as easy to assimilate as the authors would have us believe.
I find the titles somewhat confusing and the layout even more so.
These are not documents which can be picked up and understood in

five minutes – five hours would be nearer the mark. I do believe that there will be considerable benefit for the architect and client prepared to persevere in the understanding and use of them.

I think that once it is realised that the concentrated content of the schedules and conditions, which make up the bulk of SFA/92 represent only a 'shopping list', where the numbered items have only to be ringed for acceptance or crossed through for deletion, the document will prove to be far more manageable and acceptable than might be thought at first sight.

The professional institutions who represent us, after some years of relative inattention to these vital matters are now making serious attempts to keep pace with, or even get ahead of the considerable changes in methods of building procurement. The practitioner of today has the benefit of a good deal of well-publicised advice made readily available in one form or another.

Architects face a difficult future. Inadequacies of the past have caught up with us. Much ground has been given to building surveyors, unqualified designers, project managers, contractors, to name but a few.

Perhaps all this is just what is needed to give architects a renewed sense of purpose and to make a positive and realistic approach to those opportunities which still exist and, with the opening up of wider boundaries in Europe, will increase.

What I have written here is intended to explain, albeit briefly, the present situation with regard to the Appointment of an Architect. The SFA/92 Standard Forms, together with their Guides, may not be infallible, nor cover every circumstance, but clearly they represent a very considerable improvement on what was previously available. I commend, without hesitation, their study and use.

Acknowledgments

I am grateful for the advice and assistance given by the Chairman of the Architect's Appointment Review Group and to RIBA Publications and for permission to quote from the documents concerned. Their co-operation, however, does not imply that the views and advice given here are an extension of the guidance officially published as part of the SFA documents. The opinions expressed in my contribution are my own.

Reference in this chapter and additional related reading:

Architect's Appointment (1982 still current but superseded by):
Standard Form of Agreement for the Appointment of an Architect (SFA/92)

Supplementary Schedule of Service: Community Architecture
Alternative Schedule of Services: Historic Buildings: Repairs and
    Conservation Work
A Guide to the Standard Form of Agreement for the Appointment of
    an Architect
Standard Form of Agreement for the Appointment of and Architect
    Employer/Client version
    Contractor/Client version
A Guide to the Standard Form of Agreement for the Appointment of
    an Architect for Design and Build
Architect's Job Book: Volume 1: Fifth edition, 1988
Plan of Work, reprinted from the RIBA Handbook 1973 edition
RIBA Code of Professional Conduct

All are obtainable by post from: RIBA Publications Ltd, Finsbury
Mission, 39 Moreland Street, London EC1V 8BB (tel: 071 251 0791),
or for personal callers only, from RIBA bookshops.

Chapter 4

Collateral warranties

Andrea Burns

The purpose of collateral warranties

The tort of negligence: the erosion of remedies

The importance of collateral warranties derives from the erosion of
tortious remedies in law. The tort of negligence has been created
almost entirely by judges, as opposed to statute. The modern law was
founded in the case of *Donoghue v Stevenson*[1] in which it was held that
the manufacturer of an article of food, in this case ginger beer, was
under a legal duty to the ultimate purchaser or consumer to take
reasonable care that the article was free from defect likely to cause
injury. In this case there was no contract between the manufacturer
and the consumer. Lord Atkin said:

> 'You must take reasonable care to avoid acts or omissions which
> you can reasonably foresee would be likely to injure your neighbour.
> Who, then, in law is my neighbour? The answer seems to be –
> persons who are so closely and directly affected by my act that I
> ought reasonably to have them in contemplation as being so affected
> when I am directing my mind to the acts or omissions which care
> called in question.'

In the case of *Dutton v Bognor Regis UDC*[2] it was established that the
rule of law applicable in the *Donoghue v Stevenson* case was equally
relevant to buildings. The law was further extended in the case of

1   [1932] AC 562.
2   [1972] 1 QB 373.

Anns v Merton London Borough Council[3] where Lord Wilberforce described the duty of care as follows:

> 'Through the trilogy of cases in this House, *Donoghue v Stevenson* [1932] AC 562, *Hedley Byrne & Co Ltd v Heller & Partners* [1964] AC 465 and *Dorset Yacht Co Ltd v Home Office* [1970] AC 1004, the position has now been reached that in order to establish that a duty of care arises in a particular situation, it is not necessary to bring the facts of that situation within those of previous situations in which a duty of care has been held to exist. Rather the question has to be approached in two stages. First, one has to ask whether, as between the alleged wrongdoer and the person who has suffered damage, there is a sufficient relationship of proximity or neighbourhood such that, in the reasonable contemplation of the former, carelessness on his part may be likely to cause damage to the latter . . . in which case a prima facie duty of care exists. Secondly, if the first question is answered affirmatively, it is necessary to consider whether there are any considerations which ought to negative or to reduce or limit the scope of the duty or the class of person to whom it is owed or the damages to which a breach of it may give rise.'

In this case the liabilities of local authorities, contractors and consultants were greatly extended. In the law of tort there has always been distinction between the concepts of physical damage and economic loss. The law has traditionally recognised physical damage to person and property in awarding damages for the tort of negligence, but has been reluctant to recognise the careless infliction of non-physical and purely economic loss.

The major exception to this rule arose in the House of Lords decision of *Hedley Byrne & Co Ltd v Heller & Partners*[4] when it was established that a negligent misrepresentation may give rise to an action in tort for damages for financial loss. The basis of the decision was summarised by Lord Hodson:

> '. . . if in a sphere where a person is so placed that others could reasonably rely upon his judgment or his skill or upon his ability to make careful enquiry, such person takes it upon himself to give information or advice to, or allows his information or advice to be passed on to, another person, who, as he knows or should know, will place reliance upon it, then a duty of care will arise.'

This principle was extended in the case of *Junior Books v Veitchi* [5] This was a Scottish case where the House of Lords held that the

3   [1978] AC 728, [1977] 2 All ER 492.
4   [1964] AC 465, [1963] 2 All ER 575.
5   [1983] 1 AC 520, [1982] 3 All ER 201.

pursuers (owners and occupiers of the factory) were entitled to recover as damages the cost of relaying a defective floor and loss of profits whilst the floor was relaid, although the defects were not alleged to give rise, or to be likely to give rise, to any danger of personal injury or to property in the factory. Lord Frazer said: 'The proximity between the parties is extremely close, falling only just short of a direct contractual relationship.'

Lord Roskill considered the following facts as essential:

1   The appellants were nominated sub-contractors.
2.   The appellants were specialists in flooring.
3.   The appellants knew what products were required by the respondents and their main contract and specialised in the production of those products.
4.   The appellants alone were responsible for the composition and construction of the flooring.
5.   The respondents relied upon the appellant's skill and experience.
6.   The appellants, as nominated sub-contractors, must have known that the respondents relied upon their skill and experience.
7.   The relationship between the parties was as close as it could be, short of actual privity of contract.
8.   The appellants must be taken to have known that if they did the work negligently (as it must be assumed they did) the resulting defects would at sometime require remedying by the respondents expending money upon the remedial measures, as a consequence of which the respondents would suffer financial or economic loss.

It was thought at the time that the *Junior Books* decision had opened the floodgates for claims in the tort of negligence for economic loss. This was perhaps the high point of tortious liability. The decision in *Junior Books* has been severely criticised and is no longer thought to be good law following recent decisions.

There has been a batch of decisions in the late 1980s and early 1990s, severely restricting tortious remedies so that, if consumers require a certain level of performance, they must rely upon contractual remedies. The collateral warranty has come into its own.

What were these decisions which restricted liability and consequently remedies in tort? The reaction against the *Anns* and *Junior Books* decisions was very swift. In the Privy Council case of *Candlewood Navigation Corporation v Mitsui OSK Lines (The Mineral Transporter)* [6] Lord Frazer of Tullybelton said:

> 'Their Lordships consider that some limit or control mechanism has to be imposed upon the liability of a wrongdoer towards those who I have suffered economic damage in consequence of his negligence.'

6   [1986] AC 1.

In the House of Lords case of *Leigh & Sullivan Ltd v Aliakmon Shipping Co Ltd* [7] it was held that the buyers under a CIF Contract of Sale who were neither legal owners of the goods nor had any possessory title to them as the relevant time, had no right to sue the ship owners in tort. In *Muirhead v Industrial Tank Specialities Ltd* [8] again recovery of pure economic loss was disallowed and *Junior Books* was distinguished.

Robert Goff LJ said (at 528):

> '. . . it is, I think, safest for this court to treat *Junior Books* as a case which on its particular facts there was considered to be such a very close relationship between the parties that the defenders could, if the facts as pleaded were proved, be held liable to the pursuers.'

The House of Lords in *Peabody Donation Fund Governors v Sir Lindsay Parkinson & Co Ltd*[9] placed a restrictive interpretation on the nature of a local building control authority's duty. The local authority would not be liable if the building were defective nor would it be liable for pure economic loss.

The restrictive attitude was further extended in the case of *D & F Estates v Church Commissioners*[10] The case reached the House of Lords and concerned the defective plastering of a flat. D & F Estates had a lease of the flat and were joint plaintiffs with Mr and Mrs Tilman, who controlled the company and, for a time, occupied the flat. They sued Wates (the builders), the freeholders (who were the Church Commissioners for England) and the property developers, Hyde Park Property Developers Ltd.

The defective plastering was carried out by Wates' sub-contractor. The allegation was that Wates and the Church Commissioners were both under a duty to D & F Estates to supervise the work of the building sub-contractor and were responsible for the failure to supervise effectively.

Both D & F Estates and Mr and Mrs Tilman claimed damages against the Church Commissioners and Wates for failing to warn them before 1980 that the plaster work in the flat was defective and liable to fail.

Mr and Mrs Tilman claimed damages against the Church Commissioners and Wates for the inconvenience caused to them during remedial works in 1980. It was held that the damages suffered consisted of pure economic loss which was not recoverable in tort. In the absence of a contractual duty, a statutory duty, or a special relationship of proximity, a builder owes no duty of care in tort in

7 [1986] AC 785.
8 [1986] 1 QB 507.
9 [1985] AC 210.
10 [1989] AC 177.

respect of the quality of his work. This principle, of course, extends to architects and thus a future purchaser's tenants and bank have been keen to ensure an architect provides them with a contractual remedy, ie a collateral warranty.

The *D & F Estates* case was followed by *Murphy v Brentwood District Council* [11] In this case, seven Law Lords departed from the *Anns* decision and overruled *Dutton v Bognor Regis UDC*. There have been other cases emphasising this trend, for example, *Department of the Environment v Thomas Bates.* [12]

This is not an attempt at an exhaustive description of case law in the tort of negligence; it is merely an explanation by way of illustration of how tortious remedies have been eroded, thereby placing greater emphasis upon contractual remedies.

Collateral warranties have become an essential part of building projects. During the boom period of the late 1980s very many of these documents were signed by professionals, contractors and suppliers in a variety of forms; some standard but most non-standard. Most have flaws and one view is that there will, in the future, be a proliferation of litigation concerning these forms, which are now lying dormant in people's cupboards. There have been many attempts to standardise these documents and certain standard forms are considered later in this chapter.

To whom might a warranty be given?

Without collateral warranties or the assignment of contractual rights, a person who subsequently acquires an interest in a particular development has little or no protection at law if it is subsequently found that one of the parties involved in the building project has been negligent or has acted in breach of contract.

The purpose of a collateral warranty is the establishment of a contractual link between the giver of the warranty and the beneficiary. Therefore, if an architect enters into a collateral warranty with his client's bank then this constitutes a contract. If the bank does not have the benefit of a collateral warranty and the developer goes into receivership or liquidation, the bank has very little remedy against the architect responsible for the design of the particular scheme. It is now, therefore, commonplace for banks to require collateral warranties prior to advancing any moneys.

There have been a plethora of documents known as 'collateral agreements', 'duty of care letters' or 'collateral warranties' and often these terms are used without due regard to the strict legal meaning of the phrases.

11 [1990] 3 WLR 414.
12 [1990] 3 WLR 457.

There are standard forms of warranties, agreed by the industry, which consultants may be asked to sign; one for the benefit of funds and the other for the benefit of purchasers and/or tenants. Both warranties were agreed by the British Property Federation, The Association of Consulting Engineers, The Royal Incorporation of Architects in Scotland, The Royal Institute of British Architects and the Royal Institution of Chartered Surveyors. These will be examined in some detail at a later stage in this chapter and are reproduced in full together with Important Additional Notes for Clients of the British Property Federation at Appendices A and B.

The National Federation of Housing Associations has a recommended form of collateral warranty for housing associations. It is published with a guide to collateral warranties aimed at housing association development staff, their consultants and house builders. The form of warranty is for use in the context of design and build projects and there are accompanying notes on how to complete the form; which is reproduced at Appendix C.

Invariably, an architect will be requested by his client to enter into a collateral warranty with the client's bank or other funding institution. What other warranties will an architect be asked to sign and with whom? He may be asked to enter into a direct warranty with the eventual purchaser of the completed development. This may be assignable to subsequent purchasers. Furthermore, an architect may be asked to enter into a collateral warranty with a tenant either of a whole building or with tenants of parts of multi-let buildings. Is such a request justified? It is often argued that such a request is justified by virtue of the purchaser having made a substantial investment in a building. He needs to know that he would have remedies should he suffer a loss if there are defects in the building. It is often the case in this country that lettings are on the basis that a tenant will enter into a full repairing and insuring lease. Such leases can be long leases of up to 25 years with upward rent reviews only. The tenant therefore stands to lose, should there be defects in the building, in that he would be obliged to rectify such defects. Should he not be afforded the benefit of a warranty from the architect who designed the building? If the building is multi-let then it is likely that the landlord will be responsible for repairs but will recoup the costs from the tenants by virtue of the service charge. Therefore, again, the tenants stand to lose if there are defects in the building. Consultants often refuse to enter into collateral warranties with a number of tenants upon the basis of increased liability. It is common for an architect to enter into a collateral warranty with a first purchaser or first tenant, although architects and their insurers are becoming rather more cautious about the form of such warranties and the potential liability they import.

Is there any need for an architect to be concerned by the proliferation of collateral warranties? Does it increase his liability?

The answer to this question must be 'yes'. Not only will the architect have a contract with the developer but also he may have contracts with the developer's bank, the purchaser of the freehold, the tenant or perhaps tenants if the building is multi-let. If the warranty is assignable then he could be in contract with various previously unidentified third parties. Although his liability is not necessarily extended by assignment in itself in that the limitation period will be increased, he has no choice concerning the person to whom he is contractually liable. His liability for economic loss will be his main concern as will his ability to obtain professional indemnity insurance to cover this liability. The Form of Agreement for Collateral Warranty for purchasers and tenants Co Wa/P&T states: 'It is essential that the number of warranties to be given to tenants in one building should sensibly be limited.'

Is it reasonable for an architect to be liable to all these third parties without being paid any further fee by them?

Insurance

The giving of a collateral warranty by an architect is a matter which will usually be viewed as a material fact by an insurer and it should therefore be disclosed. It is essential for architects to include within their proposal form a note to the effect that collateral warranties will be given in the ordinary course of business. Many architects are asked to sign collateral warranties. This can cause difficulties for the architect, who is keen to please his developer client and do all that is necessary to progress the particular project, but is also wary of his own position, particularly vis-a-vis his insurers.

In times of recession, market conditions are tight and an architect may very well be requested to sign a collateral warranty which at other times he would not consider. He must always have regard to his insurance and in particular to the following points:

(i)   Any warranty should be qualified by the words 'reasonable skill and care'. If there is no such qualification then the architect may be exposed to an obligation of strict liability, eg the architect would be liable for design if it did not work, whether or not he had exercised reasonable skill and care in its formulation. In other words, this is a fitness for purpose warranty. It is extremely unlikely that fitness for purpose warranties would be covered by his professional indemnity policy.

(ii) Professional indemnity insurers are likely to object to any form of performance guarantee, any liability for liquidated and ascertained damages or any penalty.

(iii) Professional indemnity insurers usually object to the assignment of the warranty to more than one party. This can provide difficulties especially in relation to banks who wish to have the freedom to manoeuvre if a developer goes into liquidation in that then they have to step in and try to sell the development. They wish to sell the development with the benefit of collateral warranties from the contractor and professional team which can be further assigned by the purchaser.

(iv) Professional indemnity insurers usually insist that all other parties to the project, being members of the professional team, as well as the contractor, give collateral warranties in a similar if not the same form. This can be difficult to achieve, in practical terms.

(v) There is usually a warranty exclusion in a professional indemnity policy to the effect that the insurance does not cover any increase in the insured's liability by virtue of his entering into contracts such as collateral warranties. Invariably, collateral warranties which are satisfactory to a third party will extend an architect's liability. In some cases it is possible to negotiate a modification of this clause with professional indemnity insurers. Obviously, if the policy does contain a warranty exclusion and professional indemnity insurers refuse any modification of it, the architect must think seriously before entering into any form of collateral warranty since he may have to bear any claims arising without the benefit of insurance. In some circumstances, his insurance policy may be jeopardised in its entirety.

It has to be borne in mind that professional indemnity policies are usually on a 'claims made' basis. This means that what is covered are claims made during the policy period. If, for example, an architect designs a building and inspects the development as it is constructed over a three-year period commencing in 1994, practical completion is due to be attained in 1997. If the developer, or anyone to whom an architect has given a collateral warranty, whether it be a purchaser, tenant or fund, discovers in 1998 a defect in the building which is allegedly a design defect caused by the architect's negligence and issues proceedings against the architect, the architect will notify his insurers in 1998. The policy which will be current when the notification is made in 1998 will be the relevant policy. The following points are therefore relevant:

(i)   The architect may have changed insurers since he executed the collateral warranty in 1994. His present insurers may hold views which differ from those insurers who approved the warranty in 1994.

(ii) The architect may no longer be insured in 1998, having retired from his practice at the end of the project or having decided to 'go bare' since the premiums were greater than he could realistically afford.

(iii) Alternatively, the architect may have increased his cover from £5m to £12m.

(iv) Circumstances are viewed as at the time when the claim is made. Underwriters' attitudes to warranties may have changed by 1998. There may be a prohibition by insurers against an architect entering into collateral warranties at all, in which case the architect may find himself uninsured.

The effect of the claims made basis is that the warranty is considered at the time the claim is made and not when the warranty was given by the architect. It is therefore difficult, if not impossible, for an architect to be confident that he will be insured should a claim be made against him. The fact that he is increasing his liability by entering into collateral warranties can only cause him greater, and not less, unease. It is very rare for insurers to say categorically that they will provide professional indemnity insurance for any particular warranty in relation to any particular project, even if it is in the standard form adopted by the industry. Architects should enquire of their insurers as to cover. Every time an architect renews his insurance he should check with his insurers whether he will be covered for warranties, not only those which he proposes to sign currently or in the future but those which he has signed in the past and upon which claims could be made, ie those where the limitation period has not expired.

Bearing in mind the potential exposure it is perhaps unfair to expect an architect to enter into collateral warranties, especially since he derives little or no commercial benefit by virtue of so doing. If he is sued under one of these forms he may very well find himself with no insurance cover which could lead to financial ruin.

The assignment of collateral warranties

It is important for a building owner that the benefit of his contracts with the consultants and the benefit of any collateral warranties are assignable to future purchasers.

There are two types of assignment: legal and equitable. For an assignment to be a legal assignment it must comply with s 136 of the Law of Property Act 1925 which states:

> 'Any absolute assignment by writing under the hand of the assignor (not purporting to be by way of charge only) of any debt or other legal thing in action, of which express notice in writing has been given to the debtor, trustee or other person from whom the assignor would have been entitled to claim such debt or thing in action, is effectual in law (subject to equities having priority over the right of the assignee) to pass and transfer from the date of such notice –
>
> (i)   the legal right to such debt or thing in action

(ii) all legal and other remedies for the same; and
(iii) the power to give a good discharge for the same without the concurrence of the assignor.'

Thus, for a first purchaser to assign a collateral warranty to a second purchaser s 136 requires that:

1.   The assignment is in writing and signed by the first purchaser.
2.   It is absolute and without qualification. It cannot be by way of charge.
3.   That express notice is given to the person who gave the collateral warranty. For example, where the collateral warranty is given by an architect, the architect must be given express written notice of the assignment.

An effective legal assignment gives the assignee a legal right to sue in his own name. Equitable assignments are less certain and should only be relied upon if a legal assignment is defective.

In many cases there are restrictions within the collateral warranty upon assignment. Suppose there is no such restriction? Is the warranty then freely assignable? There are two restrictions as a matter of law.

First, a personal contract is not assignable. The test as to whether the contract is personal is whether from an objective point of view the assignment makes any difference to the person on whom the obligation lies *Tolhurst v Associated Portland Cement Manufacturers Ltd* [13] This was a contract concluded with the plaintiffs for the supply of chalk from certain quarries for 50 years. It was held to be assignable to a successor of the original contracting company because, on its true construction, there was nothing in the contract which involved a personal element so as to preclude the assignment of the benefit of the contract in the sense of the supply of chalk to a different company. There was also nothing in the contract which expressly prohibited assignment. As Lord McNaughten said (at 420):

'It seems to me that the contract is to be read and construed as if it contained an interpretation clause saying that the expression "Tolhurst" should include Tolhurst and his heirs, executors, administrators and assigns owners and occupiers of the Northfleet Quarries, that the expression "the company" should include the company and its successors and assigns owners and occupiers of the Northfleet Cement Works and that the words "his" and "their" should have a corresponding meaning. That, I think, was the plain intention of the parties.'

An architect may, from a subjective point of view, mind whether his obligations are due to a first or subsequent purchaser. However, from

13 [1903] AC 414.

an objective point of view, it is likely that a court would say that it would make no difference. Therefore, it is likely that collateral warranties are not personal and the benefit can be assigned if there is no express prohibition against assignment, although as a cautionary note the Court of Appeal in the case of *Southway Group Ltd v Wolff* [14] indicated that contracts for the construction or alteration of buildings may or may not be personal in their nature.

A bare right of action or right to litigate cannot be assigned. This offends against the rules of maintenance and champerty. It is a fundamental principle of the English legal system that a bare right to litigate cannot be assigned. In the case of *Trendtex Trading Corporation v Credit Suisse* [15] it was decided that if the assignment is of a property right or interest, or if the assignee has a genuine commercial interest in taking the assignment and in enforcing it for his own benefit, it will not be struck down as savouring of maintenance. The assignment of any collateral warranty should take place as a condition of the sale of the property in an attempt to avoid the pitfalls of the *Trendtex* case.

It is far more preferable, in the interests of certainty, to set out the parties' rights of assignment and this is generally the case in relation to collateral warranties, especially those in standard form.

Two important cases concerning rights of assignment are *Linden Gardens Trust Ltd v Lenesta Sludge Disposals*[16] and *St Martins Corporation Ltd and St Martins Property Investments Ltd v Sir Robert McAlpine & Sons Ltd* [17]. These were both considered by the House of Lords and judgment was delivered in July 1993. In both these cases the developer entered into a standard form of JCT Contract with the contractor which had the following clause dealing with assignment:

> '17(1) The Employer shall not without the written consent of the Contractor assign this Contract.
>
> (2) The Contractor shall not without the written consent of the Employer assign this Contract, and shall not without the written consent of the Architect (which consent shall not be unreasonably withheld to the prejudice of the Contractor) sub-let any portion of the Works.
>
> Provided that it shall be a condition in any sub-letting which may occur that the employment of the sub-contractor under the sub-contract shall determine immediately upon the determination (for any reason) of the Contractor's employment under this Contract.'

14 [1991] 57 BLR 33.
15 [1982] AC 679.
16 [1993] 3 WLR 408.
17 [1993] 3 WLR 408.

In both cases there was a purported assignment. In the *Linden Gardens* case there was an assignment of all rights of action against Lenesta Sludge Disposals Ltd, the latter being an asbestos contractor who had been in direct contract with the developers. There was also an assignment of all other rights of action currently vested in the assignors which were incidental to their leasehold interest in the premises.

The assignees were Linden Gardens Trust and they were substituted for Stock Conversion as plaintiffs in the proceedings. The question which arose was whether they were entitled to recover damages against the defendants by virtue of the assignment:

(i)   where the loss was incurred by Stock Conversion prior to the said Deed of Assignment,

(ii) where the loss was incurred by Linden Gardens subsequent thereto.

The second question which arose was whether Stock Conversion were precluded from lawfully assigning rights of action to Linden Gardens against the second defendants by clause 17(1) of the contract between Stock Conversion and the second defendants.

There were similar preliminary issues in the *St Martins* case. The difference in that case however was that the cause of action against McAlpines, the contractor, arose after the date of the deed of assignment. In the *Linden Gardens* case, the deed of assignment post-dated the issue of High Court proceedings.

The Court of Appeal had held that the prohibition on assignment prevented the benefit of the contracts, in the sense of the benefit of the right to call for their performance, from being assignable. However, on their true construction the contracts did not preclude the assignment of benefits arising under the contracts nor assignment of claims for damages under the contracts where the cause of action had arisen at the date of the assignment.

In the *Linden Gardens* case it was held that the breach in question occurred before the assignment. The Court of Appeal held that the claims were therefore validly assigned. The House of Lords came to a different conclusion and held that the clause prohibited the assignment not only of the benefits of the contractor's obligations of performance, but also of accrued rights to sue for breaches already committed.

In the *St Martins* case it was held by the Court of Appeal that when the contract was assigned by the assignor to the assignee no breach had occurred and therefore no cause of action was vested in the assignee. The express prohibition against assignment therefore precluded any such assignment without McAlpine's consent. The effect of the contractual prohibition was that the assignment was invalid and ineffective to transfer anything. The right to have the contract performed could not be assigned without consent, and no assignable claim for damages or for any other chose in action under the contract had vested in the corporation. The effect of this finding was that such cause of action as existed remained vested in the assignor corporation. Whilst it had not expended any sums in the remedial works and had sold the building for its full market value it was however liable under the assignment to indemnify the assignee in respect of the cost of the remedial works. The Court of Appeal found that such loss was not too remote and that the assignor could recover damages from McAlpine. McAlpine appealed to the House of Lords. Their appeal was dismissed but the House of Lords adopted different reasoning from the Court of Appeal. They held that the case was an exception to the general rule that a plaintiff can only recover damages for his own loss. An original party to the contract can, if both parties so intend, be treated as having entered into the contract for the benefit of all persons who may acquire an interest in goods or property and is entitled to recover damages for the actual loss sustained by those for whose benefit the contract is entered into. (*Dunlop v Lambert*[18] and *Albacruz v Albazero, the Albazero*[19] applied).

The appeal has raised problems concerning assignment but these are capable of cure by clear and explicit drafting. The questions raised by this appeal regarding the assignment clause in building contracts have direct relevance to collateral warranties and terms of appointment. It is also clear that where consent is required, it is important to obtain such consent prior to assignment to avoid complications such as arose in this case.

Limitation

What is the difference between a warranty which is simply signed and one which is executed as a deed?

The answer is found in ss 5 and 8 of the Limitation Act 1980. Actions against an architect in contract must be commenced within six years of the date on which the cause of action accrued, or 12 years if the engagement was by deed. The question then arises as to when the cause of action accrued. It is likely that a cause of action will accrue from the date of breach of any of the duties set out in the document appointing the architect. If there is no document, it will be necessary to look at the surrounding circumstances of the engagement, including what was said at the time of the engagement, the terms of the building contract and the services to be performed by the architect as anticipated by the parties.

The law has been criticised in that the limitation period can be doubled by a simple procedure, ie execution by deed, which is now considered to be archaic.

The period can be longer where the employer can rely on the provisions of the Limitation Act 1980 relating to fraud, deliberate concealment or mistake.

In relation to tort, actions must be commenced within six years of the cause of action accruing. This is also subject to the provisions of the Limitation Act 1980 with regard to fraud, deliberate concealment or mistake.

18 (1839) 6 Cl & F 600.
19 [1977] AC 744, HL.

The position is further complicated by the Latent Damage Act 1986 which deals with claims in tort. This Act introduced a 15-year long-stop. The plaintiff's right to bring an action is barred after 15 years from the relevant breach of duty. There are certain exceptions to the long-stop provisions which may extend a defendant's exposure to liability. The Latent Damage Act also extended the limitation period for claims in tort by the provision of a limitation period of three years commencing from the date of discoverability. This amendment was made in the light of dissatisfaction resulting from the case of *Pirelli v Oscar Faber & Partners*[20]. Lord Fraser commented in *Pirelli*:

> 'Part of the plaintiff's argument in favour of the date of discoverability as the date when the right of action accrued was that date could be ascertained objectively. In my opinion that is by no means necessarily correct. In the present case, for instance, the judge held that the plaintiffs as owners of the chimney, built in 1969, had no duty to inspect the top of it for cracks in spring 1970. But if they had happened to sell their works at that time, it is quite possible that the purchaser might have had such a duty to inspect and, if so, that would have been the date of discoverability. That appears to me to show that the date of discoverability may depend on events which have nothing to do with the nature or extent of the damage.'

The three-year period commences from the 'earliest date on which the plaintiff or any person in whom the cause of action was vested before him first had both the knowledge required . . . and a right to bring such an action'.

This analysis of limitation periods is not intended to be exhaustive. It merely illustrates the complications which can arise and frequently do arise in construction disputes. There have been many proposals for reform and, indeed, contractually it is possible to have an express limitation period in a contract. This could, for example, be six years from practical completion. A report published by the Department of Trade and Industry entitled 'Professional Liability: Report of the Study Team' recommended ten years from practical completion. This coincides, of course, with the usual period of latent defects insurance commonly referred to as decennial insurance.

The new Black Book, 'Standard Form of Agreement for the Appointment of an Architect' has the following provision in the memorandum of agreement:

> '5. No action or proceedings for any breach of this Agreement shall be commenced against the Architect after the expiry of_____ years from completion of the Architect's Services, or, where the services specific to building

20   [1983] 2 AC 1.

projects Stages K-L are provided by the Architect, from the date of practical completion of the Project.'

The architect is left to fill in the blank and, effectively, to agree the limitation period as a matter of contract. Stages K-L relate to operations on site and completion and it is extremely restrictive for the client if he cannot bring proceedings after the date of practical completion.

Consideration

A subsidiary point with regard to documents that are deeds is that they require no consideration. In the case of *Beoco Ltd v Alfa Laval Co Ltd* [1] the agreement was under hand as opposed to by deed. The sub-contractor had entered into an agreement with the main contractor by virtue of which they agreed to execute a collateral warranty with the developer. The contract was dated 29 November 1984. It was not until 15 months later, on 4 February 1986, that the collateral warranty agreement was executed.

The sub-contractors alleged that the only consideration for the collateral warranty was past consideration, which was no consideration.

The only consideration relied upon by the plaintiff was the granting by the developer of approval of the appointment of the first defendants.

It was held by Judge Bowsher QC that the approval of the developer only became perfected on the giving of the warranty and the consideration stated in the document was not past consideration but was effective and valuable consideration. The consideration clause in the warranty was as follows:

> 'NOW in consideration of the Purchaser granting his approval to the Managing Contractor for the Managing Contractor to enter into an agreement with the Contractor/Vendor the Contractor/Vendor hereby furnishes the Purchaser with the following Warranties.'

The court rejected the contention of the sub-contractor that the warranty was unenforceable for lack of consideration. To put the matter beyond reasonable doubt it is a simple matter to include a nominal consideration of, say, £1.

Limitation of liability

In the *Beoco* case, referred to above, the sub-contractors attempted to limit their liability under the warranty which stated that they would perform the contract works strictly in accordance with the terms and

1   (1992) unreported.

conditions of purchase. They also warranted that they would execute complete and maintain the contract works in accordance with the conditions of purchase. The conditions of purchase attempted to impose a time limit shorter than the usual limitation period and attempted to limit the sub-contractors' liability. In particular clause 7 stated as follows:

> *'Limitation of liability*
> The Vendor's liability covers only such loss or damage as he could reasonably have foreseen at the time of the formation of the contract. The Vendor shall in no event be liable to pay compensation for indirect or consequential damages. The total aggregate liability of the Vendor for any loss, damage or compensation whatsoever related to the contract shall never exceed an amount equivalent to 15% of the total contract price save and except for delay in delivery of the goods in which case the liability shall not exceed £ Sterling 1,000,000.'

The sub-contractor submitted that on a correct construction of the collateral warranty they could be under no greater liability to the developer than they could have been to the main contractor under the terms of the purchase order because:

(i)   The sub-contractor warranted that they would perform the contract works 'strictly in accordance with the terms of the conditions of purchase'.

(ii) The indemnity under clause 2(b) of the collateral warranty was limited to '. . . damages. . . incurred by the Purchaser (the Developer) by reason of any breach of these warranties for which the Contractor/Vendor has undertaken liability under the conditions of purchase'.

(iii) Clause 2(c) of the warranty prevented the sub-contractor from relying on their tender to exclude or limit liability for breach of the warranties and this suggested that they could rely on the terms of the purchase order to limit liability.

The judge did not accept these submissions. He said that to impose a time limit shorter than the usual limitation period on the liabilities under the warranties would require clear words. Such clear words were not found in the collateral warranty agreement. The obligation to execute and perform contract works in accordance with the terms of the purchase order did not import limitations on the effects of breach contained in the purchase order. An agreement to perform or execute works in accordance with the conditions of purchase only referred to performance. It said nothing about the consequences of failure to perform in accordance with the conditions of purchase. The closing words of clause 2(b) were not, in the judge's view, appropriate to import a restriction of amount; they simply identified the warranties referred to in the conditions of purchase.

This decision could be relevant to the position of an architect, for example, where a main contractor is employed on a design and build contract and they sub-contract a certain amount of the design to an architect. The architect may negotiate with the design and build contract or his terms and conditions and the limitations upon his liability. If he wishes these to be imported into a collateral warranty with the developer then very clear words indeed are necessary. A mere reference to carrying out certain works in accordance with the conditions agreed between architect and the contractor would not suffice. The limitations upon liability must be explicit.

Standard form warranties

Form of Agreement for Collateral Warranty CoWa/F

This form of warranty was first produced in 1990 and it is now in its third edition. The form is intended for use where the warranty is given to a company providing finance for construction and development.

The warranty was produced following the proliferation of forms and protracted negotiations which took place in the construction industry. Thousands of pounds were spent in legal fees by parties arguing over such matters as rights of assignment, liability for consequential loss and so on. When it was first published it was hailed as a solution to previous problems. However, it is true to say that it has not been readily accepted either by banks and financial institutions or by consultants. Either banks put forward their own document drafted by their lawyers or they make substantial amendments to the printed form. Consultants are understandably wary in their acceptance of forms which are different from those negotiated by their professional body and by the industry.

In the form, the consultant is called 'The Firm', the developer 'The Client' and the financier is defined as 'The Company which term shall include all permitted assignees under the agreement'. Some of the more important clauses are discussed below.

The primary obligation of the firm is contained in clause 1 as follows:

'1. The Firm warrants that it has exercised and will continue to exercise reasonable skill [and care] [care and diligence] in the performance of its duties to the Client under the Appointment. In the event of any breach of this Warranty:
(a) the Firm's liability for costs under this Agreement shall be limited to that proportion of the Company's losses which it would be just and equitable to require the Firm to pay having regard to the extent of the Firm's responsibility for the same and on the basis that [*insert*

the names of other intended warrantors] shall be deemed to have provided contractual undertakings on terms no less onerous than this Clause 1 to the Company in respect of the performance of their services in connection with the Development and shall be deemed to have paid to the Company such proportion which it would be just and equitable for them to pay having regard to the extent of their responsibility;

(b) the Firm shall be entitled in any action or proceedings by the Company to rely on any limitation in the Appointment and to raise the equivalent rights in defence of liability as it would have against the Client under the Appointment.'

The accompanying Commentary reads:

'This [Clause] confirms the duty of care that will be owed to the Company. The words in square brackets enable the Clause to reflect exactly the provisions contained in the terms and conditions of the Appointment.

Paragraphs (a) and (b) qualify and limit in two ways the firm's liability in the event of a breach of the duty of care.

1(a) By this provision the Firm's potential liability is limited. The intention is that the effect of "several" liability at Common Law is negated. When the Firm agrees – probably at the time of appointment – to sign a warranty at a future date, the list should include the names, if known, or otherwise the description or profession, of those responsible for the design of the relevant parts of the Development and the general contractor. When the warranty is signed, the list should be completed with the names of those previously referred to by description or profession.

1(b) By this clause, the Company is bound by any limitations on liability that may exist in the conditions of Appointment. Furthermore, the consultant has the same rights of defence that would have been available had the relevant claim been made by the Client under the Appointment.'

The client has the same rights of defence but perhaps not set-offs or counterclaims in relation to unpaid fees. It is obviously important for the architect to ensure that his appointment is in an acceptable form as there are clearly implications which impact upon this collateral warranty.

This clause can be criticised on several bases. First, any bank or other fund accepting a warranty must ensure that it has all the documents, specifications, drawings, copies of variations and other details in relation to the development in order that, if necessary, it may prove negligence as against a particular consultant at a future date. It is virtually impossible to achieve a comprehensive knowledge of the development in practice.

Clause 1(a) amounts to an attempt at a net contribution clause. It remains to be seen whether a court would interpret this as such. For example, if all the other firms and companies set out in the agreement were insolvent or were simply not sued by the fund, would a court hold that the architect was only 10% liable and if so, how would it reach such determination if the other parties involved in the development were not before the court? It is submitted that the court would be reluctant to determine the liability of a third party not before it and would be reluctant to give effect to this clause. A satisfactory way of achieving the aim of this clause would be by way of statute.

Clause 2 of the warranty (which should be deleted where the firm is a quantity surveyor) states as follows:

> '2. Without prejudice to the generality of Clause 1, the Firm further warrants that it has exercised and will continue to exercise reasonable skill and care to see that, unless authorised by the Client in writing or, where such authorisation is given orally, confirmed by the Firm to the Client in writing, none of the following has been or will be specified by the Firm for use in the construction of those parts of the Development to which the Appointment relates:-
> (a) high alumina cement in structural elements;
> (b) wood wool slabs in permanent formwork to concrete;
> (c) calcium chloride in admixtures for use in reinforced concrete;
> (d) asbestos products;
> (e) naturally occurring aggregates for use in reinforced concrete which do not comply with British Standard 882: 1983 and/or naturally occurring aggregates for use in concrete which do not comply with British Standard 8110:1985.'

Further specific materials may be added by agreement.

In general this clause does not cause a great deal of difficulty. Sometimes the fund will require a warranty that none of the substances has been or will be specified by the firm or used in the construction of the development. The firm may object on the basis that its duty is to monitor and inspect the development as opposed to an obligation of constant supervision. Concealed use of such materials by a contractor could possibly occur, hence the very careful restriction in terms of this particular warranty. Sometimes the firm may modify some of the descriptions of the materials, for example, in (d) asbestos products, they may wish this to be confined to blue as opposed to white or other types of asbestos.

Clause 8 states as follows:

'8. The copyright in all drawings, reports, models, specifications, bills of quantities, calculations and other similar documents provided by the Firm in connection with the Development (together referred to in this Clause 8 as "the Documents") shall remain vested in the Firm but, subject to the Firm having received payment of any fees agreed as properly due under the Appointment, the Company and its appointee shall have a licence to copy and use the Documents and to reproduce the designs and content of them for any purpose related to the Premises including, but without limitation, the construction, completion, maintenance, letting, promotion, advertisement, reinstatement, refurbishment and repair of the Development. Such licence shall enable the Company and its appointee to copy and use the Documents for the extension of the Development but such use shall not include a licence to reproduce the designs contained in them for any extension of the Development. The Firm shall not be liable for any such use by the Company or its appointee of any of the Documents for any purpose other than that for which the same were prepared by or on behalf of the Firm.'

The usual starting point for a fund is that they require the copyright to be vested in them. Most architects oppose this. This clause does include a fairly wide licence in that the company and its appointee (whoever that might be) has licence to copy and use the documents and to reproduce the designs contained in them for any purpose related to the premises including, but without limitation, the construction, completion, maintenance, letting, promotion, advertisement, reinstatement, refurbishment and repair of the development subject, of course, to the consultants having received their fees. If the developer defaults upon his loan, it is somewhat unlikely that he will have paid his consultants, so that the fund will have to meet any deficiency as a condition precedent to receiving the benefit of the licence granted by this clause. Most funds are not happy with this arrangement. The licence does not include reproduction of the designs for an extension of the development. Funds usually object to this prohibition in that should they be obliged to take over the development if the client defaults upon the finance agreement then they or their successor may wish to carry the design into the next phase of the development. Presumably this clause is designed to protect the architect so that the fund would be obliged to negotiate with him a fee for the continuation of the design into the next phase.

Funds inevitably object to the last sentence of the clause concerning liability in that it is somewhat vague. If the client has been wound up, then the fund may find it difficult to ascertain readily the purpose for which the documents were prepared and provided. They can, of course, have regard to the appointment and tender documents but there may very well have been important meetings and discussions to which the fund was not a party.

Clause 9 concerns professional indemnity insurance and states:

> '9. The Firm shall maintain professional indemnity insurance in an amount of not less than [insert amount] pounds (£   ) for any one occurrence or series of occurrences arising out of any one event for a period of [insert period] years from the date of practical completion of the Development for the purposes of the Building Contract, provided always that such insurance is available at commercially reasonable rates. The Firm shall immediately inform the Company if such insurance ceases to be available at commercially reasonable rates in order that the Firm and the Company can discuss means of best protecting the respective positions of the Company and the Firm in respect of the Development in the absence of such insurance. As and when it is reasonably requested to do so by the Company or its appointee under the Clauses 5 or 6, the Firm shall produce for inspection documentary evidence that its professional indemnity insurance is being maintained.'

Consultants always used to object to an absolute obligation to maintain professional indemnity insurance for a certain period of years from the date of practical completion. This was on the basis that they did not know whether they would be able to obtain such insurance and, indeed, whether they would be able to afford to maintain such insurance. The problem with the clause in this agreement is that it is the product of a compromise. This is often the case when drafting is carried out by committee. Provided the firm and the company can agree upon the amount of the insurance and the number of years it has to be maintained, there is still a problem in relation to the proviso that such insurance is available at commercially reasonable rates. What are commercially reasonable rates? This is surely in the eyes of the beholder. As ever, with the word 'reasonable', what one person considers to be reasonable, another may consider to be quite out of the question. Is 'reasonable' to be construed as against the architect's turnover and profits or is it to be interpreted upon the basis of relevant prices at the relevant time? Or are both considerations to be taken into account? There is clearly a potential difficulty with such wording. The clause goes on to say that if the insurance ceases to be available at commercially reasonable rates then the firm and the company can discuss means of best protecting their respective interests. This assumes that the fund and the architect are capable of agreement. If there is no such solution, what rights does the fund actually have? The answer would appear to be very few rights indeed and funds often insist upon amendments to this clause to provide a more onerous obligation upon the architect to obtain such insurance.   Sometimes a formula is suggested for commercially reasonable rates by reference to an architect's turnover or by reference to the tender figure, both as a percentage. Of course if the firm does not maintain professional indemnity insurance and then becomes insolvent, the fund has little remedy, unless it wants to make the partners of the firm bankrupt.

Clause 11 is always controversial. It states:

> '11. This Agreement may be assigned by the Company by way of absolute legal assignment to another company providing finance or re-finance in connection with the carrying out of the Development without the consent of the Client or the Firm being required and such assignment shall be effective upon written notice thereof being given to the Client and to the Firm.'

The clause does not apply to agreements made under Scottish law. There is a special version of this clause (clause 11S) for application in Scotland.

Consultants and their insurers invariably attempt to impose restrictions upon assignment. Funds, on the other hand, say that they must be unfettered in their ability to deal with the development if the client defaults. They will frequently request amendments to the description of the type of person to whom the collateral warranty may be assigned. Often they argue that the right of assignment should be unlimited or that there should be a right to assign at least twice. This, of course, imposes no greater liability upon the architect if the limitation period is not extended. He may, however, find himself in a contractual relationship with a previously unidentified third party.

Clause 13 states as follows, and requires completion:

> '13. No action or proceedings for any breach of this Agreement shall be commenced against the Firm after the expiry of [complete number] years from the date of practical completion of the Premises under the Building Contract.'

The clause states clearly that the liability of the firm under this warranty ceases on the expiry of the period stated in the clause. The length of the period is a matter for agreement between the firm and the company.

There are then provisions for either signature under hand or under seal.

It is frequent for both consultants and funds to suggest their own amendments or supplementary clauses to the agreement, but at least this form provides a starting point for negotiation and agreement.

Form of Agreement for Collateral CoWa / P & T

This standard form of warranty is intended for use where the warranty is to be given to a purchaser or tenant of a whole building in a commercial and/or industrial development, or a part of such a building. This form is in its second edition, published in 1993, and some of the important provisions are set out and described below.

Again, in this warranty the consultant is defined as 'the Firm'. The purchaser or tenant is defined widely as being 'the Purchaser/the Tenant', which term shall include all permitted assignees under this Agreement'. The developer is called 'the Client'.

The main obligation of the firm is contained in clause 1. This is broken down into five parts:

'1. The Firm warrants that it has exercised and will continue to exercise reasonable skill [and care] [care and diligence] in the performance of its services to the Client under the Appointment. In the event of any breach terms of this warranty:
   (a) subject to paragraphs (b) and (c) of this clause, the Firm shall be liable for the reasonable costs of repair renewal and/or reinstatement of any part or parts of the Development to the extent that
      − the Purchaser/the Tenant incurs such costs and/or
      − the Purchaser/the Tenant is or becomes liable either directly or by way of financial contribution for such costs
      The Firm shall not be liable for other losses incurred by the Purchaser/the Tenant.
   (b) the Firm's liability for costs under this Agreement shall be limited to that proportion of such costs which it would be just and equitable to require the Firm to pay having regard to the extent of the Firm's responsibility for the same and on the basis that [insert the names of other intended warrantors] be deemed to have provided contractual undertakings on terms no less onerous than this Clause 1 to the Purchaser/the Tenant in respect of the performance of their services in connection with the Development and shall be deemed to have paid to the Purchaser/the Tenant such proportion which it would be just and equitable for them to pay having regard to the extent of their responsibility;
   (c) the Firm shall be entitled in any action or proceedings by the Purchaser/the Tenant to rely on any limitation in the Appointment and to raise the equivalent rights in defence of liability as it would have against the Client under the Appointment;

(d) the obligations of the Firm under or pursuant to this Clause 1 shall not be released or diminished by the appointment of any person by the Purchaser/the Tenant to carry out any independent enquiry into any relevant matter".

The general part of this clause relates to the standard of care and the Firm warrants as follows:

'1. The Firm warrants that it has exercised and will continue to exercise reasonable skill [and care] [care and diligence] in the performance of its services to the Client under the Appointment.'

The same comments apply to this wording as those in relation to the warranty to the fund set out above.

The clause then goes on to say that 'in the event of any breach of this warranty' there are four provisos. The first is contained in sub-clause (a). By this provision, the firm is liable for the reasonable costs of repair renewal and/or reinstatement of the development.

There are two main objections which can be raised to sub-clause (a).

The first is that there is no definition of 'reasonable' and no mechanism by which the same should be determined for example, by an independent expert or an expert appointed by one of the parties or otherwise.

Secondly, the costs are limited to those direct costs of repair renewal and/or reinstatement and consequential and economic losses are excluded. Thus, for example, if the tenant has to vacate and incur the cost of alternative accommodation, such costs would not be recoverable from the firm. The tenant would not be reimbursed for any loss of production or loss of profit. This clearly is very controversial.

This sub-clause is unlikely to be acceptable to a developer as some purchasers and tenants may require that the firm is liable for consequential losses. In particular, it is common for a consultant's professional indemnity insurance to provide for liability for consequential losses.

The British Property Federation's suggestion for those clients who wish to extend the consultant's responsibility to cover economic and consequential loss – and who can persuade the consultants to provide adequate insurance cover – is to delete the last sentence of clause 1(a), which reads: 'The Firm shall not be liable for other losses incurred by the Purchaser/the Tennant' and to insert instead:

'The Firm shall in addition be liable for other losses incurred by the Purchaser/the Tenant provided that such additional liability of the Firm shall not exceed £.......... in respect of each breach of the Firm's warranty contained in this Clause 1.'

The British Property Federation suggest that the sum to be inserted could be the same as the consultant's professional indemnity cover.

By proviso (b) the firm's potential liability is limited. The intention is that the effect of 'several' liability at common law is negated. When the firm agrees – probably at the time of appointment – to sign a warranty at a future date, the list should include the names, if known, or otherwise the description or profession, of those responsible for the design of the relevant parts of the development and the general contractor. When the warranty is signed, the list should be completed with the names of those previously referred to by description or profession.

This is similar to clause 1(a) of CoWa/F, set out above, and the same comments apply.

By proviso (c), the Purchaser/the Tenant is bound by any limitations on liability that may exist in the conditions of the appointment. Furthermore, the consultant has the same rights of defence that would have been available had the relevant claim been made by the client under the appointment. This is clearly intended to be a limitation upon liability. It is no doubt intended that the firm should be entitled to raise equivalent rights in defence of liability, but perhaps not set offs or counterclaims in relation to unpaid fees.

Proviso (d) is unlikely to be controversial. It simply permits the purchaser or tenant to employ an independent expert without waiving their rights against the firm.

Clause 2, which does not apply to quantity surveyors, is very similar to clause 2 of CoWa/F warranty and the same comments apply. An additional question arises and that is whether, if there is a breach, the firm is liable for consequential and economic losses, which do not appear specifically to have been excluded.

Clause 5 relates to copyright and is very similar to clause 8 of the funding warranty. The same considerations apply, although a purchaser or tenant may be less concerned to obtain the copyright than a fund.

Clause 6 is very similar to clause 9 of the funding warranty and the same considerations apply.

Clause 7 states:

> '7. This Agreement may be assigned [insert number of times] by the Purchaser/the Tenant by way of absolute legal assignment to another person taking an assignment of the Purchaser's/the Tenant's interest in the Premises without the consent of the Client or the Firm being required and such assignment shall be effective upon written notice thereof being given to the Firm. No further assignment shall be permitted.'

The important point in this clause, ie the number of times the agreement may be assigned, has to be agreed between the parties and this will be controversial. A developer, purchaser or tenant will usually require an unfettered right to assign, whereas the firm will wish to have a prohibition upon assignment. A compromise will obviously be necessary. There are special provisions for application in Scotland.

Clause 9 states:

> '9. No action or proceedings for any breach of this Agreement shall be commenced against the Firm after the expiry of [complete period] years from the date of practical completion of the Premises under the Building Contract.'

The parties can agree to their own limitation period in relation to these warranties.

There are the usual alternatives for the agreement to be executed under hand or to be executed as a deed.

National Federation of Housing Associations Form of Agreement for Collateral Warranty

This form is very similar to the British Property Federation forms. The main obligation is contained in Clause 1 as follows:

> '1   The Warrantor warrants and undertakes to the Association that it has exercised and will continue to exercise reasonable skill and care in the performance of its duties to the Main Contractor under the Warrantor's Contract provided that:
> (a) The liability of the Warrantor to the Association shall be limited to the reasonable costs of remedying the physical defects to the works caused directly by the failure of the Warrantor to exercise such skill and care and any other losses incurred by the Association howsoever arising are expressly excluded.
> (b) The Warrantor is entitled to raise against the Association the equivalent rights of defence as it might have against the Main Contractor under the Warrantor's Contract.
> (c) For the avoidance of doubt the Warrantor's liability for loss or damage shall be limited to such sum as the Warrantor ought reasonably to pay having regard to his or her responsibility for the same on the basis that all other consultants and specialists shall where appointed be deemed to have provided to the Association contractual undertakings in respect of their services and shall be deemed to have paid the Association such contributions

as may be appropriate having regard to the extent of their responsibility for such loss or damage.'

The liability of the warrantor is limited to the reasonable cost of remedying the physical defects to the works and excludes economic loss. The form has recently been amended to include the note which appears against clause 1(a) and reads as follows:

'This clause may be deleted if the Association does not wish the Warranty to be limited in this way. The effect of the deletion will be that the Warrantor will be liable for other costs such as loss of rent or decanting costs, or damage caused by the defect to other property of the Association.'

Other clauses relate to the use or prohibition of certain materials, payment of the warrantor's fees, copyright licence, and the maintenance of professional indemnity insurance and are very similar to the two other warranties discussed in this chapter.

Clause 6 is peculiar to the Housing Association warranty and states:

'6 In the event [that] the Association claims a breach of this Agreement the Association shall in so far as the alleged breach is covered by any guarantee given by or on behalf of the National House Builders Council (or other similar organisation) use all reasonable endeavours to seek rectification or remedy of such alleged breach pursuant to the said guarantee to the terms of this Agreement.'

The provisions relating to assignment are quite wide and are contained in clause 8 as follows:

'8 This Agreement may be assigned by the Association to another Housing Association by way of absolute legal assignment without the consent of the Warrantor being required and such assignment shall be effective upon written notice thereof being given to the firm.'

Alternatives to collateral warranties

Collateral warranties are clearly unsatisfactory in that they impose very great potential liability and obligation upon the architect, usually for no extra fee. They are also very difficult to negotiate, which has resulted in a proliferation of non-standard warranties many of which, it is submitted, will be a future source of work for the courts if there are disputes.

Professionals have for some time been looking at alternatives to collateral warranties.

The main alternative is latent defects insurance, also known as inherent defects insurance, decennial insurance and building users insurance against latent defects – 'BUILD'.

Latent defects insurance is relatively new to UK insurers. It has, however, been available from continental insurers for a number of years, largely as a result of it being a compulsory statutory requirement in France. Most policies tend to be for ten years and the insurance covers the defects which occur in the building without proof of fault.

The advantages

The advantage to the property developer and to the bank is that they will not have the costs aggravation and hassle of pursuing the contractor, architect or whoever else may be considered to be liable. This is particularly relevant for banks where property developers have gone into receivership or liquidation. They may not have the full facts available to them, or the time to pursue litigation or arbitration against the various parties who may be involved. Also there may be serious limitations as to liability contained in the collateral warranties.

If an appropriate policy is taken out, then it will be for the insurers to pursue the parties. Insurers usually decide whether they wish to exercise their right of subrogation and claim against the design or construction team. Insurers will bear the risk that they will lose the action and have to pay the costs and they will have to weigh up the advantages and disadvantages in settling the action out of court. The developer, building owner or bank is spared the aggravation and uncertainties of litigation. The policy can be assigned by the developer to future purchasers who may be particularly attracted by the existence of latent defects insurance. As discussed above, there may be severe restrictions and limitations upon the assignability of collateral warranties.

The disadvantages

The main disadvantage is that of cost. The cost of a latent defects policy depends upon the type of cover which is chosen but is usually calculated as a percentage of the contract sum and includes the cost of the insurance company's technical bureau monitoring the works. The cost will usually be between 1% and 2% of the construction cost. For the building owner, profit margins are vital and there must be valid justification for taking out yet another form of insurance. Will the building owner be able to recoup this extra cost? Will the building be more attractive to pension funds or banks or other institutions who fund the development? Banks and other funders might well make such insurance compulsory prior to advancing any moneys on a development. If the property developer defaults on his loan, then at least they will be able to market the property with the benefit of the insurance and, furthermore, will not have to rely upon collateral warranties which may be defective or inadequate.

A further disadvantage is that inherent defects insurance is quite difficult and expensive to obtain once the building has been erected. The decision to take out a policy should therefore be made prior to the commencement of construction. The work on site can then be monitored during the construction period.

The cover

The insurance usually provides:
(i)   A long term protection of the investment in a new building project which cannot be cancelled by insurers.
(ii)   Payment of claims on the basis of damage having occurred giving a faster settlement than if legal liability has to be proved.
(iii) The certainty that the financier, owner or tenant will obtain full recovery under the policy provided that the sums insured are adequate.
(iv)   A transfer to insurers of the risk that recovery from consultants or contractors may not be possible.
(v)   An insurance policy which is assignable to any subsequent financiers, owners or tenants.
(vi)   Cover for the costs of demolition, removal of debris and professional fees.

The insurance may be extended to include:
(i)   Cover for damage resulting from defective waterproofing to walls and roofs and underground leakage.
(ii)   The indexation of the sum insured to allow for future inflation.
(iii) The possibility of a waiver of insurers' rights of recourse to any specific parties.
(iv)   Insurance for loss of income, removal expenses and additional costs incurred in occupying alternative premises.
It is impossible to arrange a parallel policy in respect of loss of profit but, again, this would involve further costs. The policy does not extend to defects discovered prior to the date of practical completion nor does it extend to defects discovered after the period of insurance, ie outside the ten-year limit.

Owner-controlled professional indemnity insurance

A further alternative to collateral warranties is owner-controlled professional indemnity cover. The principal will arrange insurance to cover negligence of all consultants. In this way, he will not be dependent upon a particular consultant complying with his contractual liability to maintain professional indemnity insurance. The consultant may be unable (due, for example, to other claims or impecuniosity) or unwilling to insure, or the amount of the insurance may be insufficient to meet the particular claim in question.

Such a policy is a relatively new innovation and underwriters consider each proposal on its merits, with different terms and conditions being imposed for each project.

Chapter 5

Professional indemnity insurance

Peter Madge

The insurance market

The insurance market consists of insurers and underwriters who carry the risk and brokers who place the risks with them. The broker is the professional insurance adviser to the insured.

Not all insurers underwrite professional indemnity risks. Indeed there is a restricted and limited market. Nor is there such a thing as a standard insurance policy wording: the words differ from insurer to insurer.

What is considered below is, however, typical of the sort of policy that is on offer.

Because the market is a restricted one and continually changing it is sensible to use an insurance broker who has experience in this class of business.

Hard and soft markets

One of the unsatisfactory features of the insurance market in the last decade has been its cyclical nature. This is often determined by high rates of interest where insurers try to obtain large amounts of premium which they can invest. Markets are said to be 'soft' when it is a buyer's market. In a soft market there is much competition for business by insurers, premium rates are depressed, cover is widened and, usually, an insurer will hold onto his existing portfolio of business at all costs even if it means charging uneconomical premiums. Markets are 'hard' when the reverse applies. Underwriting losses force some insurers out of the market. Those that stay in can make increases in their premiums. It becomes a seller's market. Increased premiums are often coupled with restricted cover which means less exposure to the insurer. Profits begin to be made as premiums rise. As a result, other insurers come back into the market to compete for business, forcing premiums down again. The cycle repeats itself.

When a market is soft the benefit to the insured is that normally he can buy his wide form of cover at less than the true cost. The disadvantage is that as this produces normally an underwriting loss to the insurers, they deal with claims strictly on their legal merits. If there is, therefore, non-disclosure or misrepresentation on the proposal form (considered later) or a breach of the policy conditions (considered later) they are legally entitled to avoid the policy or the claim and in practice may do so.

Insurance law and utmost good faith

Insurers get the information they need to underwrite a risk from the insured. Usually he has to complete a proposal form which contains many relevant and searching questions. The insured normally knows more about his business than do the insurers.

Utmost good faith

Like other forms of contract, insurance is subject to the normal contractual rules of offer and acceptance, consideration (the premium), legality, agreement of the parties, contractual capacity of the parties and the intention to create a legal relationship. Insurance contracts, however, differ fundamentally from other commercial contracts in the sense that they are bound by the principle of utmost good faith. There is a duty on the insured to disclose to the insurer all material facts bearing on the risk.

All material facts must be disclosed

A material fact is something which would influence the judgment of a prudent insurer in agreeing to accept the risk or not and in deciding the amount of premium he would charge. The test of whether a fact is material or not is whether it would have influenced the judgment of a prudent insurer, not the particular insurer issuing the policy. Whether or not the insured considered the fact to be material is not relevant. It is the test of the prudent insurer, not the prudent insured.

The insured has a duty to disclose all material facts which have a bearing on the risk. The onus of proving that there had been a non-disclosure of information or fact is upon the insurers. The insured must disclose all those material facts which are within his knowledge, whether actual or presumed. He must disclose all those facts which he knows, or ought in the ordinary course of business affairs to know or have known about.

The proposal form

The above represents the common law position. Insurers often insist upon a proposal form being completed before insurance is offered. This asks a number of relevant questions which are material to the risk, but the important point to note is that even though a question is not asked, if there is something material to the risk then the insured must disclose it. Moreover, most proposal forms contain a declaration and warranty at the foot of the form stating that the insured has answered all questions accurately and not withheld material information. The insured has to sign this. The effect of signing this declaration and warranty is that the insured warrants the accuracy of all the answers on the proposal form and further warrants that he has not withheld or failed to disclose all material facts. A warranty in insurance law has a strict interpretation. Thus, any inaccuracy on the proposal form or non-disclosure of material information gives the insurers the right, if they so wish, to treat the policy as void. Hence the importance of making sure that all answers to questions and information shown on proposal forms are correct.

What is material?

Over the years many technical and legal rules have been established in relation to non-disclosure. Generally, the following will be held to be material and must, therefore, be disclosed:
1. Facts indicating that the subject matter of the insurance is exposed to more than the ordinary degree of risk.
2. Facts indicating that the insured is activated by some special notice as, for example, where he greatly over-insures.
3. Facts indicating that the liability of the insurer is greater than he would normally have expected it to be.
4. Facts showing that there is a moral hazard attaching to the insured suggesting that he is not a fit person to whom insurance can be granted – for example, a person with a bad criminal history.
5. Facts which to the insured's knowledge are regarded by the insurers as material.

On the other hand there are facts which, although material, may become immaterial in certain circumstances and there is, therefore, no obligation upon the insured to disclose them. For example:

1.   Facts which are already known to the insurers or which they may be reasonably presumed to know.
2.   Facts which the insurers could have discovered themselves by making some enquiries.
3.   Facts where the insurer has waived further information.
4.   Facts tending to lessen the risk – for obvious reasons, since anything that lessens the risk is beneficial to the underwriter.

The policy

The object of the policy is to protect the insured against this legal liability for claims made against him by third parties for breach of professional duty.

It is important to recognise that there are usually three stages to a professional liability claim, ie:

1.   some act or omission, eg a design miscalculation which may result in
2.   injury loss or damage to a third party which may result in
3.   a claim being made against the insured.

There is often a long time gap between the three stages. For example, a negligent design committed in 1980 may not give rise to damage until 1985 and the claimant may not decide to put in a formal claim until many years later.

As is explained below, policies protect against *claims made* during the currency of the policy. It is not a negligence-committed policy.

The policy

Policies vary from insurer to insurer. All, however, will make the proposal form, completed by the insured, the basis of the contract. Any inaccuracies on that form or any non-disclosure of material fact may make the policy void.

Most policies agree:

1.   to indemnify the insured (the firm or practice including past directors, principals or partners)
2.   against any claim made against him during the period of insurance
3.   for which he shall become legally liable to pay compensation, together with claimants' costs, fees and expenses
4.   in accordance with any judgment, award or settlement made in the United Kingdom (or any order made anywhere in the world to

enforce such judgment, award or settlement in whole or in part) in consequence of

5. any breach of professional duty of care by the assured to any claimant including breach of warranty or authority or

6. any libel, slander or slander of title, slander of goods or injurious falsehood

7. in connection with the professional business described in the policy.

The policy covers *legal* liability, not *moral* liability.

Some policies limit the cover to breach of professional duty arising out of neglect, error or omission of the insured or his employees. The professional business should be defined in terms wide enough to cover all professional activities.

Limit of indemnity

There is a limit up to which insurers will pay claims but not beyond. It is the insured's responsibility to select an adequate limit. The limit may be an *aggregate* limit covering all claims in every policy year or a limit in respect of each and every *claim* (or series of claims from the same originating cause).

Legal costs

In addition to the limit of indemnity, insurers will normally pay defence costs incurred with their consent in the investigation, defence or settlement of any claim. However, if a payment is made which is greater than the limit of indemnity insurers' agreement to pay, the legal costs are scaled down, eg if the limit of indemnity is £1m and the claim is settled for £2m then the insurer will only pay 50% of legal costs.

Claims made cover

It is important to note that the policy is a *claims made* policy. In other words it pays only for claims made against the insured during the period of insurance. It is not a negligence committed policy. *Once the policy lapses so does the cover*. Retired partners should make sure the firm's policy covers them. Sole practitioners need 'run off' cover. Liability continues into retirement.

Many policies do not define a 'claim'. Normally it is intended to mean a demand for money or services or recompense.

Main exclusions in the policy

These should be read very carefully. Normally the policy will *not* pay for:

1. Any excess or deductible, ie the first amount of each and every claim or series of claim from the same originating cause.
2. Any claim arising out of participation in any consortium or joint venture, of which the insured forms part (because the liability of the insured in any consortium or joint venture agreement can be varied or increased by the terms of the joint venture or consortium agreement).
3. Any claim arising out of any circumstance or event which has been disclosed by the insured on the proposal form or renewal declaration form (the previous policy should cover the eventuality – the insured should make sure it does by telling the insurers before the policy expires). (See Condition 2 later, p 174.)
4. Claims caused by dishonest, fraudulent, criminal or malicious act or omission of any partner, director or principal of the insured (but such conduct on the part of *employees* may be covered to the extent it gives rise to legal liability). Where it is the insured's own money or property which has been stolen, it is a fidelity guarantee policy which will apply, not a professional liability policy.
5. Any claim arising out of performance warranties, collateral warranties, penalty clauses or liquidated damages clauses unless the liability of the insured to the claimant would have existed in the absence of such warranties. Collateral warranties or fitness for purpose clauses. These clauses often extend the insured's duty which is to exercise reasonable care and skill so as to almost guarantee the work performed.

Most underwriters take the view that they are only prepared to indemnify the insured against accidental or fortuitous mistakes and not to 'guarantee' the work performed. Collateral warranties may extend the insured's duty to third parties, eg subsequent owners of the building or tenants.

The attitude of insurers to collateral warranties depends upon whether the insurance market is hard or soft.

Where the policy covers claims arising from neglect, error or omission, liability under the warranty may extend beyond these words. Where the policy protects against claims for civil liability or, as in the case of the policy form being considered, covers claims for 'any breach of professional duty' an exclusion similar to the one being considered will remove the contractual element of the claim.

The initial approach of underwriters to collateral warranties was that they were not prepared to give cover. Fortunately, this position has changed over the years since many underwriters recognise the commercial realities of life and that the insured has to sign them. But the extent of cover they are prepared to give must be considered carefully with the insurer. Statements by insurers and brokers that the policy 'subject to its terms and conditions' covers liability under the collateral warranty are misleading.

One unsatisfactory feature of the 'claims made' basis of cover is that while an existing underwriter may agree to cover collateral warranties, his cover will normally run for only one year. It is the attitude of the insurer on risk when the claim is made – which may be many years after the collateral warranty was signed – that is important.

Thus, it is important when changing insurers to make sure what the attitude of the new insurer is to all collateral warranties that have been signed in the past. How does his policy respond to them? The duty of utmost good faith described above may make it incumbent upon the insured to disclose all these warranties to the new underwriter. It follows, therefore, that full records of each warranty should be kept.

Surveys

Where the insured engages in surveys or valuation reports, there will be a policy condition regulating how such reports should be carried out. Normally such work will only be covered if carried out by a qualified architect or surveyor who has had some years' experience. In addition the survey or valuation report must contain a disclaimer to the effect that woodwork or other parts of the structure which are covered, unexposed or inaccessible have not been inspected and the report, therefore, is unable to comment on whether such property is free from defect.

Where the insured considers that high alumina cement may be present in the building, a similar clause must be included in the report to the effect that no detailed investigations have been carried out to determine whether high alumina cement was used during the construction of the building and the report, therefore, is unable to say whether the building is free from risk in this respect.

Contract terms must be communicated to the client at the outset so as to become part of the conditions of engagement. They cannot be introduced after the contract has been concluded.

Territorial limits

The policy normally covers work performed in the United Kingdom, which means England, Wales, Scotland, Northern Ireland, the Isle of Man or the Channel Islands. If work outside these limits is to be performed or the insured has offices abroad, then the insurers must be told and cover agreed.

Fees recovery extension

Often the insured has to sue his client to recover his fees. The result, normally, is a counter-claim for breach of professional duty. It may be possible to extend the policy to protect the insured against costs which are necessarily incurred on his behalf in recovering or attempting to recover professional fees.

Policy conditions

These stipulate certain things that must be done or complied with before insurers pay. They must be read with care, since any breach or non-observance of them may result in the insurers refusing to deal with any claim.

1. Once a claim is made against the insured then the insurers must be notified immediately. If the insured becomes aware from any third party that there is an intention to make a claim against him then again the insurers must be notified immediately.

2. If the insured becomes aware of any circumstance or event *which has not yet resulted in a claim* – eg a design mistake but which is likely to do so, the insured must give full details of that circumstance or event to the insurer. Once he has done so then any claim which subsequently arises from that circumstance or event, even if made many years later, will be covered under the policy in force at the date the circumstance or event *was notified*, notwithstanding that the policy may not be in force at the time of the claim. The insured should give *full details* of any circumstance or event. The condition is not an easy one with which to comply in practice because so many things may arise in a busy office which may be caught by the condition. If in doubt, the best thing to do would be to tell the insurers. Insurance, essentially, is about peace of mind. It should be remembered that the insured's new or renewal policy will exclude the claim and he will be relying upon his old policy for protection.

3. The insured should not admit liability or make any admission, arrangement, offer, promise or payment without the insurers' written consent.

4. The insured must give as much assistance to the insurers as is necessary for them to handle any claim. However, in the event of a dispute the insured will not be required to contest any legal proceedings unless a Queen's Counsel (or by mutual agreement

between the insured and the insurers a similar authority) shall advise that such proceedings could be contested with the probability of success.

5. Insurers will not exercise any right of subrogation against any employee or former employee of the insured unless there is any dishonest, fraudulent, criminal or malicious conduct on the part of that employee.

6. If any claim which is made under the policy for indemnity is false or fraudulent then the policy becomes void

7. The policy is normally governed by the law of England and any dispute or difference arising between the insured and his insurers will be referred to a Queen's Counsel to be mutually agreed between the insured and the insurers.

Alleviation of non-disclosure rule

The non-disclosure rule in insurance law is harsh. Any failure to disclose a material fact, misrepresentation or any mistake on the proposal form may make the policy void. Breach of the policy conditions may also invalidate a claim. Some policies contain a clause to the effect that the insurers will not exercise their rights to void the policy or to refuse indemnity to the insured for any breach of non-disclosure of material facts or misrepresentation or breach of policy conditions provided always that *the insured* shall establish to the satisfaction of insurers that such non-disclosure or breach or misrepresentation was innocent and free of any fraudulent conduct or intent to deceive. *The onus of proof is on the insured.* The words used differ amongst insurers. It offers valuable protection.

Chapter 6

Dispute resolution

Elizabeth Jones

Introduction

The history of dispute resolution goes back almost as far as does man himself, with trial by combat, the ducking stool and other such illuminating – and for the purposes of this chapter, irrelevant – techniques, employed in medieval times. The Anglo-Saxons had local systems of dispute settlement, based largely on the principle of jury trial, to deal with land disputes and cattle theft, English law being pre-occupied even then with property, but these were not nationally administered. The Church, however, provided the literacy and the administrative structure to create a national system of what was essentially early central government, ie direct control by the state of the activities of its subjects, the aim being, of course, to facilitate the assessment and collection of taxes which were in existence – and being collected – long before the Domesday Book.

The next development was the struggle between Church and state for pre-eminence symbolised in the Henry II/Becket saga, and the Star Chamber Court of Henry VII (which was originally welcomed as a means of direct access to Royal Authority). At the dissolution of the monasteries in the mid-sixteenth Century the state took over almost completely. The development of the legal doctrine of precedent occurred, perhaps ancillary to, and as a result of, the restriction by the common law of the powers of the Chancellor, who had exercised them – wide and undefined as they were – on the grounds of conscience. This was the forerunner of equity, the branch of law which at one time was said to vary 'with the length of the Chancellor's big toe'. Equity was designed to alleviate the rigidity of the King's Courts of King's Bench, Common Pleas, and Exchequer, and still survives today in the Chancery Division, although it is now administered by all courts.

Most litigation involving building disputes today takes place in the High Court, which is a generic term for the 'King's Court's', where sat the 'King's judges' who used to progress from to town to town for 'Assizes'. For civil matters there are now so-called District Registries of the High Court in regional centres such as Birmingham, Guildford, Manchester and Leeds.

The litigation process

Anyone who has had contact with litigation, either as plaintiff or (more usually) defendant or expert witness, will know that it is arcane, long-drawn-out, expensive, and not really the most efficient way of getting a dispute resolved, let alone achieving that nirvana sometimes called 'justice'. When explaining the court system as found in England and Wales it is necessary to preface any comments by saying that it has nothing or almost nothing to do with the abstract concept called 'justice'. In the High Court it is a process governed by a rigid and much thumbed set of rules called the Supreme Court Practice which are contained in two massive tomes known popularly as the 'White Book'. Anyone who consults the White Book on a point of practice will often find that litigation practitioners interpret the possible courses of action open to them, in terms of the way in which they conduct litigation, more restrictively than the rules would appear to require. One can either attribute this to unfamiliarity with the rules which, to be charitable, is probably not the case, or to long experience of Masters – those appointees of the Lord Chancellor who deal with the procedural points in the preparation for a large case (or Official Referees in building disputes) – refusing to make the order on the point requested because it is too outlandish or appears, without extensive argument on the merits of the case, to be too complex to deal with at that stage of the proceedings. They will also find that the affidavits which they have sworn appear not always to be read in detail, although they are usually submitted before procedural hearings, so that the Master of Official Referee can digest them at leisure.

The post of Official Referee of the Supreme Court of Justice was created by the Judicature Acts of 1873-75. At that time any question could be referred to them for query and report, and any case or matter could, with the consent of the parties – or without their consent if it involved prolonged investigation of documents or accounts, or any scientific or local investigation – be referred for trial.

The first Official Referees were appointed in 1876 and by 1884, the Official Referees could exercise all the powers of a High Court judge.

Today, most of the Official Referees' work is concerned with construction, although RSC Ord 36, in explaining Official Referees' business, states:

'The effect of the rule 1(2) is that Official Referees may try any case within the business of the Chancery and Queen's Bench Divisions unless the defendant is entitled to and insists upon a trial by jury, but while the list is not exclusive, classes of action normally tried by the Official Referees concern:

a) civil or mechanical engineering;
b) building and other construction work generally;
c) claims by and against engineers, architects, surveyors, accountants and other such specialised professional persons or bodies;
d) claims by and against local authorities relating to their statutory duties concerning the development of land or the construction of buildings;
e) claims between neighbours, owners and occupiers of land and trespass, nuisance and liability under *Rylands v Fletcher* (1868) L.R. 3 H.L. 330;
f) claims between landlord and tenant for breaches of repairing covenants;
g) claims relating to the quality of goods sold or hired;
h) claims relating to work done and materials supplied or services rendered;
i) claims involving taking of accounts especially where these are complicated;
j) claims arising out of fires;
k) claims relating to computers; and
l) claims relating to the environment.'

The London Official Referees' Courts consist of eight large and two small courts situated on the third to sixth floors of St Dunstan's House, 133-137 Fetter Lane, London, EC4.

For those not familiar with them, the stages for civil litigation in the High Court are as follows:

(a) A writ is issued by the plaintiff (ie the claimant) giving brief details of the claims and its amount. This must normally be served on the defendant within four months of the date of issue. The defendant will have 14 days from the date of service to file notice of intention to defend ie to indicate that he wishes to contest some (or all) of the claim. A limited company must engage solicitors to act for them, a private individual can act in person. A statement of claim, giving more details of the plaintiff's claim is served either at the same time as the writ or later. It must in any event be served within 14 days of issue of the writ. The statement of claim is usually drafted by counsel, ie a barrister.

(b) The defendant then has to prepare his defence, which has to be served within 14 days of notice of intent to defend having been given. Usually, in complicated cases, this time limit is extended by agreement and the defendant will serve lists of questions for 'further and better particulars' of the claim which must be answered by the plaintiff. The plaintiff can then himself ask for further and better particulars of the defence and will usually put in a reply, rebutting the defendant's argument. The aim of this exercise in exchanging pieces of paper (not always successful) is to highlight any weaknesses in the plaintiff's case (or for that matter that of the defence) to encourage the parties to settle. The defendant may serve a counterclaim.

(c) *Discovery* is the term for a process peculiar to common law based systems whereby, apart from documents claimed to be privileged, ie protected from disclosure, every relevant document relating to the case in the possession of either side must be disclosed to the other. These documents are listed in set categories and each side 'serves' their list on the other. The recipient can then either inspect the listed documents (apart from the privileged ones) or ask for photocopies of individual documents, or both. Discovery in a large case can take several months to complete and is a major source of pre-trial costs, something which at least discourages frivolous claims and defences. Unfortunately (and see the discussion below about 'front-loading' disputes), barristers and litigation solicitors are traditionally reluctant to advise on the merits of a claim until discovery is complete.

(d) *Expert witnesses* The reader may well have come into contact with the disputes process in this capacity. Experts can be appointed at any stage during the litigation process and are usually senior members of professional firms or practising academics. In major construction and other technical cases the weight placed on the expert evidence may be very great and in very complex cases more than one expert may be required. Experts' reports, once produced, are exchanged with the other side and meetings are usually held between experts 'without prejudice', either before or after exchange of reports, to clarify the issues and agree on whatever points do not need to be contested.

(e) *The trial* Settlement is most likely immediately before the start of the hearing, ideally before brief fees – the major amount of fees paid to the barrister – have been incurred. In a large trial brief fees – paid on delivery of the brief (or instructions to appear at the hearing) – can be tens of thousands of pounds. This is said by the uncharitable to be one of the reasons why counsel do not consider the merits of the case earlier. The accepted reason is that the experts' reports from both sides and the documents revealed in discovery are necessary for a proper assessment of the case.

Should a construction case arise which would appear to be Official Referee's business then a solicitor will issue his writ at the Registry at St Dunstan's House. The case will be allocated to a particular Official Referee in rotation. The judge allocated to the case will then, at least in theory, deal personally with interlocutory applications as well as the trial giving the obvious advantage of consistency and in-depth knowledge concerning the particular case. Pursuant to the court rules, the plaintiff has to make an application for directions within 14 days of the defendant giving notice of intention to defend or of the date of the order transferring the case.

For many years, Official Referees have given directions at this first hearing which are now becoming commonplace in other cases. For example, an order for directions will often include the service of a Scott Schedule, the exchange of experts reports and 'without prejudice' meetings of experts. An Official Referee will often enquire of the parties as to whether there will be any further defendants or third parties joined in the action. He will ascertain whether any preliminary issues could be tried separately, which often represents a considerable saving in costs. He will deal with the service of pleadings, discovery by way of list of documents and inspection of documents. He will invariably order the exchange by the parties of statements of witnesses of fact. RSC Order 36, r 6 was amended in October 1982 to include a specific requirement that the application for directions should include an application for a fixed date for a hearing. Thus the parties know from the outset what is the timetable for the conduct of the action and what will be the trial date.

A common form of directions is stated in the rules to be as follows:

'On the hearing of the Summons for Directions the Official Referee will usually:
1. Make orders as to pleadings.
2. Where the case involves much detail, order that one party delivers a Scott Schedule with column headings decided by the Official Referee or to be agreed between the parties, and that other parties comment upon it; alternatively the Official Referee may order a party to deliver a draft final account and other parties to comment on it; and in the further alternative the Official Referee may order that each party provides a chronicle of events.
3. Order discovery by lists, followed by inspection.
4. Make orders limiting the number of experts; requiring that those of like disciplines should meet without prejudice with a view to agreeing technical facts and narrowing issues; and that reports should be exchanged.
5. Make orders for signed statements of witnesses of fact to serve as evidence in chief to be cross served between the parties.
6. Make orders as to plans, photographs and models if parties are not agreed about them.
7. If the case is an "over 10 days case" or appears to warrant it, order a pre-trial conference to be attended by counsel and solicitors to decide among other things how the case can best

be tried. The Official Referee may order that the plaintiff's counsel provide beforehand a list of issues and proposals as to how the case should be tried and that other counsel should comment upon them.

8. When appropriate, order a view, usually after conclusion of the plaintiff's opening, but, if the subject matter of the action is likely to be altered before trial, then on a date to be arranged with his clerk.

9. Discuss with the parties the probable length of the trial and then fix a hearing date for it.

10. Give liberty to restore generally, which enables any party to restore on given written notice to the Court and to other parties of additional directions which he seeks.

11. Make orders by reference to calendar dates and not by days following events as they are less likely to be overlooked.'

The rules then go on to describe the directions which are not common form directions.

Examples of these are: buildings not to be altered until experts have had opportunities for examining them fully; joint making of trial pits or boreholes, joint laboratory analysis; where a Scott Schedule has been ordered – that parties should select representative items from it for trial; witness to be examined before trial – preferably by the Official Referee or recorder likely to conduct the trial; and arrangements for video displays and the like.

The whole emphasis in the Official Referees' Courts is towards streamlining. There are, of course, pressures upon the courts which make this aim impossible at times. Construction cases are invariably long and complicated and thus the courts can be over stretched resulting in a delay in cases coming on for trial. Cases often settle at the vary last moment and therefore other cases are booked to take place as second, third, fourth or even fifth fixtures in the event of cases having priority in relation to dates having been settled. This all results in uncertainty. Nevertheless, the Official Referees' Court strives to provide a quick method of settling disputes both in its encouragement of the parties at best to reach a settlement or, at worst, to narrow the issues prior to trial by virtue of the open system of pre-trial procedure. They encourage experts, for example, to meet without prejudice and agree a statement of what is and what is not agreed between the parties. The exchange of statements of witnesses is designed for the following beneficial purposes:

'1. The fair and expeditious disposal of proceedings and the saving of costs.

2. The elimination of any element of surprise before or at trial as to the witnesses each party intends to call at the trial or as to the substance of their evidence.

3. The promotion of a fair settlement between parties. The parties will be able to make an assessment of the strengths and weaknesses of their cases.
4. The avoidance of a trial.
5. The identification of the real issues and the elimination of unnecessary issues.
6. The encouragement of the parties to make admissions of fact, which they are often reluctant to do.
7. The reduction in the number of pre-trial applications, such as for further and better particulars or for further discovery of documents or for interrogatories.
8. The possible elimination of giving long, drawn out evidence in chief.
9. The improvement of the process of cross-examination.
10. The concentration of the parties and trial judge on the real matters in controversy between the parties.'

The witness statement served must be full and complete. It must be the 'truth, the whole truth and nothing but the truth'. The party serving the witness statement may not lead evidence from his witness, the substance of which is not included in the statement served, except as to a new matter or with the consent of the other party or with leave of the court. It is therefore essential that very great care is taken over the preparation of the witness statements. The party serving the statement may apply to the court to amend the statement to correct any error or mistake or other mistakes. The opposing party may apply to the court to amend the statement by striking out such material as they say is irrelevant or heresay evidence or expression of opinion or inadmissible evidence.

Despite the streamlining of the procedures and the open system of pre-trial procedure, the pursuit of an action in the Official Referees' Court is still likely to be very expensive indeed, as well as being time consuming for clients in that key people are likely to be taken out of the office or off site for weeks both prior to and during the trial. It has also to be borne in mind that even the successful party will have to bear some of the costs of pursuing his case – usually between one third and half of his own costs. He also runs the risk that he may lose, with the consequence that he will have to bear all his own costs plus a considerable proportion of the opposing parties' costs – usually between half and two thirds.

Given the arrival of Alternative Disputes Resolution (ADR) – which is discussed later in this chapter – there is more and more examination of the inefficiencies of the present system and Official Referees and the solicitors using their courts both have associations which, amongst other things, work to make the process more efficient. Some Official Referees' Courts now have computer screens available to assist in handling the huge amount of data which is generated by modern construction litigation and often processed, these days, by computer.

One of the expressed advantages of ADR is that it 'front-loads' the disputes process. This means that the lawyers and others involved look at the merits and causes of the dispute at the beginning of the whole process rather than at the end. Were this done as part of the litigation process, it would considerably speed matters and there are moves to use the preliminary issues procedure, whereby points of substance, decision of which might solve the whole dispute, are dealt with very early on, before discovery has taken place. In some common law jurisdictions the hearing of preliminary issues is mandatory and acts as a very good way of compulsorily 'front-loading' the litigation. In my experience, solicitors and counsel here are usually reluctant to apply for a hearing of any preliminary issues which there might be on the grounds that 'you might lose' and if you do ' you will be in a less good position to settle than before'. This, of course, is on the basis that the legal costs and expenditure in management time involved in taking a large case to trial act as a disincentive of the highest order to anything other than the settlement of the case. It is difficult to see that the system is likely to change appreciably in the near future, although there is evidence that the judiciary would like to see greater 'front-loading' of disputes, and in at least one case known to the writer a hearing of preliminary issues has been ordered by the Official Referee, regardless of the wishes of the parties.

One of the areas of litigation in which architects are (unfortunately) most likely to become involved is that of professional negligence claims. Even if they are not the 'chief' defendant, they may very well find themselves joined as parties simply in order to bring in their insurers, especially where the other defendants are financially stretched developers or contractors, whose pockets are, in the time-worn phrase, 'not so deep'. In one unfortunate case[1] the consulting engineer was left holding the proverbial baby as his co-defendants went into liquidation, and another recent case[2] was based on the premise that a potential corporate defendant was deliberately put into liquidation to avoid having to face a claim.

The great problem with litigation in these situations is that the size of the claims are often very high, the subject matter is very complex and the costs of fighting a case as a defendant also very high. If there is any sort of likelihood of liability, the advice will be, eventually, to settle rather than risk an expensive and unsuccessful battle, and this will often leave a defendant who *thinks* he has a good case not only feeling extremely dissatisfied but with a large excess to pay. His insurers, who are probably not very interested in the technical pros and cons, will feel that they have done a good commercial deal and the

1 *Eckersley v Binnie & Partners* [1988] CILL 388.
2 *Mowlem (John) & Co plc v Eagle Star Insurance* (18 December 1992, unreported) noted in [1993] BLM (March 3).

plaintiff, who may, to a great or lesser extent, be 'trying it on' anyway, will feel well satisfied. If one is a plaintiff, on the other hand, particularly one claiming money owed in a dispute, it is all too easy to feel that the system is stacked against one. Perhaps one of the greatest faults in both litigation and arbitration is that, in their wish to achieve as near perfection as possible – enormous attention to detail, hundreds of hours spent copying, sorting, collating (a whole industry of 'para-legals' or 'litigation support staff' has grown up around modern litigation) – these systems have missed the point. Whilst it may be appropriate in a criminal, or personal injuries case to turn over every stone in the pursuit of truth and justice, in most commercial disputes everyone, including the litigants, really know that it is six of one and half a dozen of the other (or something often approximating to that), in practice if not in law, and the last thing either side really wants, unless it is a point of principle, or cash flow, is to spend pounds (and hours of management time) on a long and costly arbitration or court case. Hence the interest in ADR, of which more anon.

Arbitration

Arbitration evolved as an alternative to litigation for the settlement of commercial disputes privately and, originally, informally and speedily. There is a view that it evolved from the medieval concept of law merchant or *lex mercatoria* which was used in Medieval Europe and whose enforcement by the disputants was sought otherwise than in the local jury courts (too parochial) or the King's Courts (too national). There is a report [3] of an application to the Court of Star Chamber in 1478 by 'an alien merchant who has come to conduct his case here' and who 'ought not to be held to await trial by twelve men and other solemnities of the law of the land . . . but ought to be able to sue here . . . '. Shakespeare knew the term – ' . . . that old common arbitrator, time, will one day end it'[4] and it is generally thought to be Latin in origin. Fowler defines an arbitrator as someone who 'decides an issue referred to him by the parties and is accountable if he fails to act judicially or to observe a procedure prescribed by statute. An arbiter acts arbitrarily; an arbitrator must not'.[5]

'Look-sniff' arbitrations carried out in the field of commodities are still instant 'yes-no' operations. Maritime arbitrations, equally, are very streamlined still. Not so most arbitrations concerned with the construction industry. It may be a function of the complexity and

3 See R Baden-Hellard *Managing Construction Conflicts* (1988) p 21.
4 Trolius & Cressida IV v 224-5.
5 *Fowler's Modern English Usage* (2nd edn (revsd), 1983) p 34.

value of the matters now dealt with in construction arbitrations or of the increasing tendency of the courts to claim jurisdiction over arbitration decisions where points of law are concerned, but the general rule in these arbitrations is for them to be conducted by lawyers with all the procedures of major litigation such as discovery, inspection of documents, witness statements, etc, thus in fact, making the process – it is widely acknowledged – less quick, cheap and efficient, in some cases, than the litigation it has replaced.

Now, of course, litigants attempting to use the Ord 14 (summary judgment) and Ord 29 (interim payment) procedures of the High Court are often defeated on the ground that the contract provides for arbitration of all disputes and the slightest hint of a 'genuine' dispute (as opposed to mere refusal to pay on a certificate) is enough to have the matter adjourned pending arbitration. ADR clauses or references to agreed 'experts' are now being written into many standard form contracts, so matters should improve. At present, arbitration lacks much of the flexibility which can result from intelligent use by judge, Official Referee or Master of his powers to issue directions to pressurise the parties into concentrating on the merits of their case. The arbitrator on the other hand is usually a non-lawyer who may be overawed by the battery of City law firms arrayed by the parties and thus intimidated into not using his powers. Indeed, in multi-partite disputes, arbitration can actually be less flexible than litigation, since it does not strictly provide for more than two parties to be involved – creating a situation where, for example, other parties to the dispute cannot be joined as 'third parties' as they would be in litigation. This can lead to expensive duplication of proceedings, unless the parties consent to a multi-party arbitration, but these are extremely unusual.

Arbitration procedures are – or perhaps under the influence of lawyers, have become – surprisingly like those of litigation without, in most cases, the range and flexibility of the White Book procedures. Bernstein in his *Handbook of Arbitration Practice*[6] says that 'subject always to any restrictions imposed upon him by the arbitration agreement and by the requirements of natural justice the arbitrator controls the procedure of the arbitration . . . ' However, the Court of Appeal has endorsed the adversarial, rather than the continental inquisitorial system even for arbitration[7] in spite of some very distinguished advocates of the latter: 'Arbitrators should not allow themselves to be dominated by English procedures. In long and complex cases the continental inquisitorial procedure is often more effective than our adversarial system . . .'[8]

Traditionally, there are two types of procedures: 'documents only', and the usual oral hearing. A documents only arbitration is exactly what is says and may be accompanied by written statements,

6 Sweet & Maxwell 1987.
7 Donaldson LJ in *Clutton v Saga Holidays* [1986] 1 All ER 84.
8 Kerr LJ at a seminar entitled 'Forum London' in 1981.

discovery and inspections. With an oral hearing there can be pleadings with an agreed bundle of documents, statements of case and replies in lieu of the traditional pleadings, expert evidence only, experts agreeing a list of common points etc. In practice, most large construction arbitrations resemble High Court proceedings to such an extent that the only difference is less flexibility, the lack of a forceful judge and privacy. Little wonder that commercial people have turned to the concept of ADR with such interest, if not actual enthusiasm. ADR is aiming to be what arbitration should have been: a quick, efficient and cheap way of resolving commercial disputes.

There are now proposals for a new Arbitration Act, promoted, rather unusually, by a collection of private 'interested parties' – barristers, solicitors, and others such as the Chartered Institute of Arbitrators. The Bill is intended to be more than mere consolidation of existing law: the Acts of 1950, 1975 and 1979 and the relevant provisions of the Courts and Legal Services Act 1990. For example, the need to refer to the litigator's bible, the White Book, is to be reduced – a welcome change – and the aim is to state in statutory form the more important general principles of English arbitration law. The proposal has now been adopted by the Department of Trade and Industry and once the drafting has been finalised is expected to become law sometime in 1994.

Alternative disputes resolution

Alternative Disputes Resolution (ADR) should really include arbitration, since what it is strictly 'alternative' to, it is suggested, is litigation. ADR is fundamentally an American concept, although it is now practised in the Far East, Australia and the UK, and many commercial lawyers would say they had spent their time practising ADR by settling disputes round a table on an informal basis for years.

The main acknowledged methods of ADR are listed below.

The mini-trial

A mini-trial is essentially a hearing in front of decision makers, from the (usually two) disputing parties who also have an agreed 'neutral' presence. It can take place after the commencement of court proceedings and even after discovery and inspection. Each party has a lawyer who makes a presentation plus a reply to the presentation of the other party. 'Core bundles' may be put in evidence together with a written statement of limited length. The decision makers then consider the matter with or without the participation of the neutral.

The 'neutral', otherwise known as the conciliator or mediator, is a key figure in ADR. Sir Laurence Street, former Chief Justice of New South Wales has suggested that the qualities of a neutral are impartiality, objectivity, intelligence, flexibility, articulacy, forcefulness and persuasiveness, empathy, being a 'good listener', imaginative, respected in the community, sceptical, honest, reliable, non-defensive(?), having a sense of humour, patience, perseverance and optimism – perhaps a shorter way of describing the job is that it requires the wisdom of Solomon and the patience of Job!

Mediation

Mediation also involves representatives from each side of a dispute sitting down with a neutral. The terms 'mediation' and 'conciliation' are often used interchangeably. Generally, a mediator will speak to each party separately in order to help them define their case and will not disclose confidential information to the other party. Roget gives alternatives for mediator as 'advocate, arbiter, arbitrator, go-between, honest broker, interceder, intermediary, judge, middleman, moderator, negotiator, peacemaker, referee, umpire'[9], which probably covers most of the shades of meaning associated with the process. The word 'conciliation' on the other hand has 'appeasement, disarming, mollification, pacification, placation, propitiation, reconciliation, and soothing'[10], which perhaps points up the difference.

Witnesses are usually not present although reference may be made to what they are likely to say. A presentation is made at the beginning of the session, which is likely to last a day (or at most two). A mediation, like other ADR methods, does not commit the parties to making any settlement of their dispute. Often, in a mediation run by institutions such as the Centre for Disputes Resolution (CEDR) no settlement is reached at the 'hearing' itself, but the process of communication started at the mediation, continues and may result in eventual settlement. A copy of the CEDR rules are set out in Appendix D by way of illustration of the procedures which can be used in ADR.

Conciliation

This process is often difficult to distinguish from mediation, although many bodies including the International Court of Arbitration, now have 'Rules of Conciliation' and the UN, endorsing the UNCITRAL Conciliation Rules said[11]:

9 *New Collins Thesaurus* (1987).
10 Ibid.
11 United Nations Commission on International Trade Law Resolution of 4 December 1980.

'The General Assembly

Recognising the value of conciliation as a method of amicably settling disputes arising in the context of international commercial relations.

Convinced that the establishment of conciliation rules that are acceptable in countries with different legal social and economic systems could significantly contribute to the development of harmonising international relations . . .

1. Recommends the use of the Conciliation Rules of the United Nations Commission on International Trade Law in cases where a dispute arises in the context of international commercial relations and the parties seek an amicable settlement of that dispute by recourse to conciliation.'

'Mediation' and 'conciliation' are therefore used interchangeably. The International Chamber of Commerce in Paris has Rules of Conciliation. In Australia there is a Commercial Dispute Centre in Sydney which goes under the somewhat unfortunate acronym of 'ACDC'. In the United States the American Arbitration Association and many others provide conciliation services. In the Far East, Hong Kong has a requirement for conciliation enshrined in its legislation and in the UK ACAS has for many years had, again, a statutory role to play in labour disputes. Another acronym is BATNA – Best Alternative To A Negotiated Agreement (which is presumably borrowed from the environmentalists' BATNEEC – (Best Available Technology Not Entailing Excessive Cost).

Conclusion

Dispute resolution by the end of the 1990s is likely to be an appreciably different animal from that of the 1970s and 1980s. Court procedures are likely to be more streamlined – there is already a proposal that barristers and judges should no longer wear wigs. Cynics have suggested that the failure by government thus far to fund ADR in the area of commercial disputes is a calculated attempt to reduce the costs of the legal system – if major commercial disputes are decided privately rather than through the court system, the courts will be relieved of the cost of servicing them and the lists be less full. The problem is that a two-tier NHS/private type court system would polarise the legal profession even further between those who service the large commercial clients and those who do the family, legal aid and personal injury work and standards of administration in the lower civil courts are already the subject of complaint.

Otherwise where to? Computers in court, a White Book with an intelligible index, a logical room layout to the offices in Law Courts in the Strand? The possibilities are endless. Perhaps what should genuinely be hoped for is a more efficient system which reduces delays and costs of hearings themselves and forces the parties' legal representatives to consider the merits earlier rather than at the door of the court.

Appendix A

Form of Agreement for

Collateral Warranty
for purchasers & tenants | CoWa/P&T |

The forms in this pad are for use where a warranty is to be given to a purchaser or tenant of a whole building in a commercial and/or industrial development, or a part of such a building. It is essential that the number of warranties to be given to tenants in one building should sensibly be limited.

General advice

1. The term "collateral agreement", "duty of care letter" or "collateral warranty" is often used without due regard to the strict legal meaning of the phrase. It is used here for agreements with tenants or purchasers of the whole or part of a commercial and/or industrial development.

2. The purpose of the Agreement is to bind the party giving the warranty in contract where no contract would otherwise exist. This can have implications in terms of professional liability and could cause exposure to claims which might otherwise not have existed under Common Law.

3. The information and guidance contained in this note is designed to assist consultants faced with a request that collateral agreements are entered into.

4. The use of the word 'collateral' is not accidental. It is intended to refer to an agreement that is an adjunct to another or principal agreement, namely the conditions of appointment of the consultant. It is imperative therefore that before collateral warranties are executed the consultant's terms and conditions of appointment have been agreed between the client and the consultant and set down in writing.

5. Under English Law the terms and conditions of the consultant's appointment may be 'under hand' or executed as a Deed. In the latter case the length of time that claims may be brought under the Agreement is extended from six years to twelve years.

6. Under English Law this Form of Agreement for Collateral Warranty is designed for use under hand or to be executed as a Deed. It should not be signed as a Deed when it is collateral to an appointment which is under hand.

7. The acceptance of a claim under the consultant's professional indemnity policy, brought under the terms of a collateral warranty, will depend upon the terms and conditions of the policy in force at the time when a claim is made.

8. Consultants with a current indemnity insurance policy taken out under the RIBA, RICSIS, ACE or RIASIS schemes will not have a claim refused simply on the basis that it is brought under the terms of a collateral warranty provided that warranty is in this form. In other respects the claim will be treated in accordance with policy terms and conditions in the normal way. **Consultants insured under different policies** must seek the advice of their brokers or insurers.

9. **Amendment to the clauses should be resisted.** Insurers' approval as mentioned above is in respect of the unamended clauses only.

Commentary on Clauses

Recital A.

This needs completion.

When this warranty is to be given in favour of a purchaser or tenant of part of the Development, the following words in square brackets must be deleted.

["The Premises" are also referred to as "the Development" in this Agreement.]

Care must be taken in describing "the Premises" accurately.

When this warranty is to be given in favour of a purchaser or tenant of the entire development, the terms "the Premises" and "the Development" are synonymous.

The following words in square brackets must be deleted

[forming part of. ....

at. .... ("the Development").]

Recitals B & C

These are self explanatory but need completion.

Clause 1

This confirms the duty of care that will be owed to the Purchaser/the Tenant. The words in square brackets enable the clause to reflect exactly the provisions contained within the terms and conditions of the Appointment.

Paragraphs (a),(b) and (c) qualify and limit in three ways the Firm's liability in the event of a breach of the duty of care.

1 (a) By this provision, the Firm is liable for the reasonable costs of repair renewal and or reinstatement of the Development insofar as the Purchaser/the Tenant has a financial obligation to pay or contribute to the cost of that repair. Other losses are expressly excluded.

1 (b) By this provision the Firm's potential liability is limited. The intention is that the effect of "several" liability at Common Law is negated. When the Firm agrees - probably at the time of appointment - to sign a warranty at a future date, the list should include the names, if known, or otherwise the description or profession, of those responsible for the design of the relevant parts of the Development and the general contractor. When the warranty is signed, the list should be completed with the names of those previously referred to by description or profession.

1 (c) By this clause, the Purchaser/ the Tenant is bound by any limitations on liability that may exist in the conditions of the Appointment. Furthermore, the consultant has the same rights of defence that would have been available had the relevant claim been made by the Client under the Appointment.

1 (d) This states the relationship between the Firm and any consultant employed by the Purchaser/the Tenant to survey the premises.

Clause 2

As a consultant it is not possible to give assurances beyond those to the effect that materials as listed have not been nor will be specified. Concealed use of such materials by a contractor could possibly occur, hence the very careful restriction in terms of this particular warranty. Further materials may be added.

Clause 3

This obliges the consultant to ensure that all fees due and owing including VAT at the time the warranty is entered into have been paid.

Clause 4

This is included to make it clear that the Purchaser/the Tenant has no power or authority to direct or instruct the Firm in its duties to the Client.

Clause 5

Reasonable use by the Purchaser/the Tenant of drawings and associated documents is necessary in most cases. By this clause, the Purchaser/ the Tenant is given the rights that might be reasonably expected but it does not allow the reproduction of the designs for any purpose outside the scope of the Development.

Clause 6

This confirms that professional indemnity insurance will be maintained in so far as it is reasonably possible to do so. Professional indemnity insurance is on the basis of annual contracts and the terms and conditions of a policy may change from renewal to renewal.

Clause 7

This allows the Purchaser/the Tenant to assign the benefit of this Warranty provided it is done by formal legal assignment and relates to the entire interest of the original Purchaser/Tenant. By this clause any right of assignment may be limited or extinguished. If it is to be extinguished the word "not" shall be inserted after "may" and all words after "the Purchaser/ the Tenant" deleted. If it is agreed that there should be a limited number of assignments, the precise number should be inserted in the space between "assigned" and "by the Purchaser/the Tenant".

Clause 7S

This is applicable in Scotland in relation to assignations. Completion is as for Clause 7.

Clause 8

This identifies the method of giving Notice under Clause 7 & 7S.

Clause 9

This needs completion. The clause makes clear that any liability that the Firm has by virtue of this Warranty ceases on the expiry of the stated period of years after practical completion of the Premises. (Note: the practical completion of the Development may be later).

Under English law the period should not exceed 6 years for agreements under hand, nor 12 years for those executed as a Deed.

In Scotland, the Prescription and Limitations (Scotland) Act 1973 prescribes a 5 year period.

Clause 10 and Attestation below

The appropriate method of execution by the Firm and the Purchaser/the Tenant should be checked carefully.

Clause 10S and Testing Clause below

This assumes the Firm is a partnership and the Purchaser/the Tenant is a Limited Company. Otherwise legal advice should be taken.

Published by
The British Property Federation Limited
35 Catherine Place, London SW1E 6DY Telephone: 071-828 0111

© The British Property Federation, The Association of Consulting Engineers, The Royal Incorporation of Architects in Scotland, The Royal Institute of British Architects and The Royal Institution of Chartered Surveyors. 1992.

ISBN 0 900101 08 7

N.B. The above advice and commentary is not intended to affect the interpretation of this Collateral Warranty. It is based on the terms of insurance current at the date of publication. All parties to the Agreement should ensure the terms of insurance have not changed.

British Property Federation

35 Catherine Place, London SW1E 6DY
Telephone: 071-828 0111
Facsimile: 071-834 3442

MODEL FORM OF COLLATERAL WARRANTY
FOR PURCHASERS AND TENANTS – CoWa/P&T

IMPORTANT ADDITIONAL NOTES FOR CLIENTS

Clients will generally wish to include in their Conditions of Engagement for Consultants, a clause to the effect that the consultant shall be prepared to enter into a stated number of collateral warranties in favour of possible purchasers, a number of tenants in a multi-occupied building and possibly to a funding institution. Model forms of the collateral warranty to be used should be attached to the conditions of engagement, and should be completed so that the consultant is aware of his obligations and liabilities at the time he quotes his fee for the project. CoWa/F should be used for funding institutions as a model.

This model form of collateral warranty for purchasers and tenants, "CoWa/P&T", has been agreed by the BPF, the ACE, the RIAS, the RIBA and the RICS after consultation with the Association of British Insurers. It will be acceptable to many purchasers and tenants. It should be noted that in its unamended form it is acceptable to the main insurers of the three professional organisations. However, some purchasers and tenants may demand additional features. These are listed below but it should be remembered that insistence upon them may negate the consultant's professional indemnity insurance.

In this model form for purchasers and tenants, CoWa/P&T, the following points should be noted in addition to the deletions and additions noted in the printed guidance notes.

1.   Economic and Consequential Loss

Clause 1(a) limits the consultant's liability to the recovery of costs of repair, renewal and/or reinstatement of any part or parts of the Development if the consultant has been in breach of the warranty, i.e. negligent. The clause continues by saying that the consultant shall not be liable for any other losses. In other words, if the defect caused by the consultant's negligence causes consequential loss such as loss of profit, loss of production, the cost of removal to, and the renting of, alternative premises etc. then the consultant's liability for them is **excluded.**

Some purchasers and tenants will wish to hold the consultants responsible for "consequential loss". Some consultants may be able to extend their professional indemnity cover to include "consequential loss" and some may be able to obtain additional but separate cover for these losses. In both cases, however, there will almost certainly be a limit to the extent of the consultant's liability. Those clients who wish to extend the consultant's responsibility to cover economic and consequential loss – and who can persuade the consultants to provide adequate insurance cover – should **delete** the last sentence of Clause 1a which reads:

"The Firm shall not be liable for other losses incurred by the Purchaser/the Tenant".

British Property Federation Limited
Registration No. 778293 England. Registered office, as above

Over . . . /

The following sentence should be **inserted** in lieu:

> "The Firm shall in addition be liable for other losses incurred by the Purchaser/the Tenant provided that such additional liability of the Firm shall not exceed £.................................... in respect of each breach of the Firm's warranty contained in this Clause 1".

The figure to be inserted as the limit is often the same as the consultants' professional indemnity cover.

2.   Assignment – Clause 7

Purchasers and Tenants will wish to have the facility to assign their collateral warranties when selling their property or assigning their leases. On the other hand, insurers will wish to limit the number of assignments because this limits their liability. Clients must give careful consideration to completion of Clause 7.

Consultants who wish to deny any assignment will attempt to insert "not" between "This Agreement may" and "be assigned", in line 1 of Clause 7. This would be   **unacceptable** to most purchasers and tenants. Clients are therefore advised to draw a line between "may" and "be assigned".

There is a further space in line 1 of Clause 7 between "be assigned" and "by the Purchaser/the Tenant". This enables the client to insert the number of assignments which may be allowed by the consultant. Ownership of premises does not change frequently, nor are leases often assigned. A reasonable number inserted in this space would meet most requirements of purchasers or tenants.

3.   Limitation on Liability

Clause 9 removes all doubt about the period of liability under the agreement. "6 years" should be inserted for agreements under hand and "12 years" if the original appointment is executed as a Deed and the agreement is also to be executed as a Deed. Requests from consultants to include shorter periods should be resisted.

21st February 1992
The British Property Federation

Warranty Agreement   CoWa/P&T

THIS AGREEMENT

(In Scotland, leave blank. For applicable date see Testing Clause on page 4)

is made the .... day of 199

BETWEEN:-

(insert name of the Consultant)

(1) ....

of/whose registered office is situated at ....

.... ("the Firm"), and

(insert name of the Purchaser/the Tenant)

(2) ....

whose registered office is situated at ....

....

(delete as appropriate)

("the Purchaser"/"the Tenant" which term shall include all permitted assignees under this Agreement).

WHEREAS:-

(delete as appropriate)

A. The Purchaser/the Tenant has entered into an agreement to purchase/an agreement to lease/a lease with

....

.... ("the Client") relating to

(insert description of the premises)

....

....

....("the Premises")

(delete as appropriate)

[forming part of...

(insert description of the development)

....

....

(insert address of the development)

at ....

.... ("the Development").]

(delete as appropriate)

["The Premises" are also referred to as "the Development" in this Agreement.]

(insert date of appointment)
(delete/complete as appropriate)

B. By a contract ("the Appointment") dated ....
the Client has appointed the Firm as [architects/consulting structural engineers/consulting building services engineers/   surveyors] in connection with the Development.

C. The Client has entered or may enter into a contract ("the Building Contract") with

(insert name of building contractor or "a building contractor to be selected by the Client")

....

....

....

for the construction of the Development.

SPECIMEN

NOW IN CONSIDERATION OF THE PAYMENT OF ONE POUND (£1) BY THE PURCHASER/ THE TENANT TO THE FIRM (RECEIPT OF WHICH THE FIRM ACKNOWLEDGES) IT IS HEREBY AGREED as follows:-

(delete as appropriate to reflect terms of the Appointment)

1. The Firm warrants that it has exercised and will continue to exercise reasonable skill [and care] [care and diligence] in the performance of its services to the Client under the Appointment. In the event of any breach of this warranty:

    (a) subject to paragraphs (b) and (c) of this clause, the Firm shall be liable for the reasonable costs of repair renewal and/or reinstatement of any part or parts of the Development to the extent that

    - the Purchaser/the Tenant incurs such costs and/or
    - the Purchaser/the Tenant is or becomes liable either directly or by way of financial contribution for such costs.

    The Firm shall not be liable for other losses incurred by the Purchaser/the Tenant.

    (b) the Firm's liability for costs under this Agreement shall be limited to that proportion of such costs which it would be just and equitable to require the Firm to pay having regard to the extent of the Firm's responsibility for the same and on the basis that ....

    ....

(insert the names of other intended warrantors)

    ....
    ....
    ....
    ....

    .... shall be deemed to have provided contractual undertakings on terms no less onerous than this Clause 1 to the Purchaser/the Tenant in respect of the performance of their services in connection with the Development and shall be deemed to have paid to the Purchaser/the Tenant such proportion which it would be just and equitable for them to pay having regard to the extent of their responsibility;

    (c) the Firm shall be entitled in any action or proceedings by the Purchaser/the Tenant to rely on any limitation in the Appointment and to raise the equivalent rights in defence of liability as it would have against the Client under the Appointment;

    (d) the obligations of the Firm under or pursuant to this Clause 1 shall not be released or diminished by the appointment of any person by the Purchaser/the Tenant to carry out any independent enquiry into any relevant matter.

(delete where the Firm is the quantity surveyor)

2. [Without prejudice to the generality of Clause 1, the Firm further warrants that it has exercised and will continue to exercise reasonable skill and care to see that, unless authorised by the Client in writing or, where such authorisation is given orally, confirmed by the Firm to the Client in writing, none of the following has been or will be specified by the Firm for use in the construction of those parts of the Development to which the Appointment relates:-

    (a) high alumina cement in structural elements;

    (b) wood wool slabs in permanent formwork to concrete;

    (c) calcium chloride in admixtures for use in reinforced concrete;

    (d) asbestos products;

    (e) naturally occurring aggregates for use in reinforced concrete which do not comply with British Standard 882: 1983 and/or naturally occurring aggregates for use in concrete which do not comply with British Standard 8110: 1985.

(further specific materials may be added by agreement)

    (f)

    In the event of any breach of this warranty the provisions of Clauses 1a, b, c and d shall apply.]

CoWa/P&T   2nd Edition   Page 2
© BPF, ACE, RIAS, RICS, RIBA 1993

3.   The Firm acknowledges that the Client has paid all fees and expenses properly due and owing to the Firm under the Appointment up to the date of this Agreement.

4.   The Purchaser/the Tenant has no authority to issue any direction or instruction to the Firm in relation to the Appointment.

5.   The copyright in all drawings, reports, models, specifications, bills of quantities, calculations and other documents and information prepared by or on behalf of the Firm in connection with the Development (together referred to in this Clause 5 as "the Documents") shall remain vested in the Firm but, subject to the Firm having received payment of any fees agreed as properly due under the Appointment, the Purchaser/the Tenant and its appointee shall have a licence to copy and use the Documents and to reproduce the designs and content of them for any purpose related to the Premises including, but without limitation, the construction, completion, maintenance, letting, promotion, advertisement, reinstatement, refurbishment and repair of the Premises. Such licence shall enable the Purchaser/the Tenant and its appointee to copy and use the Documents for the extension of the Premises but such use shall not include a licence to reproduce the designs contained in them for any extension of the Premises. The Firm shall not be liable for any use by the Purchaser/the Tenant or its appointee of any of the Documents for any purpose other than that for which the same were prepared by or on behalf of the Firm.

(insert amount)

(insert period)

6.   The Firm shall maintain professional indemnity insurance in an amount of not less than pounds (£   ) for any one occurrence or series of occurrences arising out of any one event for a period of   years from the date of practical completion of the Premises under the Building Contract, provided always that such insurance is available at commercially reasonable rates. The Firm shall immediately inform the Purchaser/the Tenant if such insurance ceases to be available at commercially reasonable rates in order that the Firm and the Purchaser/the Tenant can discuss means of best protecting the respective positions of the Purchaser/the Tenant and the Firm in the absence of such insurance. As and when it is reasonably requested to do so by the Purchaser/the Tenant or its appointee the Firm shall produce for inspection documentary evidence that its professional indemnity insurance is being maintained.

(insert number of times)

(delete if under Scots law)

7.   This Agreement may   be assigned   by the Purchaser/the Tenant by way of absolute legal assignment to another person taking an assignment of the Purchaser's/the Tenant's interest in the Premises without the consent of the Client or the Firm being required and such assignment shall be effective upon written notice thereof being given to the Firm. No further assignment shall be permitted.

(insert number of times)

(delete if under English law)

7S. *The Purchaser/the Tenant shall   be entitled to assign or transfer his/their rights under this Agreement   to any other person acquiring the Purchaser's/the Tenant's interest in the whole of the Premises without the consent of the Firm subject to written notice of such assignation being given to the Firm in accordance with Clause 8 hereof. Nothing in this clause shall permit any party acquiring such right as assignee or transferee to enter into any further assignation or transfer to anyone acquiring subsequently an interest in the Premises from him.*

8.   Any notice to be given by the Firm hereunder shall be deemed to be duly given if it is delivered by hand at or sent by registered post or recorded delivery to the Purchaser/the Tenant at its registered office and any notice given by the Purchaser/the Tenant hereunder shall be deemed to be duly given if it is addressed to "The Senior Partner"/"The Managing Director" and delivered by hand at or sent by registered post or recorded delivery to the above-mentioned address of the Firm or to the principal business address of the Firm for the time being and, in the case of any such notices, the same shall if sent by registered post or recorded delivery be deemed to have been received forty eight hours after being posted.

(complete as appropriate)

9.   No action or proceedings for any breach of this Agreement shall be commenced against the Firm after the expiry of   years from the date of practical completion of the Premises under the Building Contract.

(delete if under Scots law)	[10. The construction validity and performance of this Agreement shall be governed by English law and the parties agree to submit to the non-exclusive jurisdiction of the English Courts.
(alternatives: delete as appropriate)	[**AS WITNESS** the hands of the parties the day and year first before written.
(for Agreement executed under hand and NOT as a Deed)	Signed by or on behalf of the Firm ....
	in the presence of: ....
	Signed by or on behalf of the Purchaser/the Tenant ....
	in the presence of: ....]
(this must only apply if the Appointment is executed as a Deed)	[**IN WITNESS WHEREOF** this Agreement was executed as a Deed and delivered the day and year first before written.
	by the Firm
	....
	....
	....
	....
	by the Purchaser/the Tenant
	....
	....
	....
	....]]

SPECIMEN

(delete if under English law)	10S. *This Agreement shall be construed and the rights of the parties and all matters arising hereunder shall be determined in all respects according to the Law of Scotland.*
	IN WITNESS WHEREOF these presents are executed as follows:-
	SIGNED by the above named Firm at ....
	on the ....day of ....Nineteen hundred and...............................
	as follows:-
	...(Firm's signature)
	Signature ....Full Name ....
	Address ....
	...Occupation ....
	Signature...Full Name ....
	Address ....
	...Occupation ....
	SIGNED by the above named Purchaser/Tenant at..
	on the ....day of ....Nineteen hundred and...............................
	as follows:-
	For and on behalf of the Purchaser/the Tenant
	...Director/Authorised Signatory
	...Director/Authorised Signatory]

Appendix B

Form of Agreement for

Collateral Warranty
for funding institutions | CoWa/F |

The forms in this pad are for use where a warranty is to be given to a company providing finance for a proposed development. They must not in any circumstances be provided in favour of prospective purchasers or tenants.

General advice

1. The term "collateral agreement", "duty of care letter" or "collateral warranty" is often used without due regard to the strict legal meaning of the phrase. It is used here for agreements with a funding institution putting up money for construction and development.

2. The purpose of the Agreement is to bind the party giving the warranty in contract where no contract would otherwise exist. This can have implications in terms of professional liability and could cause exposure to claims which might otherwise not have existed under Common Law.

3. The information and guidance contained in this note is designed to assist consultants faced with a request that collateral agreements be entered into.

4. The use of the word "collateral" is not accidental. It is intended to refer to an agreement that is an adjunct to another or principal agreement, namely the conditions of appointment of the consultant. It is imperative therefore that before collateral warranties are executed the consultant's terms and conditions of appointment have been agreed between the client and the consultant and set down in writing.

5. Under English Law the terms and conditions of the consultant's appointment may be "under hand" or executed as a Deed. In the latter case the length of time that claims may be brought under the Agreement is extended from six years to twelve years.

6. Under English Law this Form of Agreement for Collateral Warranty is designed for use under hand or to be executed as a Deed. It should not be signed as a Deed when it is collateral to an appointment which is under hand.

7. The acceptance of a claim under the consultant's professional indemnity policy, brought under the terms of a collateral warranty, will depend upon the terms and conditions of the policy in force at the time when a claim is made.

8. Consultants with a current indemnity insurance policy taken out under the RIBA, RICSIS, ACE or RIASIS schemes will not have a claim refused simply on the basis that it is brought under the terms of a collateral warranty provided that warranty is in this form. In other respects the claim will be treated in accordance with policy terms and conditions in the normal way. **Consultants insured under different policies** must seek the advice of their brokers or insurers.

9. **Amendment to the clauses should be resisted.** Insurers' approval as mentioned above is in respect of the unamended clauses only.

Commentary on Clauses

Recitals A, B and C are self-explanatory and need completion. The Consultant is described in the form as "The Firm". The following notes are to assist in understanding the use of the document.

Clause 1
This confirms the duty of care that will be owed to the Company. The words in square brackets enable the clause to reflect exactly the provisions contained within the terms and conditions of the Appointment.

Paragraphs (a) and (b) qualify and limit in two ways the Firm's liability in the event of a breach of the duty of care.

1 (a)   By this provision the Firm's potential liability is limited. The intention is that the effect of "several" liability at Common Law is negated. When the Firm agrees - probably at the time of appointment - to sign a warranty at a future date, the list should include the names, if known, or otherwise the description or profession, of those responsible for the design of the relevant parts of the Development and the general contractor. When the warranty is signed, the list should be completed with the names of those previously referred to by description or profession.

1 (b)   By this clause, the Company is bound by any limitations on liability that may exist in the conditions of the Appointment. Furthermore, the consultant has the same rights of defence that would have been available had the relevant claim been made by the Client under the Appointment.

Clause 2
As a consultant it is not possible to give assurances beyond those to the effect that materials as listed have not been nor will be specified. Concealed use of such materials by a contractor could possibly occur, hence the very careful restriction in terms of this particular warranty. Further materials may be added.

Clause 4
This obliges the consultant to ensure that all fees due and owing including VAT at the time the warranty is entered into have been paid.

Clause 5
This entitles the funding organisation to take over the consultant's appointment from the client on terms that all fees outstanding will be discharged by the funding authority (see Clause 7).

Clause 6
This affects the consultant's right to determine the appointment with the client in the sense that the funding authority will be given the opportunity of taking over the appointment, again subject to the payment of all fees which is the purpose of **Clause 7**.

Clause 8
Reasonable use by the Company of drawings and associated documents is necessary in most cases. By this clause, the Company is given the rights that might be reasonably expected but it does not allow the reproduction of the designs for any purpose outside the scope of the Development.

Clause 9
This confirms that professional indemnity insurance will be maintained in so far as it is reasonably possible to do so. Professional indemnity insurance is on the basis of annual contracts and the terms and conditions of a policy may change from renewal to renewal.

Clause 11
This clause indicates the right of assignment by the funding institution.

Clause 11S
This is applicable in Scotland in relation to assignations.

Clause 12
This identifies the method of giving Notice under Clauses 5, 6, 11 & 11S.

Clause 13
This needs completion. The clause makes clear that any liability that the Firm has by virtue of this Warranty ceases on the expiry of the stated period of years after practical completion of the Premises. (Note: the practical completion of the Development may be later).

Under English law the period should not exceed 6 years for agreements under hand, nor 12 years for those executed as a Deed.

In Scotland, the Prescription and Limitations (Scotland) Act 1973 prescribes a 5 year period.

Clause 14 and Attestation below
The appropriate method of execution by the Firm, the Client and the Company should be checked carefully.

Clause 14S and Testing Clause below
This assumes the Firm is a partnership and the Client and the Company are Limited Companies. Otherwise legal advice should be taken.

Published by
The British Property Federation Limited
35 Catherine Place, London SW1E 6DY Telephone: 071-828 0111

© The British Property Federation, The Association of Consulting Engineers, The Royal Incorporation of Architects in Scotland, The Royal Institute of British Architects and The Royal Institution of Chartered Surveyors. 1992.

ISBN 0 900101 08 6

N.B.   The above advice and commentary is not intended to affect the interpretation of this Collateral Warranty. It is based on the terms of insurance current at the date of publication. All parties to the Agreement should ensure the terms of insurance have not changed.

Warranty Agreement　　CoWa/F

Note

This form is to be used where the warranty is to be given to a company providing finance for the proposed development. Where that company is acting as an agent for a syndicate of banks, a recital should be added to refer to this as appropriate.

THIS AGREEMENT

(In Scotland, leave blank. For applicable date see Testing Clause on page 5)

is made the .... day of .... 19 ....

BETWEEN:-

(insert name of the Consultant)

(1) ....

of/whose registered office is situated at ....

.... ("the Firm");

(insert name of the Firm's Client)

(2) ....

whose registered office is situated at ....

.... ("the Client"); and

(insert name of the financier)

(3) ....

whose registered office is situated at ....

("the Company" which term shall include all permitted assignees under this agreement).

WHEREAS:-

A. The Company has entered into an agreement ("the Finance Agreement") with the Client for the provision of certain finance in connection with the carrying out of

(insert description of the works)

....

....

(insert address of the development)

at...

....

....("the Development").

(insert date of appointment) (delete/complete as appropriate)

B. By a contract ("the Appointment") dated ....
the Client has appointed the Firm as [architects/consulting structural engineers/consulting building services engineers/　　　　　surveyors] in connection with the Development.

(insert name of building contractor or "a building contractor to be selected by the Client")

C. The Client has entered or may enter into a building contract ("the Building Contract") with

....

....

....

for the construction of the Development.

CoWa/F　3rd Edition
© BPF, ACE, RIAS, RIBA, RICS 1992

SPECIMEN

NOW IN CONSIDERATION OF THE PAYMENT OF ONE POUND (£1) BY THE COMPANY TO THE FIRM (RECEIPT OF WHICH THE FIRM ACKNOWLEDGES) IT IS HEREBY AGREED as follows:-

(delete "and care" or "care and diligence" to reflect terms of the Appointment)

1. The Firm warrants that it has exercised and will continue to exercise reasonable skill [and care] [care and diligence] in the performance of its duties to the Client under the Appointment. In the event of any breach of this warranty:

    (a) the Firm's liability for costs under this Agreement shall be limited to that proportion of the Company's losses which it would be just and equitable to require the Firm to pay having regard to the extent of the Firm's responsibility for the same and on the basis that ......

(insert the names of other intended warrantors)

    ....
    ....
    ....
    ....shall
    be deemed to have provided contractual undertakings on terms no less onerous than this Clause 1 to the Company in respect of the performance of their services in connection with the Development and shall be deemed to have paid to the Company such proportion which it would be just and equitable for them to pay having regard to the extent of their responsibility;

    (b) the Firm shall be entitled in any action or proceedings by the Company to rely on any limitation in the Appointment and to raise the equivalent rights in defence of liability as it would have against the Client under the Appointment;

(delete where the Firm is the quantity surveyor)

2. [Without prejudice to the generality of Clause 1, the Firm further warrants that it has exercised and will continue to exercise reasonable skill and care to see that, unless authorised by the Client in writing or, where such authorisation is given orally, confirmed by the Firm to the Client in writing, none of the following has been or will be specified by the Firm for use in the construction of those parts of the Development to which the Appointment relates:-

    (a) high alumina cement in structural elements;

    (b) wood wool slabs in permanent formwork to concrete;

    (c) calcium chloride in admixtures for use in reinforced concrete;

    (d) asbestos products;

    (e) naturally occurring aggregates for use in reinforced concrete which do not comply with British Standard 882: 1983 and/or naturally occurring aggregates for use in concrete which do not comply with British Standard 8110. 1985.

(further specific materials may be added by agreement)

    (f)

    ]

3. The Company has no authority to issue any direction or instruction to the Firm in relation to performance of the Firm's services under the Appointment unless and until the Company has given notice under Clauses 5 or 6.

CoWa/F 3rd Edition
© BPF, ACE, RIAS, RIBA, RICS 1992

Page 2

4. The Firm acknowledges that the Client has paid all fees and expenses properly due and owing to the Firm under the Appointment up to the date of this Agreement. The Company has no liability to the Firm in respect of fees and expenses under the Appointment unless and until the Company has given notice under Clauses 5 or 6.

5. The Firm agrees that, in the event of the termination of the Finance Agreement by the Company, the Firm will, if so required by notice in writing given by the Company and subject to Clause 7, accept the instructions of the Company or its appointee to the exclusion of the Client in respect of the Development upon the terms and conditions of the Appointment. The Client acknowledges that the Firm shall be entitled to rely on a notice given to the Firm by the Company under this Clause 5 as conclusive evidence for the purposes of this Agreement of the termination of the Finance Agreement by the Company.

6. The Firm further agrees that it will not without first giving the Company not less than twenty one days' notice in writing exercise any right it may have to terminate the Appointment or to treat the same as having been repudiated by the Client or to discontinue the performance of any services to be performed by the Firm pursuant thereto. Such right to terminate the Appointment with the Client or treat the same as having been repudiated or discontinue performance shall cease if, within such period of notice and subject to Clause 7, the Company shall give notice in writing to the Firm requiring the Firm to accept the instructions of the Company or its appointee to the exclusion of the Client in respect of the Development upon the terms and conditions of the Appointment.

7. It shall be a condition of any notice given by the Company under Clauses 5 or 6 that the Company or its appointee accepts liability for payment of the fees and expenses payable to the Firm under the Appointment and for performance of the Client's obligations including payment of any fees and expenses outstanding at the date of such notice. Upon the issue of any notice by the Company under Clauses 5 or 6, the Appointment shall continue in full force and effect as if no right of termination on the part of the Firm had arisen and the Firm shall be liable to the Company and its appointee under the Appointment in lieu of its liability to the Client. If any notice given by the Company under Clauses 5 or 6 requires the Firm to accept the instructions of the Company's appointee, the Company shall be liable to the Firm as guarantor for the payment of all sums from time to time due to the Firm from the Company's appointee.

8. The copyright in all drawings, reports, models, specifications, bills of quantities, calculations and other similar documents   provided by the Firm in connection with the Development (together referred to in this Clause 8 as "the Documents") shall remain vested in the Firm but, subject to the Firm having received payment of any fees agreed as properly due under the Appointment, the Company and its appointee shall have a licence to copy and use the Documents and to reproduce the designs and content of them for any purpose related to the Premises including, but without limitation, the construction, completion, maintenance, letting, promotion, advertisement, reinstatement, refurbishment and repair of the Development. Such licence shall enable the Company and its appointee to copy and use the Documents for the extension of the Development but such use shall not include a licence to reproduce the designs contained in them for any extension of the Development. The Firm shall not be liable for any such use by the Company or its appointee of any of the Documents for any purpose other than that for which the same were prepared by or on behalf of the Firm.

9. The Firm shall maintain professional indemnity insurance in an amount of not less than
    (insert amount)   pounds (£   )
    for any one occurrence or series of occurrences arising out of any one event for a period
    (insert period)   of   years from the date of practical completion of the Development for the purposes of the Building Contract, provided always that such insurance is available at commercially reasonable rates. The Firm shall immediately inform the Company if such insurance ceases to be available at commercially reasonable rates in order that the Firm and the Company can discuss means of best protecting the respective positions of the Company and the Firm in respect of the Development in the absence of such insurance. As and when it is reasonably requested to do so by the Company or its appointee under the Clauses 5 or 6, the Firm shall produce for inspection documentary evidence that its professional indemnity insurance is being maintained.

10. The Client has agreed to be a party to this Agreement for the purposes of acknowledging that the Firm shall not be in breach of the Appointment by complying with the obligations imposed on it by Clauses 5 and 6.

(delete if under Scots law)

[11. This Agreement may be assigned by the Company by way of absolute legal assignment to another company providing finance or re-finance in connection with the carrying out of the Development without the consent of the Client or the Firm being required and such assignment shall be effective upon written notice thereof being given to the Client and to the Firm.]

(delete if under English law)

[11S. *The Company shall be entitled to assign or transfer its rights under this Agreement to any other company providing finance or re-finance in connection with the carrying out of the Development without the consent of the Client or the Firm being required subject to written notice of such assignation being given to the Firm in accordance with Clause 12 hereof.*]

12. Any notice to be given by the Firm hereunder shall be deemed to be duly given if it is delivered by hand at or sent by registered post or recorded delivery to the Company at its registered office and any notice given by the Company hereunder shall be deemed to be duly given if it is addressed to "The Senior Partner"/"The Managing Director" and delivered by hand at or sent by registered post or recorded delivery to the above-mentioned address of the Firm or to the principal business address of the Firm for the time being and, in the case of any such notices, the same shall if sent by registered post or recorded delivery be deemed to have been received forty eight hours after being posted.

(complete as appropriate)

13. No action or proceedings for any breach of this Agreement shall be commenced against the Firm after the expiry of   years from the date of practical completion of the Premises under the Building Contract.

(delete if under Scots law)

[14. The construction validity and performance of this agreement shall be governed by English Law and the parties agree to submit to the non-exclusive jurisdiction of the English Courts.

(alternatives: delete as appropriate)

[**AS WITNESS** the hands of the parties the day and year first before written.

(for Agreement executed under hand and NOT as a Deed)

Signed by or on behalf of the Firm ....

in the presence of: ....

Signed by or on behalf of the Client ....

in the presence of: ....

Signed by or on behalf of the Company ....

in the presence of: ....]

(this must only apply if the Appointment is executed as a Deed)

[**IN WITNESS WHEREOF** this Agreement was executed as a Deed and delivered the day and year first before written.

by the Firm

....

....

....

by the Client

....

....

....

by the Company

....

....

....]]

SPECIMEN

(delete if under English law) [14S. *This Agreement shall be construed and the rights of the parties and all matters arising hereunder shall be determined in all respects according to the Law of Scotland.*

IN WITNESS WHEREOF these presents are executed as follows:-

SIGNED by the above named Firm at ....

on the ....day of...........................Nineteen hundred and................................

as follows:-

....*(Firm's signature)*

Signature ....*Full Name* ....

Address ....

....*Occupation* ....

Signature ....*Full Name* ....

Address ....

....*Occupation* ....

SIGNED by the above named Client at ....

on the ....day of...........................Nineteen hundred and................................

as follows:-

For and on behalf of the Client

....*Director/Authorised Signatory*

....*Director/Authorised Signatory*

SIGNED by the above named Company at ....

on the ....day of...........................Nineteen hundred and................................

as follows:-

For and on behalf of the Company

....*Director/Authorised Signatory*

....*Director/Authorised Signatory*]

Appendix C

NFHA Recommended Form of Agreement for Collateral Warranty

THIS AGREEMENT

is made the .... day of 199

BETWEEN:

.... of/whose registered office

is situated at .... ('the

Association'), and ....

whose registered office is situated at ....

.... ('the Warrantor')

WHEREAS:

A   The Association has entered into an agreement with ....

....

....('the Main Contractor') dated the ....

day of .... 199..... ('the Main Contract') under which the Main
Contractor has agreed to procure, manage, organise and
supervise the design and construction of certain works as
therein described ('the Works') at [...

...........................] in accordance with the terms of the Main
Contract.

B   The Main Contractor has pursuant to the terms of the Main
Contract appointed the Warrantor as[...

....] to act as such in relation to the
Works as described in and upon the terms and conditions
contained in the copy contract annexed hereto ('the Warrantor's
Contract').

Now in consideration of the payment of one pound (£1) by the
Association to the Warrantor (receipt whereof is hereby
acknowledged by the Warrantor).

IT IS HEREBY AGREED AS FOLLOWS:

1   The Warrantor warrants and undertakes to the Association that
it has exercised and will continue to exercise reasonable skill
and care in the performance of its duties to the Main Contractor
under the Warrantor's Contract provided that:

Notes on how to complete the form

Date agreement is made.

Name and address of housing association.

Name and address of firm that is providing the warranty for their design.

Insert name of builder or main contractor and date of the contract between them and the housing association.

Insert site name and address as it is described in the main contract.

Insert the type of service that is appropriate (eg, architects, quantity surveyors, surveyors, engineers, landscape architects, sub-contractors, suppliers).

The housing association must pay the warrantor £1 as consideration for this warranty.

7

(a) The liability of the Warrantor to the Association shall be limited to the reasonable costs of remedying the physical defects to the works caused directly by the failure of the Warrantor to exercise such skill and care and any other losses incurred by the Association howsoever arising are expressly excluded.

This clause may be deleted if the association does not wish the Warranty to be limited in this way. The effect of the deletion will be that the Warrantor will be liable for other costs such as loss of rent or decanting costs, or damage caused by the defect to other property of the association.

(b) The Warrantor is entitled to raise against the Association the equivalent rights of defence as it might have against the Main Contractor under the Warrantor's Contract.

(c) For the avoidance of doubt the Warrantor's liability for loss or damage shall be limited to such sum as the Warrantor ought reasonably to pay having regard to his or her responsibility for the same on the basis that all other consultants and specialists shall where appointed be deemed to have provided to the Association contractual undertakings in respect of their services and shall be deemed to have paid to the Association such contributions as may be appropriate having regard to the extent of their responsibility for such loss or damage.

2 The Warrantor further warrants that where applicable having regard to the provisions of the Main Contract they have exercised and will continue to exercise reasonable skill and care to see that unless authorised by the Association in writing none of the following have been or will be [used or] specified by the Warrantor for use in the construction of those parts of the Works to which the Warrantor's Contract relates:

Delete [ ] if the Warrantor is a designer only (applicable for a Contractor).

a) any materials which at the time they are specified do not comply with the applicable British Standard specification from time to time in force.

b)

....

....

....

....

....

....

Insert any materials or specific items that the housing association does not wish to have included in the building which are not already covered by British Standard specification, eg, asbestos-based products. Care should be taken not to provide a partial list.

3 The Warrantor acknowledges that the Main Contractor has paid all fees and expenses properly due and owing to the Warrantor under the Warrantor's Contract up to the date of this Agreement. The Association has no authority to issue any direction or instruction to the Warrantor in relation to the Warrantor's Contract.

8

4   The Association and its appointees shall have a licence to copy and use all drawings, reports, specifications and other documents relating to the Works and for the extension of the Works but such use shall not include a licence to reproduce the designs contained in them for any extension of the Works. The Warrantor shall not be liable for any such use by the Association or its appointees of any drawings and other documents for any purpose other than that for which the same were prepared and provided by the Warrantor.

5   The Warrantor shall maintain professional indemnity insurance

in the amount of not less than ....

....

....pounds (£.....................)
for any one occurrence or series of occurrences arising out of any one event for a period of (six/twelve) years from the date of practical completion of the Works for the purpose of the Main Contract provided always that such insurance is available in the market at commercially reasonable rates. The Warrantor shall immediately inform the Association if such insurance ceases to be available at commercially reasonable rates. As and when it is reasonably requested to do so by the Association or its appointee the Warrantor or its insurance agent shall produce for inspection documentary evidence that its professional indemnity insurance is being maintained.

Insert the amount of professional indemnity insurance. Housing associations will want to consider this carefully and to set a level that is not prohibitively high but is sufficient to cover any claims against the particular warrantor. This would normally be similar to the cover recommended by the Housing Corporation under a traditional contract commission.

Delete six/twelve years depending on whether the main contract is under hand or deed.

6   In the event of the Association claims a breach of this Agreement the Association shall in so far as the alleged breach is covered by any guarantee given by or on behalf of the National House Builders Council (or other similar organisation) use all reasonable endeavours to seek rectification or remedy of such alleged breach pursuant to the said guarantee to the terms of this Agreement.

7   References to the Warrantor mean as the case may be the sole trader, partnership or company which carries on the business of the Warrantor.

8   This Agreement may be assigned by the Association to another Housing Association by way of absolute legal assignment without the consent of the Warrantor being required and such assignment shall be effective upon written notice thereof being given to the firm.

9   No liability shall attach to the Warrantor hereunder after the expiry of (six/twelve) years from practical completion of the relevant part of the Works.

Delete six/twelve years depending on whether the main contract is under hand or deed.

9

[AS WITNESS the hands of the parties the day and year first before written.

Signed by or on behalf of the Association ....

.... in the

presence of ....

For Agreement under hand.

Signed by or on behalf of the Warrantor ....

in the presence of ....

....]

The warranty should be properly executed, in the same manner as the main contract and all the other collateral warranty agreements.

or

[IN WITNESS WHEREOF this Agreement was executed as a Deed and delivered the day and year first before written.

For Agreement executed as a Deed.

by the Association

....

....

....

....

by the Warrantor ....

....

....

....]

10

Appendix D

C E D R

CENTRE FOR
DISPUTE
RESOLUTION

100, FETTER LANE, LONDON EC4A 1DD
TELEPHONE: 071-430 1852/071-831 2852/071-831 2853 FAX. 071-430 1846

CEDR ALTERNATIVE DISPUTE RESOLUTION PROCEDURES

GUIDELINES FOR MEDIATION

The essence of mediation (broadly synonymous with conciliation) and other ADR procedures is that they are flexible and based on the agreement of the parties. It is therefore not appropriate to have rigid procedures. CEDR suggests that the parties work with CEDR to develop a procedure which will suit their circumstances and needs. The following are suggested guidelines.

1. **Appointment**

   1.1   If so required CEDR will nominate individuals whom it can recommend to act as mediators or work with the parties to select a mutually acceptable mediator of their choice. In exceptional disputes it may be beneficial to have two mediators.

   1.2   The role of the mediator is vital to the success of the process; his qualities and talents are therefore extremely important. It is essential that he is:

        (i)   impartial

        (ii)   articulate and intelligent

        (iii)   a good listener and patient

        (iv)   a good problem solver who can move away from positions to interest based bargaining

        (v)   creative

        (vi)   tenacious - able to keep the parties talking where it appears to be in their interest to do so.

   1.3   The role of the lawyers (or other professional advisers) representing their clients is also important. Their function is to ensure that their clients are properly and fully advised of the effect of any proposed settlement and open to present their client's case. It is their role and not the mediator's to protect their client's interests.

2. **Initial Procedure**

   If approached by one party only, CEDR will undertake to facilitate a mediation by approaching other parties to the dispute.

3. Once the mediator has been agreed by the parties they will agree a mutually convenient time to meet with the mediator for the purposes of having a preliminary discussion to agree the following:

   3.1   Information to be exchanged between the parties before the mediation.

   3.2   Materials to be provided to the mediator. The mediator will often direct that the parties deliver a concise statement of their case putting a limit on the length of the statement.

CEDR is an independent organisation
supported by industry and professional advisers and founded to promote and encourage more effective commercial resolution of disputes

Registered in England as European Dispute Resolution Limited number 2422813. Registered office 100 Fetter Lane, London EC4 1DD

3.3	The period of time each party requires to present their case (the emphasis is on brevity) and the date of the mediation.
3.4	The parties may agree before or during a mediation that they would like the mediator to make non-binding recommendations after the mediation setting out terms for a settlement of the issues between them. It will be for the parties to decide whether to reach agreement based on those recommendations.
3.5	Who is going to represent the party at the mediation. It is advisable that a party should have a management representative with authority to settle and a professional adviser.
3.6	A decision will be made as to whether the mediator needs the assistance of an independent expert.
3.7	The parties will usually agree to refrain from or to stay ongoing proceedings during the mediation process.
3.8	The parties will sign a confidentiality agreement and confirm that the procedure is without prejudice to contemplated or ongoing proceedings.
3.9	The mediator will agree not to serve as an arbitrator or expert in relation to any issues in the case in any ongoing or future proceedings.

4. The Mediation

The object of mediation is to explore settlement options with a particular emphasis on business solutions._ The procedure is business-like and non-adversarial. Each party has the opportunity to present their case without interruption and the mediator is entitled to ask for clarification where issues are unclear. Each party shall have not more than three advisers present.

5.1 After the open presentations to the mediator, the parties separate with one or both retiring to private rooms. A record of the presentations will not be kept although persons attending may keep notes. The mediator will then talk with each party in turn, seeking to learn more about the issues dividing the parties and to discover any matters which each side may feel reluctant to discuss in front of the other party.

5.2 The mediator will not disclose matters told to him in confidence without that party giving permission. The mediator will, however, seek to persuade the parties, where he perceives it to be in their interest, to allow him to make certain disclosures if he believes this will give the parties a better understanding of their dispute and therefore improve their opportunity to find an acceptable settlement.

5.3 The mediator will expect to move between the parties developing common points, carrying offers and suggestions, pressing each side to justify or modify its position until a point is reached where terms of settlement can be agreed.

6. It is for the parties to settle their own dispute - the mediator does not make any ruling or finding. He may, however, make recommendations to help them do so. If settlement is achieved, he will advise the parties to draw up an agreement with the help of the professional advisers summarising the terms of the settlement.

7. Confidentiality

By taking part in the Executive Tribunal Procedure, the parties undertake to each other that:

7.1	the entire procedure is and will be kept confidential;
7.2	the parties, their representatives and advisers and the Neutral will keep confidential all statements and all other matters including any settlement agreement except when and insofar as disclosure is necessary to implement and enforce the settlement agreement;
7.3	the procedure will be treated as being on the same basis as without prejudice negotiations in an action in the courts (or similar proceedings) and all such documents, submissions and statements produced for the purposes of the Procedure will be inadmissible and not subject to discovery in any arbitration, legal or any other similar proceedings save that evidence that is otherwise admissible or discoverable will not be rendered inadmissible or non-discoverable by reason of its use in connection with this procedure.

7.4   The Neutral will be disqualified from acting as a witness, consultant or expert for any party in any subsequent proceedings connected with the dispute and his opinions/recommendations/ statements will be inadmissible in any arbitration legal or other proceedings relating to the matter.

8. Costs

Unless the parties otherwise agree, the fees and expenses of the mediator as well as any other administrative expenses of the procedure will be borne equally by the parties and each party will bear its own costs.

9. Termination Procedure

The procedure shall terminate if and when a party serves on the other party or parties and on the mediator a written notice of withdrawal from the procedure.

10. Protection of CEDR and the Mediator

The parties will agree in writing that neither CEDR nor any mediator appointed by CEDR shall be liable to the parties for any act or omission whatsoever in connection with the services to be provided by them.

Index

213